1895

Pedagogy of Praxis

SUNY Series, Teacher Empowerment and School Reform
Henry A. Giroux and Peter L. McLaren, Editors

Pedagogy of Praxis

A Dialectical Philosophy of Education

Moacir Gadotti

Preface by Paulo Freire
Translated by John Milton

STATE UNIVERSITY OF NEW YORK PRESS

Published by
State University of New York Press, Albany

For information, address State University of New York
Press, State University Plaza, Albany, N.Y., 12246

Production by E. Moore
Marketing by Dana E. Yanulavich

Library of Congress Cataloging-in-Publication Data

Gadotti, Moacir
    Pedagogy of praxis : a dialectical philosophy of education /
Moacir Gadotti ; preface by Paulo Freire ; translated by John
Milton.
        p.   cm. — (SUNY series, teacher empowerment and school
reform)
    Includes bibliographical references (p.).
    ISBN 0-7914-2935-0 (alk. paper). — ISBN 0-7914-2936-9 (pbk. :
alk. paper)
    1. Education—Philosophy.   2. Dialectic.   3. Critical pedagogy-
-Philosophy.   4. Pragmatism.   5. Educational equalization-
-Philosophy.   I. Title.   II. Series: Teacher empowerment and school
reform.
LB880.G24   1996   95-32347
                                                                CIP

10   9   8   7   6   5   4   3   2

Human history as the history of the freedom of men and women could be summarised as the history of inequality and the struggle against inequality. In this struggle, education has a major role.

To Claude Pantillon (1938–1980),
Master and friend.

Contents

PETER L. McLAREN

Foreword

BEYOND HUMANISTIC EDUCATION: A DISCUSSION WITH MOACIR GADOTTI

Moacir Gadotti is one of Brazil's most important philosophers of education and educational activists. Director of the Paulo Freire Institute in São Paulo, and a close colleague of Paulo Freire, Professor Gadotti also teaches at the University of São Paulo, specializing in Philosophy of Education and History of Pedagogical Ideas. He was Chief of Cabinet under Paulo Freire, during the time that Freire served as Secretary of Education of the City of São Paulo. Professor Gadotti also worked as the general coordinator of MOVA-SP (Literacy Movement of the City of São Paulo). Currently, he is regional director of ICEA (International Community Education Association) in Latin America. He has published numerous books, including the recent *Reading Paulo Freire: His Life and Work*. Moacir Gadotti is one of the best known and respected educators in Brazil. He has published articles and books in Japanese, French, Italian, Spanish, English, German and Swedish.

While the following dialogue was completed through correspondence, it first began at the University of São Paulo, in Brazil, in 1994 during a visit sponsored by Movimento Boneco, a radical student group which had brought me to Florianopolis to teach a course at the University of Santa Catarina. Later, members of Movimento Boneco arranged for me to lecture in Porto Alegre, to visit Paulo Freire and to deliver several lectures in São Paulo. During this time, I was pleased to find myself again in the wonderful company of Moacir Gadotti, whom I had the opportunity to meet previously in Portugal and Malaysia. I was anxious to discuss with Professor Gadotti his new book, the translation of which I had recently read with great interest. In this book, Professor Gadotti develops an extremely innovative educational proposal, the axes of which include the critical training of educators and the construction of popular public schooling or citizen schools within an integrative-dialectical educational perspective. What is especially significant about Gadotti's book is its tremendous erudition with respect to philosophical analyses as well as social theoretical and concrete concerns. For North American educators who are largely unfamiliar with the writings of Marx, Hegel, Feuerbach, Lefebvre, Gramsci, Dewey, Marcuse, Poulantzas and other important thinkers, Gadotti's book will serve as an indispensible introduction to the critical education tradition.

One of the problems with working in colleges of education throughout North America is that prospective teachers and graduate students—through no fault of their own—are rarely ever provided with courses that engage the history of dialectical thought, neo-Marxist approaches to social and educational change, and the criticalist tradition in social theory. Fortunately, we have in Gadotti's writings an important challenge to the current content of our graduate programs in education. Gadotti's work makes no claims to have solved the problems of educational or social reform in the context of Brazil or elsewhere, and that is part of its dialectical strength. While Gadotti offers us a praxis without guarantees, he also offers us a profound challenge to rethink the Marxist problematic in our contemporary postmodernist juncture. Such a rethinking will prove to reinvigorate current North American struggles for liberation, especially in its reminder that we must not only become critically conscious agents of change, but we must also be able to organize collectively in order to be able to organically transform our public educational institutions. The following conversation touches upon some of the themes and issues explored by Gadotti throughout the pages of this book.

McLAREN: I have found your work to be invigorating and exciting. It has much to say to North American educators, and particularly educators in the United States. I'm delighted that your work is now appearing more often in English. Your current projects are particularly important, specifically your *Pedagogy of Praxis*. Why *Pedagogy of Praxis*? Is it not better to call your pedagogy a "Pedagogy of Dialogue," following in the tradition of the pedagogy of Paulo Freire?

GADOTTI: It's true. Everything began with the pedagogy of dialogue. Let's begin with a discussion about dialogue and then it will become clear why I've chosen to call my pedagogy a pedagogy of praxis. Dialogue is a practice as old as education. However, it only began to take on greater importance as a central educational idea with the "new school" movement [progressivism] toward the end of the last century. The theoreticians behind this movement took antiauthoritarian positions, opposing the traditional school which was supported by a conception of education centered on the authority of the teacher. The so-called "new schoolists" attempted to find more democratic relationships inside a free, creative and spontaneous school where there was no fear of freedom. The development of the public school and educational sciences—especially psychology and sociology—brought a new understanding of the child, and of the relationship between education and society. These developments of dialogue contributed enormously to the spread of theories.

McLaren: Can you share some of the main themes of your *Pedagogy of Praxis* in terms of the way it both critiques and extends the pedagogy of dialogue?

Gadotti: We can see two main themes or lines in the pedagogy of dialogue: the liberal line, based on the development of the educational sciences and on the principles of liberal democracy, and the religious one, which came through Judaeo-Christian humanistic philosophy and existentialism. Up to now, the idea of dialogue has been understood as a privileged relationship between two people, as Socrates understood it, a relationship which is reciprocal and with equality of conditions. This is, however, an aristocratic conception of dialogue. As such, it will sharply contradict the concrete conditions of pedagogical praxis which is embedded in social inequality with all kinds of barriers preventing the dialogical ideal. Since the 1960s, new social conditions allowed the concept of dialogue to take a new form. It became a political factor in educational relationships.

McLaren: And now we come to the pedagogical idea of Paulo Freire.

Gadotti: Yes. For Paulo Freire, dialogue is not just the encounter of two subjects who look for the meaning of things—knowledge—but an encounter which takes place in praxis—in action and reflection—in political engagement, in the pledge for social transformation. A dialogue that does not lead to transformative action is pure verbalism. Dialogue has a clear political connotation. Freire surpasses the somewhat mystical and ingenuous dialogical vision of Martin Buber, and of the metaphysical conception of Georges Gusdorf. For Freire, the focus of dialogue is predominantly social, while in Buber, it is basically individual. For Gusdorf, dialogue is seen as a privileged relationship between educator and pupil, who meet as master and disciple, and who, witnessing the truth between themselves, recognize themselves as human beings. Paulo Freire also distances himself from Carl Rogers. The existentialist and therapeutic vision of Rogers shows men and women confronting the hostility of the world alone. The initial aims of the pedagogy of dialogue were to establish friendly relationships between masters and disciples at work. Now it is different. The aim of dialogue is to affect directly social relationships. Self-determining pedagogy aims at preparing for social self-determination.

McLAREN: This is very important, Moacir. I've always seen Freire's conception of dialogue this way, and have always attributed it to Freire's dialectical ethics of imagination. It is interesting to compare Freire's view of dialogue to that of Emmanuel Levinas or Mikhail Bakhtin. In other words, dialogue needs to be seen as praxiological and not as an equal linguistic/intersubjective exchange. What are the determinations and overdeterminations surrounding the logics of signification? We need to ask such questions. Dialogue is always dialectically bound. It is always dialectically related to social, political, cultural, and gendered relations. Tell me, Moacir, what are some of the criticisms of the pedagogy of dialogue?

GADOTTI: The first criticisms of the pedagogy of dialogue came from positivists, especially economists of education, who argued that this pedagogy was too impregnated with humanistic concepts, not scientific enough, and could not meet the demands of the educational bureaucracy. The pedagogy of dialogue does not concern itself with questions such as supervision or the norms and control of the efficiency of educational systems. In fact, it would not be able to quantify the efficiency of dialogue in the classroom. This is, however, one of its central points! Criticism of the pedagogy of dialogue was also made from within as it analyzed its own practice, and gradually renewed itself as it came up against its own limits, becoming more dialectic than dialogical. It is a slow movement of self-renewal, which is the result of practical engagement and not just of mere mental exercises.

McLAREN: How familiar these criticisms appear to me! These are the same kinds of criticisms that are directed at my own work, and the work of other criticalists. When we develop our pedagogy from a conception of the sociality of language; when we base our pedagogies on a dialogics that is meant to work toward the liberation of socially, culturally and economically subjugated and peripheralised peoples; when we ground our pedagogies not in the politics of centrism nor consensus nor harmony, but in the multiple voicings of an oppositional dialogics, when we locate communication within an arena of race, class, and gender struggle—then it seems as though our critics begin to mobilize in full force to denounce us as unscientific, as politically biased, as assuming a form of semantic and social authority that must be condemned in favor of an objective approach to pedagogy. Yes, all of this sounds all too familiar. How can we understand dialogue in education today?

GADOTTI: This was the question that I asked myself in 1985 when I decided to reread critically my first book, *Teaching Communication*, published for the first time in 1975 with an excellent preface from Georges Gusdorf. This was the third time I had asked this question in a systematic way. First, I had done it with my preface to Paulo Freire's *Education and Change*, published in 1979, and in the following year, with the publication of my second book, *Education and Power*. When writing a preface for Paulo Freire, I attempted to show the insufficiency of a conception of dialogue based just on unity and reciprocity. I tried to give a dialectic interpretation to the dialogue, in other words, conceiving it at the same time as a unity and an opposition. In this preface, I showed that, in a society marked by antagonism, dialogue could represent just a romantic utopia when it comes from the oppressed, or it could be part of a cunning trap when part of the oppressor. The dialogue could take place inside the school, in the classroom, or in small groups, but not in global society.

McLAREN: I agree with you. Dialogue is too often thought of as occurring in a charmed circle of interlocutors. Language is not just a transparent reflection of the social, but rather refracts the social. Because language is fundamental to dialogue, it must always be seen as being informed by a multiplicity of interests. However, for many of our critics, we should keep on talking until meaning is stabilized and centrally purged of all dissonance. We should, in their view, join the universal conversation in which, as long as we avoid looking at the extralinguistic contexts of dialogue which are connected to the cultural logics of imperialism—all contradictions will be resolved and we will all be miraculously transformed into Americans! Do you intend, thus, to condemn all dialogue, or to restrict the forms that it can take in the school?

GADOTTI: No. By this, I don't mean to exclude all dialogue. Dialogue, however, cannot exclude conflict lest it be considered ingenuous dialogue. People act dialectically. What gives strength to dialogue between the oppressed is its bargaining force when faced by the oppressor. It is the development of the conflict with the oppressor that maintains the cohesion of the relationship between the oppressed and the oppressor. This dialogue-conflict and contradictory dimension of educative action had escaped the pioneers of the pedagogy of dialogue. In teaching, a purely unitary vision of dialogue would make the essential differences between pupil and teacher disappear. When these differences are not considered to be a unity in opposition, this could result in a loss of interest and frustration on the part of teachers who expect favorable conditions for a friendly relationship, and, instead, find an adverse reality. The result could be the opposite—the return to an authoritarian school. Facing the failure of dialogue, the teacher resorts to his or her authority. Conflict also exists in pedagogical relationships. This doesn't annul dialogue, but rather is part and parcel of it. Therefore, it is necessary that it must be faced and worked with.

McLaren: It seems to me that one of the goals of dialogue is to destabilize and unsettle the operative logic of dialogue as the creation of sameness, as the smoothing over of conflict, and as the masking of the necessity of paradox in every act of enunciation, of camouflaging the fact that the sign is the locus of multiple conflicts that disrupt the unitary cohesiveness of the sign community. Dialogue becomes exploitative when the oppressor becomes the omniscient narrator of other peoples' lives, and when the oppressor tries to seize ownership of the sign by creating and monopolizing the contexts and circumstances in which dialogue takes place. Can you point out the contributions of a pedagogy of dialogue to contemporary educational thought?

Gadotti: Well, when the pedagogy of dialogue posed the question of the democratization of school relationships, many new paths were followed. The pedagogy of dialogue contributed to the democratization of teaching when considering the democratic relationship between teachers and pupils and the democratic relationships inside the school itself; it exposed authoritarian relationships in the school. This pedagogy was able to show the institutional, bureaucratic and authoritarian relationships, the antidialogue, which predominate in any society constituted by classes. The pedagogy of dialogue, coherent with its principle, has changed with its own practice. Its initial humanistic and philosophical roots improved when it related to economics and politics, both necessary instruments for the comprehension of the new questions which were being posed, such as school management and participation in school government.

McLaren: Paulo Freire also emphasizes the problematizing characteristic of dialogue and the relationship of educational work to the transformation of society.

Gadotti: Of course. It is perfectly legitimate to consider the pedagogical work of Paulo Freire as a particular manifestation of dialectical thought. Paulo Freire captures this historical and political feeling of knowledge and of educational theory, this critical and revolutionary role, that Marx, in the postface to the second edition of *Capital*, attributes to theory.

McLaren: How does *Pedagogy of Praxis*, analyze these questions?

Gadotti: First of all, *Pedagogy of Praxis* is not a book of speculations about education. It is a demonstration, the result of a lived practice. It is the result of an intense engagement in the educational problems of my country and other countries. It is also part of a political pedagogical itinerary, nourished by certain beliefs and by a definitely hopeful ethics—that is, the joy of being part of a generation of educators who looked for new paths and who tried to open them in discussion, and who didn't take the easy way out.

McLaren: One urgent educational discussion today is centered on the relationship between technical competence and the political compromise of the educator. Is this issue important in your work?

Gadotti: My book was born from discussions like this. I attempted not to remain in the pure and simple practical debate, but rather to look for an explicative theory, reasons to put forward, which could, before anything else, give me the necessary courage to like the profession that I had chosen, to love it, so that it could nourish me with the hope that, in spite of everything, it could contribute to build a better world. I repeat that it is not a metatheory, nor is it speculation about the phenomenon of education. It is a book about themes which have been lived through and discussed with a large number of educators. The pedagogy which now I call a "pedagogy of conflict"—and which I more and more call a "pedagogy of praxis"—reflects my current educational practice.

McLaren: Do you think that the Marx's ideas can inspire a pedagogy, even after the fall of the Berlin Wall?

Gadotti: Pedagogy of praxis is not a pedagogy that has been invented out of nothing. It already has a history. It has been inspired by dialectics. Because of this, it is not necessary to go back to the sources of dialectical thinking, particularly Marxism. However, I have tried to make a nonpositivist reading of Marx. The positivist structuralist reading of Marx characterizes Marx as a popular educator, and as a revolutionary and militant thinker. On the contrary, a pedagogical and critical reading looks for the political educator in him, with an ethics founded on equality between human beings. It looks to a rigor in language, a passion, and a Utopia. I am not attempting to find in Marx a reply to all contemporary problems or, on the other hand, to totally deny his contribution. What I am attempting is to understand him historically and critically. Only in this way can he have some validity for educators today.

MCLAREN: I agree with you that a pedagogy of praxis must engage Marx in a fundamental way. It must continue to engage Marx and to reinvent him for these new times we are now facing together as agents, as educators, and as cultural workers. Now, I return to my first question. Why do you give this book the title of *Pedagogy of Praxis?*

GADOTTI: Since 1978, I have been identified with the *pedagogy of conflict*, an expression which I myself coined in the same year, referring to a pedagogy which was inspired by Marxism. Conflict is a category that I continue to claim as essential to all pedagogy. The role of the educator is to educate. Educating presupposes a transformation, and there is no kind of peaceful transformation. There is always conflict and rupture with something, with, for instance, prejudices, habits, types of behaviors, and the like. In this book, I make frequent references to the pedagogy of conflict. It continues to be my pedagogy, the pedagogy that I try to practice, despite recognizing its difficulties. We are not always willing to confront the conflict. We are not always willing to take on the onus of involving ourselves with the risks that accompany our taking part. However, it is only by taking on this risk that we can become educators. The educator is he or she who doesn't remain indifferent and neutral when faced with reality. He or she tries to intervene and learn with the changing reality. Thus, conflict is at the heart of all pedagogy.

MCLAREN: Why not give your book the title *Pedagogy of Practice* or *Pedagogy of Conflict?* Why did you insist on giving it the title *Pedagogy of Praxis?*

GADOTTI: Well, I discussed the issue of the title with my colleague at the Paulo Freire Institute, Dr. Carlos Alberto Torres, professor at the Graduate School of Education and Information Studies at UCLA, to keep the title as *Pedagogy of Praxis*, not practice. He agreed. The notion of "praxis" in traditional Western philosophy is more analytically complex than is the notion of practice or conflict per se. Indeed it is more appealing for those who would like to consider the relationships between theory and practice as blended together in the notion of *praxis*, a dialectical concept.

MCLAREN: Couldn't pedagogy of praxis be confused with pedagogy of action, as defended by the New School movement?

GADOTTI: Yes. In fact, *Praxis* in Greek literally means *action*. Thus, it could be considered to be a new version of the pragmatic pedagogy that understands praxis as a strictly utilitarian practice, and reducing the true to the useful. However, today—and contrary to the New School—the pedagogy of praxis evokes the radical tradition of education. In this tradition, praxis means transformative action. The kind of education that copies models, that wishes to reproduce models, doesn't stop being praxis, but is limited to a reiterative, imitative, and bureaucratized praxis. Quite different from this, transforming praxis is essentially creative, daring, critical, and reflexive. Pedagogy of praxis intends to be a pedagogy for transforming education. It originates from a branch of anthropology that considers humans to be creative beings, the subjects of history, who are transformed as they transform the world.

McLaren: Some might think that this is a pedagogy for adults.

Gadotti: Perhaps, but, on the contrary, this is a pedagogy that intends to take into account the transformations which children and youth go though during their school years. It is a pedagogy which is also appropriate for this age, which is full of conflicts, and which, because of this, is an age of fascinating transformations. As the North American educator Matthew Lipman has shown, there is no fixed age for philosophizing and critical thinking. Developing from an early age the ability to think critically and autonomously, and developing one's own ability to make decisions is the fundamental role of education for citizenship.

CARLOS ALBERTO TORRES

Foreword

DIALECTICS, CONFLICT, AND DIALOGUE

Pedagogy of Praxis is a book about and from a critical philosophy of education. However, it is, foremost, a book about people, their actions, and their consciousness. It is a book about education in the stricter sense of the term as predicated by Dewey.[1]

Gadotti starts with the premise that human history is the product of the struggle of women and men against inequality. This struggle is presented in this book in terms of a dialectic of oppositions and a pedagogy of consciousness. A pedagogy of praxis is nothing but a pedagogy of consciousness.

Dialectics in this book is understood as both a method for intellectual inquiry, and as the texture and dynamics underscoring the evolving reality of human beings, culture, and society. For Gadotti—what is influenced by the Hegelian-Marxist *weltstanchuung*—dialectical development begins with the assumptions that reality evolves from contradictions between antagonistic and nonantagonistic forces. It is always a dialectic of oppositions that constitute the dynamics of transformation of reality. Culture is always the result of the systematic accumulation of human actions and reactions. Hence as a civilizatory artifact, culture—and, by implication, human praxis—is always entangled with moral, ethical, spiritual, and material premises—and, I must add—dilemmas which underscore, but also result from, conflictive (r)evolution of any human or cultural reality. Reality is, simply put, constituted through and an outcome of historical struggles.

The Hegelian premises of "rupture, historical development, and contradiction"[2] are part and parcel of any dialectical thought about social transformation. Yet, the Marxiam philosophy of praxis, particularly after the contribution of Antonio Gramsci,[3] thinks of reality as a self-evolving process which constitutes, and is constituted

XX　　　　　　　　　　　　　　　　　　　　　　　*Foreword*

by, human beings. The dialectics of reality, both in its material and spiritual-social bases, constitute the premises, but also prime material of human beings' praxis. Not surprisingly, from a dialectical approach, a central question is the education of educators, so well articulated by Marx in his *Thesis Twelve* on Feuerbach.

A dialectical approach has been, for some time, quite at odds with recent trends in academia. This is not surprising because Marx, himself a philosopher, was very much at odds with the philosophical premises of his own time. Similarly, many of the Marxist philosophers that have revisited Marx's dialectical materialism in the twentieth century, from Karl Kautsky to Vladimir Lenin, and Mao Tse-tung; to the Marxist hegelianism of Vietnamese philosopher Tran-Duc-Tao; to the Hungarian encyclopedic philosopher, Georg Lukács, or the German, Karl Korsch; to the Italian, Antonio Gramsci; to the French philosopher, Louis Althusser; or to the founders of critical theory and the Frankfurt School, Herbert Marcuse most prominently among them—and to some extent Claus Offe and Jürgen Habermas among the contemporary scholars. All have been trail blazers living in the uncomfortable twilight of challenging the old philosophical gospel while remissibly playing the odds as prophets of a new, uncharted philosophical message.

Dialectics is indeed a philosophical perception that is at odds with the philosophical establishment.Taking stock of the introduction of Marxist philosophy in academic environments in the United States, Wartofsky argues, "Philosophy proper was largely analytic and linguistic in focus, and formalist in character. It was notable for its rigor, for close attention to details and to clarity in the logic of argument—virtues certainly. But it was also notably ahistorical, asocial, and apractical. Insofar as it was normative, the norms were methodological rather than substantive. That is, they were norms concerning the right way to proceed in argument or in theory construction, rather than norms concerning what was right or wrong in content or in practice. In fact, such substantive questions were explicitly set aside as lying outside philosophy, as 'external questions.' In this philosophical scene, Marxism could hardly be taken as a fit subject for philosophical study."[4]

This description has changed somewhat in the last few years, not as a result of a decisive introduction of Marxism as an alternative, but with the introduction, albeit limited, of poststructuralist philosophies in Departments of Philosophy, including postmodernism, feminism, and deconstructivism. Deconstructionism and postmodernism, themselves, have emerged as champions of a criticism of Marxism as a dialects of enlightenment. I suspect, however, that the changes in the last decade or so in the philosophy of education in the United States, moving in a more ecumenical and less analytical direction, have not been followed in the standard philosophical departments. In the realm of philosophy of education, it is also unclear what—if any—new directions are emerging. With the vacuum of a whole generation of philosophers of education not hired in the United States between the mid-1970s until the mid-1980s, it is hard to figure out who in the younger generation of professors and/or senior associate professors of philosophy of education are going to produce new departures. *Pedagogy of Praxis* will pose, perhaps, old challenges to new philosophers of education.

However, Gadotti, does not seek to merely extend the Hegelian-Marxist tradition, but to reinvent it. Having never had a "postmodernist" phase in his philosophical analysis—and, more importantly, writing from the contradictory reality of his motherland of Brazil—Gadotti follows the footprints of educational philosophers such as John Dewey, Paulo Freire, or Maxine Green who have tirelessly argued that the best way to honor the accomplishments of a tradition is not to canonize but to reinvent it. The dialectical conception of education that Gadotti lays out with craft and imagination sets the stage for what Gadotti calls, "an education for the future."

Writing from Brazil, Gadotti reminds us of many "uncomfortable" facts obscured rather than highlighted by the passing fads of postmodernism. Let me mention just two analytical premises that linger in the background of contemporary debates. Gadotti will argue that first, social classes still exist and class inequality is growing; and second, the process of work still constitutes a basic anthropological principle of what Existentialist philosophers called "existence" in the world. Let us discuss both themes in reverse order.

The process of work cannot be separated from the Existence, even when work might have become, in some areas of the planet, a jobless work process.[5] Existence would seem, to a certain extent, to be opposed to essence. Etymologically, to exist, signifies "to be outside of," to emerge, to transcend the projecting outward from the being in space and time. Kierkegaard tackles the Hegelian concept of mediation or synthesis of opposites and affirms existence as an immediation which excludes synthesis—for example—unity of opposites—thus disputing against "the system" as a harmonic and integrating vision of factual happening.

The *leitmotiv* of the Kierkegaard spirit is *anguish*, the vital tone of existence. Existentialism, as a philosophical direction, cannot be constrained or defined easily, let alone accomplished in a few pages. Its basic exponents—such as Kierkegaard, Heidegger, Marcel, Jaspers, Mounier, Sartre, or Merleau Ponty, among the most significant ones—have polemicized among themselves, and one can often come to lose sight of the main thread joining this movement known as "existentialism." Yet, this notion of anguish is a foundation of sorts.

When Heidegger once again took up the Kierkegaard theme almost a century later, he discovered that anguish leads human beings to experience a feeling of "self" as being there, in the world, and abandoned. It leads him to the experience of the *Dasein* (being there), as an existence estranged from its essence, or as an existence with no apparent reason.

This provokes the birth of the anxiety or worry of daily life. Thus, human existence, or *Dasein*, represents the fundamental concept of the philosophy of existence. The *Dasein* possesses temporality as its fundamental structure. The phenomenological description that Heidegger brought about, in search of the existential analytic of the *Dasein*, establishes that the latter manifests itself as being whose basic characteristics is to-be-in-the-world, with its corresponding existential behavior consisting in the faculty of *disappropriation*, an aptitude that the human existence has in order to become engrossed in things.

For Gadotti, this notion of *Dasein* is ever present in his philosophical arguments, not so much in his conceptualization, which is less prone to existentialism than to dialectics, but in the notion of critical consciousness and the education of the future as an agonic enterprise. It is agonic because it is built on doubt and, uncertainly, not on objective truth and certainty. It is agonic because, while it doubts about the premises and outcomes of instrumental action, it still searches for a form of rationality that could guide practical and political action, as a dialectical rationality. It is also agonic because it relies on dialogue, and that dialogue, by its very nature, is always risky, open-ended, and without much of an explicit curriculum. Dialogue is, at that same time, utopian and optimistic which could bring to the subjects trying to establish that dialogue among themselves a sense of agony, uncertainty, hopelessness, tragedy, or action, in the old Greek term of the word. However, agony, hopelessness, and tragedy can live together with notions of hope and utopianism in the pursuit of happiness. Dialogue, as a philosophy of existence, rejects absolutisms and essentialisms, and becomes a social construction, or a constructivist perspective in cognitive—and to some extent social—terms, which is part and parcel of the mixed bag of dichotomies that human actions always embody, namely doubt and certainty, common sense and science, and philosophy and ideology.

Praxis is, then, the natural state of human beings who attempt to be self-reflective about their own actions. It is a life world that, in the words of Maxine Green, can be characterized as a world of "unmet needs and broken promises."[6] A pedagogy of praxis for Moacir Gadotti embodies, but goes beyond, a pedagogy of conflict or a pedagogy of dialogue. It is a pedagogy of hope and action together.

Maxine Green wrote a few years ago about praxis. She wrote celebrating the philosophical contributions of the Third World to the notion of a "passionate" pluralism expanding the multicultural community. As a sharp and sensible intellectual receptive to the multiple faces of pluralism, and a good observer and frequent visitor to New York classrooms, Green had been observing for years the vital presence of the Third World's "faceless faces" in the United States. Thus, recent immigrant groups are always associated in her analysis with the social construction of "faceless faces" of groups and traditions such as African-American, Native-Americans, Latinos, and Latinas, and Asian-Americans whom, not being recent immigrants into this country, had nevertheless been cossified and reificated, exploited by a colonial policy and a colonial mentality. Many, if not most of them, have fallen by the wayside of the American dream.

Taking the notion of Third World as an existentialist rather than a geographical analytical, sociological, or normative category, Green is looking at—and dreaming of—post-Colonial philosophies. Through her philosophical quest, she reached out to the post-Colonial philosophies emerging in the post-Colonial countries, underscoring the philosophical work of individuals, scholars of color, and women who have been struggling to shake off the Colonial yoke from their own as well as our mentalities—the most insidious and difficult yoke to exorcise. Green speaks of praxis as an attempt to build humanity from the concrete conditions of our existence. She speaks with a voice that, while original, resonates with Dewey's voice of building a public as a foundation of democracy. She speaks of building community, pluralism, and multiculturalism, starting from the American *Dassein* rather from a canonical project or hypothetical essence.

With her graceful, poetic tone, Green says, "In the presence of an increasingly potent Third World, against the sounds of increasingly eloquent post-Colonial (and, now, posttotalitarian) voices, we cannot longer talk in terms of seamless totalities under the rubrics like 'free world,' 'free market,' 'equality,' or even 'democracy.' Like the 'wreckage in the mid-Atlantic,' the 'faceless faces,' and the 'unnatural silences,' the lacks and deprivations must be made aspects of our plurality as well as of our cultural identity."[7]

These words could be applied in toto to Gadotti's project of navigating the history of Western philosophy and speaking of the "faceless faces" and the silent voices. Perhaps one could argue that Gadotti did not capture the experience of all "faceless faces" and did not listen to all the silent voices. One could also argue that Gadotti doesn't have enough familiarity with the powerful contributions of feminism, particularly in the industrial advanced world, or that he is just nibbling at the margins of powerful theoretical currents such as postmodernism, deconstructionism, or the linguistic turn. Perhaps one could argue that, in his philosophical journey, Gadotti has neglected many contributions from several perspectives, and that his work should be revisited critically and, perhaps, reinvented.

Following the tradition of dialogue that he practices in his own life, Gadotti will welcome a critical engagement with his work, not as a rhetorical plot or an authoritative device, but as an authentic disposition to learn, and to engage passionately in the discourse of reason as a discourse of love. Let me relate a personal experience.

In August 1994, Moacir Gadotti presented a new book with Jose Eustaquio Romão on school autonomy[8] at the Federal University of Juiz de Fora in Minas Gerais, Brazil. I was invited to participate in a *batepapo* (a polemic dialogue) with Gadotti and the then vice provost of the university, José Eustaquio Ramão. Even in the context of the exquisite diplomatic scholarly exchanges which take place in Brazil—particularly among friends who might disagree but still love each other—I challenged his and Romão's perspectives, as philosophical libertarianism. I argued that for my taste, their open-ended position on school autonomy resembled too much the movement for vouchers in the United States. I argued that, while cherishing the notion of school autonomy, I was very worried that their position gave arguments to whither away the state and, with it, the traditional social contract of the Great Society—as limited and incomplete as it might have been in the experience of liberal-democracies-in-process in Latin America. I insisted that we cannot construct the public and the public sphere without the role of a democratic state. I challenged that, in the end, their proposal could justify a neoliberal policy, restricting equalizing actions by state intervention, and leaving education to the random rule of the market and privatization.

We agreed and disagreed before six hundred teachers who were very concerned with the new proposals for school autonomy in

Brazil. The gist of these proposals are discussed philosophically in the chapter 7 of this book. Toward the end of my intervention, I reminded Romão and Gadotti that Kant equated the principle of autonomy with free will, but that his "citizenship theory was grounded in the primacy of the practical politics of universal social obligations and rights."[9] Gadotti was ecstatic and thrilled with the statement, and, for more than a year, we have been discussing the political implications of Kant's aphorism.

Needless to say, our conversation continued throughout the whole day. The visit of foreign scholars to Brazil always entails a long list of activities. For instance, on that day, the three of us participated in four different academic activities, with the last public lecture finishing around 11:00. At that time—and in perfect Brazilian fashion—we regrouped for dinner with Jose Eustaquio Romão, Nailé Romão, and Gadotti. Amid appetizing Brazilian dishes and a good Brazilian wine, we argued back and forth about Kant's maxim and their positions until early morning. Indeed, Gadotti welcomes engaging criticisms of his work, and he would love to receive feed-back on this, his second book in English.

Gadotti's philosophical project is very close to Freire's philosophical understanding. For Paulo Freire, philosophy takes a reflexive, even critical, role in order to accompany pedagogical action. Gadotti joins Freire, as well as a host of theologians and philosophers of liberation from Latin America and elsewhere, arguing—exactly in the existential band that Maxine Green has invited us to locate ourselves—that the role of philosophical reflection also acquires a very precise dimension, that of bringing together the elements for the constitution of an anthropology—specifically, a political anthropology. This political anthropology explains to us how humanity is in the process of humanization, a problem that the educators must deal with and which leads to their own development, and again poses the question of the education of the educator.[10]

Let us not forget that Freire reserves for education the role of helping man to reflect on his ontological vocation as subject. Granted, this formulation reflects Paulo's historically embedded sexist language, and yet, properly deconstructed, there is a meaningful message. This ontological vocation of human beings as subjects and not objects of history continues to be a central dilemma of education. This is so because philosophy, science, and ideology cannot be disassociated so easily as following a set of standards of differentiation.

From critical modernist positions, reinforced by the postmodernist storm, it has always been very difficult to establish clear normative foundations for social action, differentiating what is science, what is philosophy, and what is ideology. The classical example within perspectives employing dialectics has been the argument about the primacy of class in social transformation, showing the limitations of seemingly clear-cut philosophical perspectives. Seeking to establish the premises for human liberation, orthodox Marxists have basically argued that, because the basic contradiction in capitalism is between capital and labor, the working class was the class to liberate all classes. However, orthodox Marxists did not take advantage of the strongly methodological indication of Marx and Engels that "The concrete is concrete because it is the synthesis of multiple determinations, hence unity in diversity."[11] Hence, orthodox Marxism could not theoretically include and act upon the fact that Michael Apple has noticed, while discussing the work of Basil Bernstein, that class itself is—and always was—increasingly becoming gendered and raced. Thus, Apple reminds us that "we cannot marginalize race and gender as constitutive categories in any cultural analysis. If there is indeed basic cultural forms and orientations that are specifically gendered and raced, and have their own partly autonomous histories, then we need to integrate theories of patriarchal and racial forms into the very core of our attempt to comprehend what is being reproduced and changed. At the very least, a theory that allows for the contradictions within and among these dynamics would be essential. Of course, this is one of the multiple areas where neo-Gramscian and some poststructuralist positions that have not become cynically depoliticized intersect."[12]

Despite debates about self-evolving narratives, multiple voices, and multiple rationalities, Gadotti still accepts the classical view that all ideology is a compromised thought. Ideology accompanies structure in order to sustain or modify it, and interacts in the educational project of each epoch. Freire said—pardon the sexist language again—and Gadotti will indeed endorse that! "Because he admires the world and therefore objectifies it, because he grasps and comprehends reality and transforms it in his action-reflection, man is a being of praxis. Even more so, man is praxis . . . His ontological vocation, which he ought to existentiate, is that of a subject who operates on and transforms the world. Subjugated to concrete conditions that transform him into an object, man will be sacrificing his fundamental vocation. . . . Nobody is if he prevents others from being."[13]

The best way to summarize Gadotti's views in this book is to simply say that a pedagogy of praxis will work to avoid that one person could prevent others from being.

MOACIR GADOTTI'S RESPONSE TO CARLOS ALBERTO
TORRES'S FOREWORD TO HIS BOOK, *PEDAGOGY OF PRAXIS*,
TRANSLATED BY PILAR O' CADIZ

São Paulo, 20 April 1995

Dear Carlos:

Last night I received the foreword you wrote to the book *Pedagogy of Praxis* and would like to thank you for the careful analysis you make, highlighting, in a critical and not a laudatory manner, central points of the text.

I am also pleased with your foreword because it will certainly awaken curiosity for the book and, at the same time, instigate a critical dialogue. Essentially, what you practice with this preface is a dialogical-dialectic method of a pedagogy of praxis. I liked that.

Because you instigate dialogue and request "suggestions for change and improvement," I feel comfortable making two comments.

First, you justifiably refer to my limited familiarity with feminist contributions. I agree with you. Just one explanation: in the book I carry out a kind of history of dialectic thought as it relates to education. Now, dialectic philosophy is as historical as any other philosophy, and, within that history, themes such as gender and race have only recently been incorporated (as they have even within my own history). It is precisely for this reason that I conclude the book with the question of social-cultural diversity—a chapter which could be considered post-Marxist, for Marx never had an explicit concern for the problems of gender or race, limited as he was by the data, information, and knowledge available to him at the time.

Second, I use the expression "social-cultural diversity" precisely with the intent of gathering, within a single expression, the notions of "class-gender-race." But I agree with you that, on several occasions, I have been betrayed by my own use of sexist language, language from which I have moved away in my latest texts, an effort which translates into a new practice of the pedagogy of praxis. However, it is a fact that I did not present, as I should have, the contributions of Apple, Giroux, McLaren, and others whom I am currently reading incorporating their rich discussion into my own analysis. Yet, at this point, I only cite their works in my bibliography.

As you plainly see, within the Marxist tradition, we always privilege the analyses of class struggle. In Third World countries, where social classes are more apparent, the gender and race issues that are so present in the First World are also explained economically. They become more obvious in a context in which inequalities are less severe. Yet, you are absolutely correct. As you point out, such an evolution is particularly notable in the work of Paulo Freire as well. Compare his early work with his more recent writings.

I very much like your reference to the work we did together in Juiz de Fora, which demonstrates that we—including you, Romão, Walter, Francisco, and others—are not mere academics, and that we actually practice the pedagogy of praxis. We do not merely write about it.

The issue of neoliberalism and the school for citizenship (*Escola Cidada*) has been continually debated among us. Today we have absolute certainty that the project for the *escola cidadá* has nothing to do with the neoliberal or social-democratic conception, but has everything to do with an emergent neosocialist conception. There exists a neoliberal conception/realization and a neosocialist conception/realization of the relationship between education and the State. It is with the latter conception that we align ourselves, and for which we desire to contribute from our realm of action which is education.

Your analysis in Juiz de Fora helped us to move forward. Romão is preparing a text on the differences from our proposal and neoliberalism. We are elaborating on notions such as "autonomy" and "parceria" (partnership) between the State and civil society, from a neosocialist vision, within an era of the advancement of social movements and the reorganization of the society. We are placing our stake with autonomy without divesting the State of its obligations. The problem is to adequately equalize the political direction of State agencies responsible for education and the autonomy of schools, a pattern being followed by various popular municipalities, and something which we attempted to do while in the municipal government of São Paulo, which is to say that it is not merely a theoretical question, but a practical one. It means that Lenin was right: "Theory should be a guide for action and not dogma."

I think that, in that regard, you could say that I have sought to be more didactic-prescriptive, and not so much analytical, but sought to maintain at all times a concern for the pedagogic. That is why in chapter 3, I make a critical analysis of the so called "critical pedagogy" that often gets lost in verbalism, leaving praxis aside. Now, pedagogy is essentially a social practice, and therefore political-ideological. In this chapter, I attempted to accentuate the leadership role on the part of the school and the teacher against nondirective pedagogies. But I also attempted to point out immediately the evolution of the concepts and practices of those pedagogies, which I consider to be perfectly adaptable to a dialectic conceptualization of education in the Marxist sense or a neosocialist conception. I did not economize in my own practice. I even went so far as to relate my own lived experience of pedagogic self-direction when I was undergoing my doctorate studies at the University of Geneva in Switzerland.

As a proposal for practice, I signal the emergence of the *escola cidadá* within the neosocialist view of education. The objective of that school is the democratization of power within the school and the formation of an intellectually autonomous citizen, a participative citizen who is as qualified for social life as for the life of work. School should not merely transmit knowledge, but also preoccupy itself with the global formation of students from within a vision in which the act of knowing and intervening come together in reality. That is why the *escola cidadá* defended here is conceived as a space for cultural production, and local culture as a point of departure—incorporating the culture of the community and responding adequately to the question of racial, sexual, and cultural diversity of its students— it should be both national and international in its point of arrival.

NOTES

1. John Dewey, *The Public and Its Problems.* Athens, Ohio: The Swallow Press, 1954.

2. Douglass Kellner, *Critical Theory, Marxism and Modernity.* Baltimore: The John Hopkins University Press, 1989. 10.

3. Raymond A. Morrow and Carlos A. Torres, *Social Theory and Education: A Critique of Theories of Social and Cultural Reproduction.* Albany, N.Y.: SUNY Press, 1995. 249–281.

4. Marx W. Wartofsky, "Marx among the Philosophers," in B. Oll-man and E. Vernoff, *The Left Academy, Marxist Scholarship on American Campuses.* New York: McGraw-Hill, 1982. 117.

5. Stanley Aronowitz and William DiFazio. *The Jobless Future: Sci-Tech and the Dogma of Work.* Minneapolis: University of Minnesota Press, 1994.

6. Maxine Green, "The Passions of Pluralism: Multiculturalism and the Expanding Community." *Journal of Negro Education,* vol. 61: 3, 1992. 258.

7. Ibid.

8. Moacir Gadotti and Jose Eustaquio Romão, (*eds.*) *Local government and education.* São Paulo: Cortez Editora, 1993.

9. Ian Culpitt, *Welfare and Citizenship: Beyond the Crisis of the Welfare State?* London, Newbury Park, and New Delhi: Sage Publications, 1992.6.

10. Following the fundamental contours of Freirean anthropology, it is understood that we would not be able to defend the thesis that the "edu-cator" is the most mature subject in the educator-learner relationship or, with his concrete action, he or she always produces the humanization of the learner. Given that humanization is a dialectical and intersubjective process, both the educator and the learner, inserted in the same pedagogical circle, interhumanize one another consistently in a dialectic of alternating influence, based on and basing itself on the process of the humanization of human beings.

11. Karl Marx, *Grundisse.* New York: Vintage Books, 1973. 101.

12. Michael W. Apple, "Education, Culture, and Class Power: Basil Bernstein and the Neo-Marxist Sociology of Education." *Educational Theory,* 42: 2, Spring 1992. 143.

13. Paulo Freire, "la concepción problematizadora de la educación y la homanización." *Cristianismoy Sociedad.* Montevideo, 1968, 18.

Preface

I met Moacir Gadotti in the 1970s in Geneva. I was in exile, wandering around the world as the special consultant for the World Council of Churches—finding my experiences at this time in *Pedagogy of Hope*—and Gadotti was writing his doctoral dissertation at the University of Geneva. We had weekly meetings in my office, where we talked openly and took part in a critical dialogue on some of the themes which he examines with such lucidity in this book, his best so far.

Pedagogy of Praxis is not a book by someone who is hiding either himself or something else. Instead, it is written by someone who risks being uncovered and, in so doing, explains the reasons why events and truths are covered up. It is also a book in which a worried philosopher lives within a shrewd and attentive historian. There is dichotomy between the thinker who deeply reflects and the historian who locates the object in space and time. Historian and philosopher work together without making any easy concessions which would result in the negation of one or the other. On the contrary, they take part in a dialogue to be able to accurately illuminate the object which attracts them and which gives itself to them to be revealed.

The discourse and the revealing and modest language with which Gadotti constructs makes him, for me, a progressively postmodern thinker. He is a thinker who knows that, if he has truths, he can't be too certain of them. The only certainty is the uncertainty that seems to be absolutely certain.

In no way can Gadotti deny the thinker or the historian working within him, and the reader should follow him. He or she should accept his invitation to think about the object and to situate and date it. It is impossible to situate or date an object without understanding its reason for being.

As with any other book, *Pedagogy of Praxis* cannot be read nor studied without prejudices, but the taste for curiosity is not just that of the spontaneous unmethodical taste which one feels for a stronger color or a more impressive form. It should be read with an epistemological curiosity—that which moves us to look for the *raison d'être* of the object.

One of the most positive elements of this book is that it is a daring text. It has willpower. It shows its face, and it takes a stand but doesn't exude arrogance. It doesn't even suggest that its position is the only position with no other possible solutions. This displays its postmodernity once again. Between the lines, we can find the author's hope that its readers will take on a position as producers of the understanding of their own text instead of simply looking at it as something that was left for them to discover.

Finally, a word about my way of writing prefaces—which may neither be the best nor the worst, but is my own way—is in order.

As a preface writer, I feel that my task is that of quite simply inviting probable readers to assume their intimacy with the book, and to promise to "rewrite" it. As I respect readers—and myself, too—I would never invite them to hand themselves over to a book which seemed to be a disappointment unless I told the truth. As there would be no sense in this, in these cases I prefer to refuse.

But I loved *Pedagogy of Praxis*.

Introduction

WHY PEDAGOGY OF PRAXIS

We must begin with the pedagogy of dialogue as introduced into the history of pedagogical thought by the "new school" movement and by the development of the educational sciences.

In fact, the development of the educational sciences—especially psychology and sociology—toward the end of the last century brought a new understanding of the child and the relationship between education and society. Educational psychology showed that, despite previous beliefs, the child is a complete human being with his or her own needs and is very different from an adult. Children are not miniature adults. Sociology of education introduced the concept of the training of the human being in order to exercise democracy. It also questioned the old theory that education is limited only to the influence of the older generation upon the younger.

The idea of dialogue in education cannot be discussed without mentioning the educational philosophy of the "new school" movement. It had an idealistic concept of dialogue and of education itself, of the equality of educational opportunities, and of the furtherance of humanity through education. Phenomenology supplied the anthropological bases for the new pedagogical practices. See, for example, Martin Buber (1878–1966) with his "dialogical principle" in his work *You and I* (1923); and later, Georges Gusdorf (1912-) with the phenomenology of the "master-disciple relationship" developed in his book *Why Teachers?* (1963).

However, since the 1960s, the new social conditions allowed a new concept of dialogue, assuming a more political connotation. The idea of the neutrality of the educational action which oriented the educational theory of the old school—and which had initially not been questioned by the new school—became problematic for the supporters of the new school. Among them was the Brazilian educa-

tor Anisio Teixeira (1900–1971), who had been influenced by the
North American philosopher and educator John Dewey (1859–1952).

The pedagogy of dialogue is a historical pedagogy. As with any
other pedagogy, it is always in evolution. Its main supporters were
under the influence of the thinking of their times and of the historical conditions of their pedagogical practice. It grew during the pro-
longed period of warfare with constant upheavals which involved
almost the whole world in the first half of the twentieth century, and
at the peak of a sociohistorical movement of reaction to authoritarianism. The race between catastrophe and education—foreseen at
the beginning of the century by H. G. Wells—was won by catastrophe.

In this historical context of the failure of education and of new
hopes, the concept of a pedagogy of dialogue, acquires new systematization with the word of Paulo Freire (1921), a major figure in this
movement. As a successor of Anisio Teixeira and the "new schoolists,"
Freire provides the best example of a renewed understanding of the
notion of dialogue in the tradition of the "new schoolists." Since his
first works—*Education as a Practice of Freedom* (1967) and *Pedagogy of the Oppressed* (1970)—Freire has given dialogue a clear political character. In his work, the dialogue of the oppressed, oriented
by a critical conscience of reality, tries to surpass the conflict between the oppressed and their oppressors. He conceives dialogue
as an educator who takes the side of the oppressed. This position
is the opposite of the educator who proclaims neutrality or doesn't
take sides.

Pedagogy of dialogue reached its most elaborate point with the
nondirective educational philosophers and with the self-determining
socialists. In this case, the aim of education is social self-determination.
The training and work of educators is part and parcel of a pedagogical
and political strategy of social transformation in which education
should be an important factor. Among the main representatives of
this perspective, are Michel Lobrot, author of *Institutional Pedagogy*,
who, in turn, was a disciple of Celestin Freinet (1896–1966), author
of *Education through Work*.

In a society marked by antagonism, dialogue could represent
just a romantic utopia when it comes from the oppressed, or it could
be part of a cunning trap when it comes from the oppressor.

> The dialogue could take place inside the school, in the class-
> room, in small groups, but not in global society. Within a
> macroeducational vision, where pedagogical education is not
> limited to school, the organization of society is also the task of

the educator. In order to do this, his strategy, his method, is much more that of disobedience, *conflict, suspicion,* than that of dialogue . . . Dialogue cannot exclude conflict lest it be considered ingenuous. They act dialectically: what gives strength to dialogue between the oppressed is its force of bargain when faced by the oppressor. It is the development of the conflict with the oppressor that maintains the cohesion of the relationship between the oppressed and the oppressor. (Gadotti in Freire 1979, 12–13)

This dialogue-conflict dimension of education had escaped the pioneers of the pedagogy of dialogue. An emphasis should be placed not just on the equality between the educator and the pupil, but also on the *differences.* The first conception of dialogue overemphasized unity and equality, devaluing the differences. What takes place in teaching practice is that someone teaches and someone learns; that someone provokes an act of learning, and stimulates it, witnesses it, and soon—that is, there are different roles—and that there is also an educational relationship in both those who educate and in those who are learning.

We have already surpassed the phase of the mechanical imposition of the teacher's knowledge. Dialogue is definitively incorporated into the task of learning and of knowing. In the act of knowing and of thinking—as the Spanish philosopher Eduardo Nicol argued in *The Principles of Science* (1965), there is always in a dialogical relationship with the other. Knowledge must have an expression and a communication. It is not a solitary act. In addition to the historical, gnoseological, and logical dimensions of the relationship, there is a fourth element—namely, the dialogical dimension. This dimension indicates the social and interdisciplinary characteristics of knowledge, going beyond the disciplinary barriers of the different types of knowledge.

The pedagogy of dialogue, coherent with its principles has changed with its own practice. Its initial humanistic and philosophical roots improved when it related to economics and politics, both necessary instruments for the comprehension of the new questions which were being posed, such as school management and participation in school government.

Beginning from the analyses of the *theory-practice relationship* in the history of pedagogy, Wolfdietrich Schmied-Kowarzik tries to show this evolution of dialogical-dialectical pedagogy from Aristotle to Paulo Freire. He emphasizes the characteristic of dialogue, how it makes all relationships problematic and hence an object of critique. He also shows the relationship of educational work with the transformation of society in the work of Paulo Freire. He says that Freire defines education as the "basically dialectic experience of the human liberation of mankind, which can only take place together, in the critical dialogue between educator and pupil . . . a moment of the total dialectal experience of the humanization of mankind." (Schmied-Kowarzik 1983, 70)

Schmied-Kowarzik demonstrates why he calls this pedagogy dialectic, avoiding an interpretation that frequently occurs, according to which dialectics are reduced to the logic of knowledge which is a rigorous form of thinking or a pure philosophy of language. Schmied-Kowarzik analyzes the differences found in this respect in Hegel and Marx.

> For both Hegel and Marx, dialectics is not just a methodical form of thinking, but rather the actual movement of the historical coming of humanity—even more than this, the movement of the world in process. The basic opposition between both, however, lies in the different values they give to the theory that understands this dialectic movement. For Hegel, the task of philosophy is just to recover for our comprehension *a posteriori* a dialectic process of already complete training. Here, one sees Hegel's fundamentally affirmative and bourgeois characteristic of dialectics. Marx, on the other hand, attributes a basically revolutionary role to the theory which understands past history, so that it itself must be included dialectically and practically in the yet unfinished process of the training of man. (Schmied-Kowarzik 1983, 36).

According to this conception of dialectics, it is perfectly legitimate to consider the pedagogical work of Paulo Freire as a particular manifestation of dialectical thought. Paulo Freire captures this historical and political feeling of knowledge and of educational theory, this "critical and revolutionary role" (Marx 1980 1:17) that Marx, in the postface to the second edition of *Capital*, attributes to theory.

Pedagogical theories suffer, together with practice, from certain distortions which can completely disfigure them. Thus, the word *dialogue* can hide elements such as complacency and complicity, in which the demands and the compromise with teaching content and education completely disappear. The word *dialogue* can also be used as a pretext for absenteeism or a negative form of domination, allurement, and seduction, with the aim of reaching a false conclusion, a unity without tensions, or a dialogue without opposition.

The pedagogy of dialogue has made an enormous contribution to the development of contemporary pedagogy and to the understanding of the institution of school. It has demystified the natural superiority of the master, and the idea of the moral superiority of some individuals over others either because they have superior positions or because they are more competent. In this aspect, the pedagogy of dialogue has made a great advance in relation to the critique of bourgeois education which was started by Marxist analysis in the second half of the nineteenth century. However, in the twentieth century, *dialectical pedagogy* has gone further than the *pedagogy of dialogue.* Dialectical pedagogy has looked at the relationships of education and society differently as it has placed the theme of power as a central theme of pedagogy.

The question of education was never separate from the question of power. Those who still insist that education is a technical question are, in fact, hiding a political project behind their technical argument. Education has always been the extension of a political project. It is, thus, that we find it as much in Plato as in Jean-Jacques Rousseau and John Dewey.

The relationship between education and power has accompanied the development of all history of pedagogical ideas. What is new in each period is that this relationship is seen in a different way and provokes new questions. Education is not a process that is always repeated in the same way. There is a historical reading which is different in each epoch from that which one understands and from that which one desires of education.

Modern pedagogies—both traditional and new kinds—have excessively centered education on the bipolar relationship between the educator and the pupil. Even the most recent pedagogies, which have discussed directivity and nondirectivity, have failed to escape this reductionism.

The contributions from political science, economics, and sociology have gradually enabled educational systems to be focused from a new perspective, that of educating the educators. The school is no longer considered to be an island of purity dreamed of by educators who had seen education as the way of redemption for humanity. In a world in which social, ethnic, and cultural conflicts are more and more visible, the school cannot remain immune. Education has now become the arena in which education itself is denounced, and the school has become an institution in conflict like any other. The established powers fear the school, mainly the university, because of its critical potential, and because of its capacity for social mobilization. This conflict is visible today in the fact that the school, organized as an apparatus of reproduction, is rethinking society, and uniting *pedagogical and social struggles.*

There is a crisis as to the goals of education, which is not merely a reflection of the crisis of society. The crisis of education is a result of the reeducation of educators as trained and professional educators, in a period in which they stopped being schoolmasters to become badly paid teachers of the masses. After learning from the streets, educators have discovered that they had excessive confidence in the school and in school reforms. Thus, they asked themselves about their functions within society and about the aims of their practices. This question cannot be resumed just in knowing whether education reproduces or can transform society. The relationship between education and power is much more complex.

Normally, when one talks about power, one immediately thinks about political power, that

> . . . some wish to conquer, others struggle, some resign themselves to it, others fear it or hate it." (Lebrun 1981, 9) Power can be defined as the capacity, the potency, and the virtuality of putting an act into practice, even if it never takes place. Power is "the name attributed to a group of relationships, which are always bustling around everywhere throughout the social body: pedagogical power, patriotic power, police power, the foreman's power, the power of the psychoanalyst, the power of the priest, etc. etc. (Lebrun 1981, 20)

Hegel says that the history "of man" [sic] is the history of his freedom. Agreeing with Hegel—but not with his perception of history of man and not women—we can say that the twentieth century has represented, in this history of freedom, the century of the discovery of the plot behind power, the century of attention to power and domination. This is the century of awareness of rights, exactly when they were most disrespected. As the last century was the century of the natural science, this has been the century of the human and the social sciences. It is not yet the century of the creation of rights, just of awareness and of the defense of human rights. In this century, power—economic power especially—has been concentrated more and more in the hands of fewer and fewer people, even in the richest countries. Power has been discovered and analyzed, not just in its negative sense, of curtailing freedom, but also in the sense of its possibilities and projects.

All pedagogy refers to practice and intends to be put into practice. It makes no sense without practice, as it is the science of education. To act pedagogically is to put theory into practice *par excellence*. It is to discover and elaborate instruments of social action. In doing so, one becomes aware of the essential unity between theory and practice. Pedagogy, as the theory of education, cannot abstract itself from the intended practice. Pedagogy is, above all, a theory of praxis.

In pedagogy, the practice is the horizon, the aim of the theory. Therefore, the educationalist lives the instigating dialectic between his or her daily life—the *lived school* and the *projected school*—which attempts to inspire a new school. Pedagogical theory attempts to educate individuals as a point on the horizon but never a finished process because education is really an unending process. Educators look forward to a new reality which doesn't yet exist but which they wish to create. Education is at the same time promise and project. It is also a Utopia.

1

Dialectics: Conception and Method

In ancient Greece, the word dialectic expressed a specific manner of argumentation which consisted of discovering the contradictions which were contained in the reasoning of the opponent, thus denying the validity of his argument and surpassing it by another synthesis.

Socrates (479–399 B.C.) was considered to be the greatest dialectician of ancient Greece. Using systematic and methodical doubt, he proceded by analysis and synthesis, elucidating the terms of the questions in dispute, enabling truth to be born as if it were a birth in which he—the master—were just an instigator and provoker, and the disciple were the true discoverer and creator.

However, dialectics precedes Socrates.

Lao Tsé, author of the famous book *Tao tö King* (The Book of Tao), who lived seven centuries before Christ, is considered to be the precursor of dialectics, not because he elaborated his own laws, but because he incorporated them into his doctrine. In the form that it has reached our own days—as the logic inherent in nature, men,

knowledge, and society logic began with Zenon of Elea (340–263 B.C.)
who was well-known for his numerous paradoxes as well as his belief in dialectics as a philosophy of appearances.

Another pre-Socratic philosopher who started dialectics is
Heraclitus of Ephesus (535–463 B.C.) He believed that reality was a
constant future, in which the struggle of opposites is prevalent—
cold-heat, life-death, good-bad, health-illness, each one transforming
into the other. He said that everything changes so quickly that it is
never possible to bathe twice in the same river. The second time, the
river will not be the same, and we ourselves will have changed.

In contrast to Heraclitus, Parmenides of Elea believed that
movement was an illusion and that everything was immutable.

As we can see, the question from which dialectics originated is
that of the *explanation of the movement* and of the transformation
of things. In the metaphysical vision of things—to which dialectics
is opposed—the universe is presented as an "agglomeration of distinct things or entities, and though they are related to each other each
has its own exclusive individuality, which is independent of all other
things or entities." (Prado, Jr. 1952, 1:11) Dialectics considers that all
things are in motion, and all things are related to each other.

For Plato (420–348 B.C.), dialectics were the manner in which
one ascended to the intelligible, a *method of the rational deduction*
of things. This dialectic movement first allowed one to pass from
multiplicity to unity and, second, to discriminate between various
ideas and not confuse them. Plato used dialectics as a research technique which was applied through the collaboration of two or more
people, who would proceed through questions and replies. Knowledge should grow from this encounter as well as from collective reflection and the dispute, but not from isolation. This process would
have two key moments. The first consists of uniting disperse things
into a single idea, clarifying them and making them communicable.
The second consists in newly dividing the idea into its parts.

For Aristotle (385–322 B.C.)—whom Marx (1980 1:465) called
"the greatest thinker of ancient times"—dialectics were merely an
auxiliary to philosophy. He reduced it to a critical activity. It was
not, however, a method through which one would reach the truth. It
was just an appearance of the philosophy, a logic of the probable. For
Aristotle, the dialectic method did not lead to knowledge, but to dispute, probability, and opinion.

Aristotle managed to conciliate Heraclitus and Parmenides
with his theory on the *act* and the *potency*. According to this theory,
changes exist, but they are just updatings of potentialities which al-

ready existed but were not yet released. The pupil would be potentially educated. The education of mankind would be the process through which individuals release all their potentialities.

In the third century after Christ, with the reemergence of Platonism, the debate surrounding dialectics was also renewed. Plotinus (203–259) considered it to be part of philosophy and not just a method. However, the sense of dialectics as a method predominated in the Middle Ages as it was classified beside *rhetoric* and *grammar* as a liberal art—that is, a means of discerning the true from the false.

The philosophy considered to be a slave of theology by the Church had a low opinion of dialectics, and pejoratively compared it to sophism. In the words of Leandro Konder,

> The metaphysical conception prevailed throughout history because it corresponded, in societies divided into classes, to the interests of the dominating classes, who were always interested in making what was working now last forever. They are always interested in tying up values and concepts, like existing institutions, to prevent people from giving in to the temptation of wanting to change the existing social regime. (1981, 9)

At the beginning of the Modern Age, dialectics was considered to be useless as it was believed that Aristotle had said all that there is to say about about logic, and that there was nothing to add. Dialectics would be limited to the syllogism of one kind of logic, a logic of appearances, and there would be nothing to add. This was the opinion of Immanuel Kant (1724–1804).

However, René Descartes (1596–1650) made his contribution to the dialectical method. In order to reach the truth, he said, in his *Discourse of the Method*, that it is necessary to proceed by analyses and syntheses—*analysis*, to reach each element of the object or phenomenon studied, and *synthesis* for the reconstitution of the whole. As we shall see, Karl Marx (1818–1883) also suggested, in his dialectic method, that we should proceed through analysis and synthesis, respectively calling them "method of research" and a "method of exposition."

The dialectic conception of history, as opposed to the metaphysical conception of the Middle Ages, began to take shape with the Swiss social philosopher Jean-Jacques Rousseau (1712–1779). For Rousseau, all people are born free, and only a democratic organization of society will allow individual human beings to develop fully. The individual is conditioned by society.

However, it is only with Friedrich Hegel (1770–1831) that dialectics returned to be a central theme of philosophy. Hegel conceived it as "a scientific application of conformity to the laws, which are inherent to nature and to thought, the natural way of the determinations of knowledge, things, and, in general terms, of all which is finite." (Lalande 1960, 227) Dialectics, according to him, is the negative moment of all reality, that which has the possibility of not being, of denying itself. However, for Hegel, reason is not just the understanding of reality as Kant wanted, but reality itself. The rational is real, and the real is rational. The idea—the reason—is the world itself in evolution. The change of the world of ideas is the actual change in history and in the world. Because of this, universal history is, at the same time, the domain of the mutable, and the manifestation of reason.

Hegel arrived at the real starting from the abstract. Reason dominated the world, and has, as its function, unification, conciliation, and the maintenance of the order of the whole. This reason is dialectics—that is, it proceeds through unity and opposition of opposites. Thus, Hegel takes up, again, Heraclitus's concept of unity of opposites.

Hegel conceived the rational process as a dialectic process in which contradiction is not considered to be illogical and paradoxical, but is considered to be the real engine of thought, and, at the same time, the engine of history, as history is no more than the manifestation of ideas. Thought is not considered to be a static entity. It evolved through contradictions which have been surpassed, from that of the thesis (affirmation) to that of the antithesis (negation), and thence to synthesis (conciliation). A proposition (thesis) cannot exist without opposition to another proposition (antithesis). The first proposition will be modified in this process, and a new proposition will come about. The antithesis is contained in the thesis itself, which is, therefore, contradictory. The conciliation existing in the synthesis is provisional, as it, in itself, will be transformed into a new thesis.

With Ludwig Feuerbach (1804–1872), dialectics gained a new defender. For Feuerbach, mankind projects into heaven the dream of justice that he can never make happen on earth—that is, the poor man has a rich God. Therefore, God is an imaginary projection of humanity which believes it has been deprived of something, thus becoming alienated. Therefore, to deny the existence of God is to affirm oneself as a human being.

MARXIST DIALECTICS

However, it was just with Marx and Friedrich Engels (1820–1895) that dialectics acquired a philosophical (material dialectics) and scientific (historical materialism) status.

Marx renewed Hegel's idealism with materialistic realism.

In the social production of their lives, men contract determined necessary relationships independent of their will. These are the relationships of production which correspond to a determined phase of the development of their productive material force. The whole of these relationships of production form the economic structure of society, the real base on which the legal and political superstructure will be built and which will have determined corresponding forms of social consciousness. The means of production of material life conditions the general process of social, political and spiritual life. It is not the consciousness of man that determines his being, but, on the contrary, it is his social being that determines his consciousness. (Marx and Engels 1977a, 1:301)

Hegel's dialectics were limited to the world of the spirit. Marx inverted this, introducing it into the material. For Marx, dialectics explained the evolution of the material, of nature, and of mankind itself. It is the science of the general laws of movement, both in the external world and in human thought. This Hegelian origin of Marxist thought is recognised by Lenin when he affirms in his *Philosophic Notebooks* (Lenin 1973, 1700), the *Capital* cannot be understood without first having read and understood all of Hegel's *Logic*.

For Marx and Engels, the principles of Hegelian dialectics are pure laws of thought. Leonardo Konder states, "It was necessary to avoid the dialectics of human history being analysed as if they had absolutely nothing to do with nature, as if man did not have an irreducibly natural dimension and had not begun his trajectory in nature." (1981, 9)

Marx's dialectics is not merely a method to arrive at the truth. It is a conception of man, society, and the realtionship between man and the world.

In opposition to the idealistic philosophers, Marx doesn't start off from a conceptual scheme, which is theoretically made up a priori, trying to identify the essence. Neither does he take, as a starting point, phenomena which are isolated in themselves, as the empiricists did. He criticises both of these positions and takes a new path.

This is particularly seen in *Capital*. Marx is worried about understanding the process of the historical formation of the capitalist mode of production, not as if it were a finished form of the relationship between man and society, but rather as a *fieri*, on a becoming. For Marx, facts in themselves do not exist differently to empiricism, which wants to make us believe in the existence of facts which can be examined neutrally and disconnected from the historico-economic, psychological, and political contexts of humanity. It is not the human consciousness, as idealism believes, nor pure reality, as empiricism believes, but mankind itself which acts as beings in producing itself, through its own activity and its own way of life—that is, through the means of production of mankind's material life. The condition for mankind to become individuals—because each person is not an adult but becomes one—is that of work. Mediation between mankind and the world is made though material activity.

> To Hegel, the life-process of the human brain, i.e., the process of thinking, which, under the name "the Idea," he even transforms into an independent subject, is the demiurgos of the real world, and the real world is only the external, phenomenal form of "the Idea" with me, on the contrary, the ideal is nothing else than the material world reflected by the human mind, and translated into the forms of thought. (Marx 1906, 25)

What distinguished Marx and Hegel in this point is the explanation of movement. Both argue the point that movement takes place through the opposition of contrary elements—that is, through contradiction. However, while Hegel localizes contradictory movement in logic, Marx places it right inside the thing itself, in the phenomenon, material, or thought. Mao Tse-tung (1893–1976) summarized Marx's thinking in this respect.

> The material-dialectic conception understands that, in the study of the development of a phenomenon, one should start from its internal content and its relationships with other phenomena, that is, one should consider the development of phenomena as being their own necessary and internal movement. Each phenomenon will find itself in its movement, in connection and interaction with other phenomena which surround it. The fundamental cause of the development of phenomena is

not external but internal: it is to be found in the contradiction which is inside the phenomena. Inside all phenomena there are contradictions, thus their movement and development. (Tse-tung 1979, 32)

This, however, has nothing to do with knowing just how dialectics of knowledge takes place and even less to do with reducing the dialectics of nature to pure knowledge, as Hegel, for whom the world was no more than a succession of ideas, thought. Hegel, as Marx said, imagined that the world was world "through the movement of thought, but in reality he does no more than systematically reconstruct and, in relation to the absolute method, use the thoughts which have nested in the head of all men." (Marx 1965, 104)

Here, Marx doesn't want to deny the value and the necessity of subjectivity in knowledge. The world is always a vision of the world, the world reflected. However, it doesn't have an existence just in the idea. Its existence is real, material, and independent of the knowledge of this or that man. Dialectics is not a spiritual movement that operates inside human understanding. There is a reciprocal determination between the ideas of the human mind and the real conditions of man's existence.

What is essential is that dialectic analysis understands the manner in which the conditions of social existence and the different modalities of consciousness are reciprocally related, linked and determined. There is no question of giving autonomy to one or another dimension of social reality. It is clear that the modalities of consciousness are a part of the conditions of social existence. (Marx 1979, 23)

Marx did not just turn Hegelian logic "upside down" (1980, 1:12). He made profound innovations, thereby proving its veracity, and applied it to social, economic and political reality. As Henri Lefèbvre said, "the Marxist method insists, much more clearly than previous methodologies, on an essential fact: the reality to be reached through analysis, to be reconstituted through the exposition (synthesis), is always a reality in movement." (Lefébvre 1974, 36). Dialectics considers each object with its own characteristics, its own future, its own contradictions. As far as dialectics is concerned, there are no universal rules *more mathematico,* as Descartes (1971) wanted, which guarantee that, after their application, we will obtain dialectic products.

From the Marxist point of view, dialectics focuses on "the things and their conceptual images in their connections, chains, dynamics and their process of genesis and aging" (Engels 1980, 58). Dialectics considers things and phenomena not statically, but in their continuous movement, and in the struggle between their contrary qualities.

Dialectic materialism doesn't believe that material and thinking are isolated, unconnected principles, but rather as aspects of a same indivisible nature. It considers that the form of ideas is as concrete as the form of nature and studies the more general laws of the universe, laws which are common to all aspects of reality, from physical nature to thought, passing through living nature and society. Materialism presupposes that the world is a material reality—nature and society—in which man is present, and that he can get to know it and transform it.

While sciences have, as an objective, a limited aspect of the real, dialectic materialism has as its objective the conception of the world as a whole. However, dialectic materialism doesn't separate itself from science as it is thanks to science that it can develop and renew itself.

As a dialectic conception, Marxism does not separate theory (knowledge) from practice (action). "Theory is not a dogma but a guide for action." (Lenin in Politzer 1970, 23) Practice is the real criterion of the theory, as knowledge starts from practice and returns to it dialectically. Marx expressed himself in the following way in his *Second Thesis on Feuerbach:* "The question of knowing whether human thought can have an objective truth or not is not a theoretical but rather a practical question. It is in the praxis that man should demonstrate the truth, that is, the reality and power, the earthly characteristics of his thinking. The dispute on the reality or nonreality of his thinking isolated from praxis is a purely scholastic question." (Marx-Engels 1977, 12)

Because dialectics considers things and phenomena as a unity of contraries, in a chain of relationships, modifications, and continuous movement, it oppose metaphysics. Dialectics admits rest and the separation between the diverse aspects of the real as relative. Only movement is absolute, as it is constant in all processes.

Starting from the simplest element of production, which is that of goods, Marx is able to postulate general hypotheses on the dialectics of man and nature, thereby accomplishing his proposal of "man's reflections on the forms of social life." (Marx 1906, 1:87) However, as Kosik observes, "the structure of *Capital* is not a structure of logical categories to which the reality investigated and its elaboration may be submitted. The scientific reality analysed is that which is adequately expressed in the dialectic pronouncement, guided and possible to fulfill in a determined corresponding logical structure (Kosik 1969, 162). Going through the contradictions of the capitalist system of production in his massive study, the categories which form the framework of his method come to light. These categories are understood as a unity and opposition of contraries, and they are exhaustively exemplified: the simple versus the complex, the homogenuous versus the heterogenuous, the concrete versus the abstract, the quantitative versus the qualitative, form vesus content, essence versus phenomenon, the particular versus the general, the individual versus the social, necessity versus freedom, possibility versus reality, and more.

In Marx, these categories are not reduced to fixed laws of thought but are made up by fundamental elements of the explanation of the transformation of things.

Engels, in the *Dialectics of Nature* (1976), formulated three general laws of nature: the first law of the conversion of quantity into quality and vice versa; the second law of the interpenetration of opposites (the law of unity and of the strugggle of opposites); and the third law of the negation of negation.

Through the first law, it can be understood that, in nature, qualitative variations can be obtained through quantitive variations. The second law guarantees the unity and continuity of incessant change in nature and in phenomena. The third law guarantees that each synthesis is, in turn, the thesis of a new antithesis which indefinitely reproduces the process.

Taking examples from the natural sciences, Engels tried to demonstrate these general laws. However, criticisms of these classifications soon came as the laws tried to reduce a philosophy of change to fixed codes. Was Engels betrayed by Hegel's idealistic system, or did he fall into the trap of scientific positivism? Whatever was the case, it is not these laws but some general principles or characteristics of dialectics that are accepted today as a starting point by many authors who, after Marx and Engels, took on the difficult task of making more explicit what was found in them in embryonic form (Cheptulin 1982).

THE PRINCIPLES OF DIALECTICS

I would like to talk about principles rather than about laws, as they have much more to do with philosophical presuppositions than with scientific laws.

The First Principle

With the principle of *totality,* everything is related.

For dialectics, nature is presented as a coherent whole in which objects and phenomena are related to each other, reciprocally conditioning each other. The dialectic method takes this reciprocal action into account and examines objects and phenomena in an attempt to understand them in a concrete totality. "The dialectic comprehension of the totality means not just that the parts are in a relationship of internal interaction and connection with each other and with the whole, but also that the whole cannot be petrified in the abstraction which is situated over the parts, seen that the whole creates itself in the interaction of the parts." (Kosik 1969, 42)

The basic presupposition of dialectics is that the sense of things is not obtained from their individuality but, rather, from the totality, which is, according to Kosik, first the reply to the question of "What is reality?" (Kosik 1969, 34). This is what Engels calls "the law of the interpenetration of opposites," in which everything has something to do with everything else, the law of the interaction or universal connection—"the law of the reciprocal action of the universal connection," as it is called by Politzer (1970, 35)

Engels included in this law the unity and struggle of opposites. "Nothing is isolated. Isolating is a fact, a phenomenon, and to preserve it by understanding in this isolation, and to deprive it of sense, explanation and content is to artificially immobilize it, to kill it. This is to transform nature, through metaphysical understanding, into an accumulation of objects where some are exterior to others, into a chaos of phenomena." (Engels in Lefèbvre 1975, 238)

The Second Principle

This is principle of *movement* in which everything is transformed.

Dialectics considers everything in its future. Movement is a quality inherent to everything. Nature and society are not understood as fixed entities, but in continuous transformation, never definitively established, and always unfinished. The cause of this struggle is the internal struggle. "Dialectics cannot understand totality as a whole which is already made and formalized." (Kosik 1969, 49) This is what Engels calls the "law of negation of negation," and what Politzer calls "the law of universal transformation and incessant development," which is also called "the law of negation or surpassing."

This is the law of universal movement. As Leandro Konder observes,

It takes into account the fact that the general movement of reality makes sense, that is to say, it is not an absurdity, it is not exhausted in irrational, unintelligible contradictions, nor is it lost in the eternal repetition of the conflict between theses and antitheses, between affirmations and negations. An affirmation necessarily engenders its negation, but the negation is not prevalent as such: both the affirmation and the negation are renewed and what finally prevails is a synthesis, a negation of the negation. (Konder 1981, 59)

Life produces death; heat can be understood only in function of cold; and the new is born from the old.

The Third Principle

This one is that of *qualitative change.*

The transformation of things does not take place in a circular process of eternal repetition, or a repetition of the old. Qualitative changes can operate through an accumulation of quantitative elements. "The classic example is that of water: when it is being heated, the temperature goes up progressively, an elevation which constitutes a quantitative variation. But the moment comes when the temperature is constant and a qualitatively different phenomenon will take place, that of boiling." (Foulquié 1974, 62)

This is what Engels calls "the law of the conversion of the qualtity into quality or vice versa" or, according to others, "the law of leaps." Starting from a certain threshold of quantitative changes, a passing from quantity to quality takes place. For example, a small village can gradually transform into a big city.

The Fourth Principle

This is about *contradiction* and the unity and struggle of opposites.

The transformation of things is possible only because opposing forces coexist in their own interior and simultaneously move toward unity and opposition. It is this which is called "contradiction," and which is universal and inherent to all material and spiritual things. Contradiction is the essence or the fundamental law of dialectics.

It is this fourth principle which has interested so many researchers into dialectics in the twentieth century, developing what Engels had just started. The contradictory elements coexist in a structured reality, one not being able to exist without the other. The existence of the opposites is not a logical absurdity. It is founded on reality.

Through the dynamics of the contradictions which exist in each phenomenon or thing, each of the two contradictory aspects tends to transform itself into its opposite, under certain conditions. "Unity (coincidence, identity, equivalence) of the opposites is conditional, temporal, transitory, relative. The struggle of opposites which exclude each other mutually is absolute, like development and movement." (Lenin 1973, 344)

These principles can be applied to material elements, to human society, and to our own knowledge. This is why dialectics can be subdivided into three levels, as Ernest Mandel shows.

1. *Dialectics of nature,* which is entirely objective, that is, independent of the existence of man's projects, intentions, or motivations;
2. *Dialectics of history,* generally objective as a starting point, but in which men can intervene with a new project for society, the concrete fulfillment of which is connected to objective, preexisting material conditions which are independent of the will of men; and
3. *Dialectics of knowledge,* the result of a constant interaction between the objects to be known and the action of the subjects who are trying to understand them. (Mandel 1978, 116)

What are the consequences that dialectics brings for logic—that is, for the structure and functioning of mental processes?

It seems that this question has resulted in considerable errors in the history of Marxism, especially in the period of Stalinism, which attempted to make a mechanical epistemological break between it calls "bourgeois science" and "proletarian science" and between formal logic and dialectic logic.

It is necessary to recognize, together with the eminent Brazilian philosopher, Alvaro Vieira Pinto (1969, 72), that "formal logic is the logic of metaphysics, as dialectic logic is the logic of dialectics," and it is from this that we understand both the distinctions and the complementarity of the two kinds of logic.

The principle which fundamentally distinguishes them is that of contradiction. While *dialectic logic* starts from the principle of contradiction, *formal logic* starts from its opposite—that is, non-contradiction. This is because the first conceives objects and phenomena in movement, and the second conceives of them as static.

Starting from the principle that things and phenomena are static, a thing will always remain equal to itself (the law of identity); a thing cannot be equal to another (the law of non-contradiction); and it is either one thing or another (the law of the excluded third).

This type of logic is certainly valid and true—if, methodologically, we put the movement between parentheses, and if we study the phemonena in an entirely isolated way.

> If it is taken to a deeper level, formal logic doesn't forbid dialectic thinking. On the contrary, it shows its possibility, it opens up to its demands, its sphere, its trajectory: it establishes a foundation for the necessity of this thought. Formal logic defers to dialectics, through the mediation of logic. Then, this movement is inverted, and formal logic appears just as a reduction of content, an elaborated abstraction, a neutral (empty, transparent) element in every investigation. (Lefèbvre 1975, 24)

Nevertheless, formal logic shows that it is capable of classifying and distinguishing objects, but it is insufficent to understand these very objects in their real, incessant movement. Because of this, dialectics does not refuse formal logic, but includes it as an essential part of dialectic logic.

> Dialectic contradiction is a (full, concrete) inclusion of the contradictory elements in each other, and, at the same time, an active exclusion. And the dialectic method is not content just to say that contradictions exist, as sophistry, eclecticism and skepticism are able to say the same thing. The dialectic method attempts to capture the connection, unity and movement that engender, oppose and make the contradictory elements clash, that break them or surpass them. (Lefèbvre 1975, 238)

Marx and Engels, exemplifying the *law of contradiction* in social history, show the contradiction that exists between the productive forces and the relationships of production, the contradiction between the exploiting classes and the exploited classes, the contradiction between the economic base and the superstructure, between politics and ideology.

> On reaching a determined phase of development, the material productive forces of society will clash with the existing relationships of production or, if not with their legal representatives,

with the property relationships in which they have developed up until that moment. From being forms of development of the productive forces, these relationships will develop into obstacles to them, and a period of social revolution will thus begin. On changing the economic base, more or less quickly, the whole superstructure which has been built on it will find itself in a state of revolution. (Marx-Engels 1977a, 1:301)

Marx, studying the economic structure of capitalist society, concludes that the basic contradiction of this society is the basic contradiction between the social character of production and the private character of property.

In addition to this general characteristic of contradiction, its universality and the existence of a main contradiction, specific, or particular contradictions exist inside each stage of the process of development of each thing or phenomenon.

As Mao Tse-tung (1979, 30) points out in his study *On Contradiction*, in order to make the essence of each process appear, it is necessary to bring to light the specific character of two aspects of each one of the contradictions of this process—the main aspect and the secondary aspect of each contradiction—in order to verify the reciprocal action of the opposite poles of contradiction and the action of the whole of the contradictions which involve each contradiction or thing.

In every process of development of a phenomenon or thing there will always exist a main contradiction, whose existence determines the existence of others. It is also in this main contradiction that there exists one main aspect and one aspect that is necessarily secondary. It is the main aspect that plays the dominant role in the contradiction.

THE DIALECTIC METHOD

These principles of dialectics did not come about a priori. They are the result of a slow maturing of the development of modern sciences. In Marx's work, they came about only after an exhaustive analysis of the capitalist means of production, and as the consequence of a scientific analysis, as he himself states (Marx 1980, 1:84). It was only after he finished his work, that Marx could see these principles and categories, and demonstrate the path or method that he had followed, and could announce and demonstrate his natural, concrete, nonabstract method.

His total lack of scorn for the traditional academic way of thinking can be seen when he didn't announce in the preface to the first German edition of *Capital* the way in which he would treat the theme of the process of the production of capital. It was only in the postface of the second German edition (1873), after being called by some Comtist critics the greatest idealist philosopher, that he succinctly presents the dialectic fundamentals of his method.

> Of course the method of presentation must differ in form from that of inquiry. The latter has to appropriate the material in detail, to analyze its different forms of development, to trace out their inner connection. Only after this work is done can the actual movement be adequately described. If this is done successfully, if the life of the subject matter is ideally reflected as in a mirror, then it may appear as if we had before us a mere a priori construction. (Marx 1906, 1:25)

Marx formally distinguishes the method of exposition from the method of research. The exposition is the consequence of a previous piece of research of the forms of development and of the existing connections between them.

Marx is the first researcher to adopt the dialectic method formally.

> On studying a determined objective reality, he methodically analyses the contradictory aspects and elements of this reality and considers all the antagonic notions that are at play, but whose tenor no one is still able to discern. After having distinguished the contradictory aspects or elements, not neglecting their connections, and without forgetting that he is working with a reality, Marx finds the reality again in its unity, that is, in the whole of its movement. (Lefèbvre 1974, 34)

By *research method*, Marx means a detailed appropriation of the studied reality. It is the analysis that will bring the internal relationships into evidence, with each element in itself.

Each object of analysis requires a specific approach which is determined by the object itself. Each historical period has its own laws. Because of this, the analysis that is made in philosophy cannot be automatically employed in all the other sciences. The detailed analysis of a thing or phenomenon will show the particular laws that rule the beginning, development, and end of each thing or phenomenon.

By *method of exposition*, Marx understands the reconstitution, or the synthesis of the object or phenomenon under study, as an inverse process, opposed to the first in such a way that the reader will imagine that the author constructed it a priori. In the exposition, the object gradually reveals itself, according to its own peculiarities.

In relation to the form of exposition of the capitalist process of production, Marx observes in chapter 1 of book 3 of *Capital:* "The various forms of capital, as evolved in this book, thus step by step approach the form which they assume on the surface of society, in the action of different capitals upon one another, in competition, and in the ordinary consciousness of the agents of production themselves." (Marx 1906, 3:25)

It is through the dialectic method that the phenomenon or thing under study presents itself to the reader in such a way that he or she will learn about it in its totality. For this, it is necessary to successively make more wide-ranging approximations. This will make it accessible.

In a letter that Karl Marx wrote from London on 18 March 1873 to the Frenchman Maurice La Châtre, he insisted that making his work "accessible to the working class" was, for him, "the greatest motive of all." However, he warned, immediately afterword that his method of analysis and exposition—"a method that I used and one that had still not been applied to economic problems"—did not prevent the reading from being "rather tough." He concluded: "There is nothing I can do about this disadvantage, unless I warn and caution those readers who are anxious for the truth. There is no royal road to to science, and only those who are not afraid of confronting exhaustion to climb up the steep paths might reach their shining peaks." (Marx in Althusser 1979, 1:7)

As Henri Lefèbvre (1974, 35–36) has observed, before Marx, many philosophers had already made a decisive contribution to the formulation of the dialectic method. Among them were Descartes, Kant, and Auguste Comte. However, none of them had realized the importance of the contradiction that is inherent to all phenomena, facts, and things—that is, the positive and the negative, the proletariat and the bourgeoisie, and the being and nonbeing. Hegel discovered this and Marx extended it.

The difference in this particular fact between Hegel and Marx is that Hegel abstractly defines the general contradiction of history and of nature, considering movement as merely a logical transformation of ideas. Marx, on the other hand,

. . . states that the general idea, the method, doesn't dispense with the apprehension, in one's own self, of the object. The method provides just a guide and orientation for the knowledge of reality. In each reality, we need to learn its peculiar contradictions, its own peculiar internal movement, its qualities and its rapid transformations. The logical form of the method should then be subordinate to the content, to the object, to the material studied. It allows us to efficiently tackle its study, capturing the most general aspect of this reality, but never substitutes scientific research by an abstract construction. (Lefèbvre 1974, 38)

At the same time as he moves on from his critique of Hegel, Marx is opposed to vulgar or metaphysical materialism, mainly in the antidialectic form of the philosophizing of Ludwig Feuerbach, who is unable to consider the world as a process, as material involved in incessant development. The thinking of Feuerbach—which Marx in his well-known *Theses on Feuerbach* considers to be vulgar and mechanistic—is still present today in the dogmatic conception of dialectics which leads to a kind of sectarianism. Dogmatism makes do with general ideas and mystified slogans in function of which it schematizes all of reality. Any discussion, debate, and criticism becomes impossible. Mystified dialectics becomes metaphysical. As Politzer (1970, 56) says, "The sectarian reasons as if he himself had learned everything at a single sitting. He forgets that we weren't born revolutionaries; we became revolutionaries. This being so, shouldn't he get much more angry with himself than with other people? The true revolutionary is he who, as a dialectician, sets up favorable conditions for the coming of the new." (1970, 56) Note that Politzer first wrote this in 1935.

In our days, dialectics and the dialectic method have often been enthroned in the capitalist world, and reduced to consumer products, with small groups praising their revolutionary virtues. Dialectic materialism when reduced to ready-make formulas and manuals, will only end up by becoming empty of interest, and generating expectations which fail to correspond to what it really is. As Leonardo Konder states, "the principles of dialectics hardly lend themselves to any kind of codification." (1981, 60)

Presenting what can be called *"the practical rules of dialectic materialism"* always represents a risk of simplification. However, following the didactic pattern of this study, I would like to take this risk and present a summary of these rules as they appear in Henri

Lefèbvre's *Formal Logic, Dialectic Logic* (1975), reminding the reader that this is much more of an orientation than rigid and definitive norms.

These "practical rules" are as follows:

1. Direct oneself to the thing itself. As a consequence, there will be an objective analysis.
2. Learn the whole of the internal connections of the thing, its various aspects and its development and movement.
3. Learn the contradictory aspects and moments, the thing as a whole and the unity of the contradictory elements.
4. Analyze the struggle and the internal conflict of the contradictions, the movement, the tendency, what tends to be and what tends to fall into nothingness.
5. Do not forget that everything is connected to everything else, and that an insignificant, negligible interaction, as it is not essential at a given moment, may become essential at another moment or in another aspect.
6. Do not forget to be alive to the transitions, the transitions of the aspects and contradictions, the way they pass from one to another, and the future transitions.
7. Do not forget that the process of deepening knowledge— which goes from the phenomenon to the essence and from the less profound essence to the more profound essence—is infinite. One should never be satisfied with what has been obtained.
8. Get deeper than the simple observed existence, always get deep into the richness of the content, learn about connections and movement.
9. In certain phases of one's own thinking, this thinking should transform, surpass itself, modify or reject its form, remanage its content, take up again the moments that have passed and look at them again, resee them, repeat them, but just apparently, with the intention of deepening them through taking a step backward toward the previous stages and, sometimes, toward the starting point. (Lefèbvre 1975, 241)

Henri Lefèbvre ends by saying that "dialectic materialism, in this way, will turn out to be at the same time rigorous, as it is connected to universal principles, and more fertile, able to detect all the aspects of things, including the aspects through which things are vulnerable to action." (1975, 241)

DIALECTICS AND TRUTH

When dialectics becomes the fashion—and its defenders present it as the solution for all problems, mystifying it, and ignoring all the concrete conditions of each thing or philosophy—then sectarianism takes over and dialectics loses its sense.

In its mystified form, dialectics became the fashion in Germany because it seemed to transfigure and glorify the existing state of things. In its rational form it is a scandal and abomination to bourgeoisdom and its doctrinaire professors, because it includes in its comprehension and affirmative recognition of the state of things, at the same time also, the recognition of the negation of that state, of its inevitable breaking up, because it regards every historically developed social form as in fluid movement, and therefore takes into account its transient nature not less than its momentary existence, because it lets nothing impose upon it, and is in its essence critical and revolutionary." (Marx 1906, 1:25–126)

Marx tells us that his critique of political economics presents the point of view of the proletariat in the same way that classical economics presents the point of view of the bourgeoisie. Marx never hid the class perspective that oriented his research. He "believes that his science is revolutionary and proletarian, and, as such, is opposed and superior to the bourgeois and conservative science of the classical economists. The break between Marx and his predecessors is for him a break of classes inside history and economic science." (Löwy 1978, 21)

Gramsci, like Marx, warned of a new mystification of dialectics reduced to a "process of reformist evolution." (Gramsci 1968, 253) He was referring to the attempt to weaken dialectics as a theory of contradictions. Marx's philosophy was never an attempt to pacifically solve the existing contradictions in history and society.

Would dialectics be a particular theory of science and of knowledge which was aimed just at sustaining the socialist process, and, with its success or failure, would tend to disappear? Or would it be a valid instrument, above any ideology, which would reach the truth?

These questions have been widely discussed inside Marxism. The objection which is made is always the same: if dialectics represents the point of view of the proleteriat which asks: How can we then avoid relativism? How can we reconcile this partisan characteristic

with the objective knowledge of truth? How can we avoid that which
Michael Löwy calls "relativistic night," (1978, 31) in which all the
cats are dark, and we end up by denying the possibility of objective
knowledge? Löwy asks:

> Why did Marx, Lenin, Gramsci, Mao Tse-tung and others
> choose the viewpoint of the proletariat? And it is he himself
> who replies: "Because the proletariat, the universal class whose
> interest coincides with that of the great majority and whose
> aim is the abolition of all kinds of class domination, is not
> obliged to hide the historical content of its struggle; it is, as a
> consequence, the first revolutionary class whose ideology has
> the possibility of being transparent." (Löwy 1978, 34)

Two pages later, Löwy concludes that

> The point of view of the proletariat is not a suffcient condition
> for the knowledge of objective truth but it is what offers the
> greatest possibility of access to this truth. This is because truth
> is for the proletariat a means of struggle, an indispensable
> weapon for the revolution. The dominant class, the bour-
> geoisie, and also the bureaucrats, in another context, need lies
> in order to maintain their power. The revolutionary proletariat
> needs the truth."

Mikhail Gorbachev would say later, in 1987, that the revolutionary proletariat also needs, "transparency."

The Brazilian philosopher, Caio Prado, Jr., warns the reader of
Dialectics of Knowledge (1952) that, in order to understand dialectics, it is necessary to think dialectically.

On the other hand, another Brazilian philosopher, Gerd A.
Bornheim, states that, "from the historical point of view, when one
considers its genesis, dialectics is pertinent to metaphysics." (1977,
13) Bornheim demands the right to think dialectics metaphysically
and criticizes Engels, who conceives dialectics through laws and di-
ametrically opposes metaphysics to dialectics. Gramsci surpasses
this argument by conceiving dialectics as a philosophy of praxis—a
new way of thinking, and not an old rhetorical technique that "was
just useful to create a cultural conformism and a language for conversation between erudites." (Gramsci 1968, 77)

The dialectic conception of Gramsci is emerging today in the
Third World as a *new weapon for the struggle*, because it doesn't
polemicize but rather serves the elaboration of the critical thought

and self-criticism, and also serves the questioning of the present reality. As the Yugoslav thinker Mihailo Markovic says, "dialectic thought is used to unmask everything that attempts to stop development." (1968, 11)

Dialectics, as different from metaphysics, questions and contests. It constantly demands the reexamination of the theory and the critique of the practice. If it is true that theory is born from practice, and that it travels with it dialectically, trying to establish "the necessary relationship between the existing and the possible, between knowledge of the present and the vision of the future" (Markovic 1968, 13), the dialectic way of thinking will find, among the thinkers who support the point of view of the oppressed, a considerable chance to develop and to place itself more and more at the service of all of humanity.

To dialectically conceive the world does not guarantee revolutionary nor progressive behavior. We can differentiate one conception of the left from a type of behavior of the left—even recognizing all the reservations that these expressions have today in a complex world which cannot be divided into two parts.

Inside Marxist thinking, this distinction seems to be clear. Certain distortions make Marxism, not a revolutionary instrument, but, rather, a conservative instrument. Among these distortions is the so-called academic Marxism, which is mechanistic and vulgar, which has no revolutionary sense, and is often of use just to show off learning.

This bias can be seen particularly in the thinking of certain Marxist economists, who exclude all social and educational vision from Marx's work, reducing it to technical economics. These economists who—as the Brazilian educator and politician Wagner Rossi says, "separate their economics from the social whole" (1978, 1:126)—believe that "educators should concentrate on the development of educational methodologies."

On the contrary, Marx and Engels never denied the importance of the social whole, and, even during their period, they recognized that some of their followers gave more importance to economics than they themselves had done. Moved by the discussion that they had to maintain with their opponents, they needed to state the fundamental points against bourgeois ideology, and did not have time to make other dimensions clear—such as the role of the superstructures, which would later be the main worry of Gramsci.

Dialectics is, necessarily, opposed to dogmatism and reductionism. It is always open and unfinished, and will always surpass itself. All dogmatic thinking is antidialectic. Academic Marxism—reducing

Marx to a code, and transforming his thinking into a law, without adding anything to him—is, therefore, antidialectic. Criticism and self-criticism, on the other hand, are revolutionary. It is, in this manner, that we should understand the Lenin's warning that Marxism is a guide to action, and not a dogma.

With the transformations that took place in Eastern Europe at the end of the 1980s, many beliefs in socialism were destroyed, and socialism suffered a hard blow. Many Marxist intellectuals changed creed because Marxism was really no more than a creed for them. However, those who perused the research developed by Marx found nourishment for their hopes, and were not stunned by the end of socialism. Ideas are just the provisional clothing of the truth. What matters is the truth itself. The political and economic failure of a concrete fulfillment of Marxist thought doesn't invalidate its anthropological perspective for the construction of a society of solidarity.

2

A Critique of Bourgeois Education

Can dialectics inspire a pedagogy? What is a dialectic conception of education?

The answer lies, less in trying to define what this conception is, than in showing how it came about, developed what are today its main themes, and how it appears in the conflict of present-day pedagogies.

This does not mean that we must rethink all the history of educational dialectics because what we use is the viewpoint of dialectics or, rather, a dialectic reading of what education has been until today.

This is what the great Argentinian philosopher and scholar of history, Anibal Ponce, did in 1981. He showed that education, as a social phenomenon connected to the superstructure, can be understood only through a socioeconomic analysis of the society that maintains it. However, this is just the point of view of dialectics confronted by the history of pedagogical practices and educational systems. The value of Anibal Ponce's study is that he showed the

principle of the dialectics of the relationship between the consciousness and the economic structure. He demonstrated how the struggle
for the right to education and to culture has accompanied the struggle for other rights. Education is not separate from the class struggle.

This has nothing to do with systematizing the thinking of Marx
and Engles on education, as Roger Dangeville has done (Marx-Engels
1978); nor the thinking of Gramsci, as Broccoli (1977), Manacorda
(1977), and Lombardi (1971) have done. It also has nothing to do with
rethinking the history of pedagogy from the main outline of dialectics or showing the formation of what can be called a dialectic pedagogy, or pedagogy of work, nor of knowing what socialists think
about education. This would be the dialectic point of view of the history of pedagogical thinking or the pedagogical thinking of dialectics.

Four authors in this area must be mentioned.

Bogdan Suchodolski

In his book *Pedagogy and the Great Pedagogical Currents*, published in France in 1969, Suchodolski studies the nature of pedagogical problematics, opposing, in the history of pedagogical ideas, the
pedagogy of the essence, connected to the rationalist or Christian
tradition including Plato, Augustine, Thomas Aquinas, and Jesuits,
Comenius, Kant, and Fichte; and the pedagogy of existence from
Rousseau, Kirkegaard, and Nietzsche.

However, it was only in 1961, with the publication of his
study *A Marxist Theory of Education*, that Suchodolski lays out the
fundamentals of the Marxist theory of education and culture. He is
mainly worried about discovering the direction of socialist dialectics in Poland without, on the one hand, ignoring the progress that
has been reached by pedagogical sciences—the inheritance of the
whole world—in the bourgeois period, and, on the other hand, without forgetting to respond to the problems which the new society
has given to education. He defends the thesis that socialist pedagogy is the historical development of the theory and the practice of
education, solving the problems and the conflicts that idealist bourgeois education has put before the present-day society. First, he describes the pedagogical theory of Marx and Engels, especially in its
philosophical and social character. Then, he details the role of human activity, or work, in education, emphasizing the importance
that the socialist revolution has had in the world for the development of education.

Mario Alighiero Manacorda

In English title of the Book (1969), Manacorda attempts to demonstrate the existence of a Marxist conception of education that he distinguishes from the conception based on the Marxist tradition that developed in the socialist countries. He begins by examining the texts of Marx which explicitly talk about education. Although there are not very many of these writings, he gives them great importance, as they maintained a coherence through thirty years, and coincided with the crucial stages of Marx's works and of the history of the workers' movement. He particularly develops the concepts of work and of omnilaterality, confronting the thinking of Marx and of Gramsci with modern pedagogies.

Maurice Dommanget

The third—and undoubtedly one of the pioneers in the study of the main sources of socialist pedagogy—is Maurice Dommanget (1972). He tries to clearly and didactally outline the history of socialist pedagogical thinking, supplying a large amount of information about eighteen writers, including a bibliography and references that stimulate new researchers to continue the search for the roots of socialist education.

Wagner Rossi

This challenge was accepted by Wagner Rossi in his *Pedagogy of Work* (1981). As he states in the preface to the first volume, he "recovers from the history of education the contributions which, as they failed to attend to the interests of the dominators, were obscure, relegated to the second league or even entirely forgotten." (Rossi 1981 1:11)

Using the work of Dommanget as a base, Rossi identifies the roots of socialist education by looking at revolutionary pedagogical proposals proposed from utopian thinkers up to Lenin. Rossi's second volume "begins with the implantation of the first revolutionary socialist government in 1917, and discusses some of the paths which have been followed by revolutionary education up to our days. Some of the most developed syntheses of socialist education are discussed, from Pistrak to Makarenko, with the work school in the Soviet Union, right up to the dialogical and problematizing pedagogy of Paulo Freire." (Rossi 1981, 2:9)

And Another Path

In summary, we must recognize the great importance of these authors and others in the formulation of a dialectic conception of education. However, I would like to pursue another path.

Rather than a systematic exposition of the conception that Marx or Marxists have of education, I would like to continue the exposition by replying to worries, which can be made into questions such as:

- Can dialectics inspire a conception of education?
- What would be the fundamental characteristics of this conception?
- In what ways are the dialectic and bourgeois conceptions of education different?
- Is there, in Marxist dialectics, a particular conception of man and of society which give rise to a pedagogical project?

These and other questions will now be looked at as we begin again from the place where we interrupted the discussion of dialectics to look for its pedagogical extension.

WORK AS AN ANTHROPOLOGICAL PRINCIPLE

Marx never considered himself to be a philosopher in the traditional sense of the term, and his work cannot be considered as just a pure critical theory. We surely find more in it than just a critique or pure speculation.

Marx's theory equally supposes a *new anthropology*. For Marx, mankind is not just a piece of finished data. Humans produce themselves and determine themselves, when placing himself as a being in transformation or as a *being of praxis*. The development of mankind in totality will happen only when the alienation which is the result of class antagonism is overcome. Because of this, Marx says that humans can find themselves even in their own prehistory (Marx-Engels 1977a, 1:302).

It is through revolutionary praxis, as he states in his *Third Thesis on Feuerbach*, that mankind transforms itself, or, as Bogdan Suchodolski (1972) would say, people give essence to their unfinished existence.

At other times, Marx calls this activity the formation of mankind, social practice, or social work, thereby distinguishing it, without separating it, from the so-called productive praxis.

> When talking about the alteration of circumstances and of education, materialist doctrine forgets that the circumstances are altered by men and that the educator himself must be educated. Materialist doctrine should, therefore, separate society into two parts, one of which is placed above society. The coincidence of the modification of circumstances with human activity or an alteration in oneself can only be rationally understood as revolutionary praxis. (Marx-Engels 1977, 12)

For Marx, educator and pupil educate themselves together in the revolutionary praxis, through the intermediary of the world which they are transforming. This praxis should be understood as social work or, quite simply, as work.

The reeducation of the educators becomes the expression of a conception of the world, of a new anthropology, whose fundamental element is the work or transformation of the world. "The way in which individuals manifest their lives reflects exactly what they are to a great extent. What they are coincides, therefore, with their production, both with what they produce, and in the way in which they produce it. What individuals are depends, therefore, on the material conditions of their production." (Marx 1979, 46).

This is the anthropological basis of the Marxist conception of education. Individuals are what they make of themselves socially. They create themselves through their acts.

> In the social production of their own existence, men enter into necessary, determined relationships which are independent of their own will; these relationships of production correspond to a determined degree of development of their productive material force. The whole of these relationships of production make up the economic structure of society, the real base upon which the legal and political superstructure is built and to which determined social forms of consciousness correspond. The means of production of material life condition the process of social, political and intellectual life. (Marx 1979, 82)

For Marx, mankind is the process and product of its acts. These acts—which humanity constructs in each person—are not isolated acts and do not happen spontaneously. They are intimately related and conditioned by the action of each individual, by nature, by society, and by history. In this totality, what primarily unites human beings is the search for the proper means to guarantee their existence.

Mankind's praxis is, however, primarily historical, and the way in which people relate to each other and attempt to maintain the species is in *work*. It is through work that they discover themselves as a being of praxis, as individuals, and as collective beings—a unity of opposites.

The debate surrounding the relationship between humans and nature began before Marx, who singled out three of those authors for special criticism. It is on the limitations which he finds in their work that he bases his conceptions. Those three authors were Baruch Spinoza (1632–1677), who conceived of nature as a substance totally independent of man; Johann Gottlieb Fichte (1762–1814), who denied the autonomy of the subject, which he called the consciousness of oneself confronting nature; and Friedrich Hegel (1770–1831), who identified the ideas of the unity of substance (nature) and of the subject.

Marx believed that Hegel failed to identify what the relationship between human beings and nature was because he had no historical method of research and remained in pure metaphysical speculation. The starting point, he said, is neither substance—as vulgar materialists think—nor is it the consciousness of oneself, as the idealists believe. The starting point is human work. Individuals are, thus, simultaneously autonomous and social beings.

Opposing himself to nature, mankind develops its own strengths. By denying nature, they produce culture and humanize nature. "Man only develops through contradictions; soon, man can be made up through the nonhuman, initially mixed with him, and which, soon after, is differentiated from him by means of a conflict, and then dominates him through the resolution of this conflict." (Lefèbvre 1974:46)

The existence of nature outside the human race is an objective piece of data, but nature cannot be understood without humans. In the same way, people cannot be understood when separated from nature.

> Man, however, only develops in connection with this other element which he has inside himself: nature. His activity is only made and progresses by making a human world come out from the breast of nature. This is the world of products of man's hand and thought. . . . In the course of his development, man expresses himself and creates himself through this otherness, which consists of innumerable things which he has moulded. Becoming conscious of himself, as far as human thought and in-

dividuality are concerned, man cannot separate himself from objects, goods and products. He can only distinguish himself from them and even oppose them in a dialectic relationship: in a unity. . . . Man becomes human through the creation of a human world. In his work and through his work, man becomes himself, without confusing himself with his work, but without separating himself from his work. (Lefèbvre, 1974, 50–52)

It is only in this *human-world dialectic* in which people are opposed to nature, that they develop their own capacities, strengths, and senses. It is also the act of developing subjective forces that they dominate nature. Nature is certainly outside people, but it cannot be understood without them. What we know about nature is the result of a practical and theoretical practice, and a struggle between human beings and nature. The humanization of nature is made through the naturalization of man.

Work fulfills people, but it can also alienate them. Marx, In explaining the formation of the *surplus value*—the supplement of work that the capitalist does not pay and which is his source of profit or accumulation of capital—Marx elaborates on the concept of *productive work*, saying that, until then, it had been studied in abstract, and "apart from its historical forms." (Marx 1906, 1:557) Marx says that, in the capitalist form of production,

> . . . The labourer produces, not for himself, but for capital. It no longer suffices, therefore, that he should supply produce. He must produce surplus-value. That labour alone is productive, who produces surplus-value for the capitalist, and thus works for the expansion of capital. . . . To be a productive labourer is, therefore, not a piece of luck, but a misfortune. (Marx 1906, 1:558)

The technical conception of Marx on what work is leaves no doubts. However, a definition of what productive work is, from a viewpoint of quality of work rather than that of economics, implies a definition of *human necessities* and the *necessities of capital*. Although it is extremely difficult to define exactly what these necessities are, Lúcio Kowarick states,

> . . . at least in thesis, it seems possible to get an idea through a scientific analysis and not just through an ethical-moral analysis, of a number of goods and services more directed toward

satisfying human necessities as against alternatives more directed toward the maintenance and expansion of the capitalist system. (Kowarick in Villalobos 1978, 91)

The productive worker is set much more against he who has *spare time*—which is another notion developed by Marx—than against the unproductive worker. The unproductive class has much more free time as its material existence is guaranteed by the social division of work.

In the social division of work, great masses of workers, both manual and intellectual, alienate their force of work through the simple need to survive. Indeed, the worker becomes a merchandise, whose value depends merely on the amount of money—the measure of value—for which he can be exchanged. This amount is defined as "the average amount of work socially necessary to reproduce oneself. As a merchandise, people have no value in themselves. Their value derives from the relationship of exchange.

> The worker always leaves the process as he entered it, a personal source of wealth, but deprived of all the means to turn it to his own advantage. Once he alienates his own work before beginning work, once he becomes a property of the capitalist and is incorporated into capital, his work during the process is always materialized in products foreign to him. As the production process is at the same time a process of the consumption of the workforce by the capitalist, the product of the worker is continually transformed not just into a merchandise, but also into capital, into a value that sucks out the creative force of value and makes it into means of subsistence that buy people, and into means of production that use the people who produce. (Marx 1980, 1:664)

The bourgeoisie, freed through the *alienation* of the work force of the masses, does not accumulate merely material capital but also cultural capital.

Education and science become private property, and the monopoly of capital. As Roger Dangeville says,

> The whole question of education can be reduced, when all is said and done, to the relationship between the work necessary and the time for free work, to expand and not to do nothing, as the present-day society of surplus value suggests. In other

words, it can be reduced to the appropriation of free time by the bourgeoisie or by the proletariat. The antagonism between work time and free time can only be resolved by making manual work generalized for everyone. This would give everyone time free to develop. (Dangeville in Marx-Engels 1978, 48)

Under the general law of capitalism, to generate the maximum profit from the minimum expenses, the worker needs to be separated from the product. Education, science, intelligence, and art are free—but just for the capitalist.

From the brutal methods of exploitation of the capitalism of the nineteenth century, which inspired Marx to make his analyses, we have moved in the twentieth century to rationalized methods and to mass production, dividing work into multiple phases and making it repetitive, impersonal, and mechanical. If the worker of today is able to escape for a period of time from the domination of the exhausting production line, he or she is no less exploited in free time. Through the creation and incentivation of all types of necessities, workers become slaves of a society which forces them into the consumption which merely suits the interests of the capitalists.

If we count the overtime and the commuting, the so-called free time, and the second job which the majority of workers now have, free time is no more than that for sleeping, which is necessary to recover physical strength.

WORK AS AN EDUCATIVE PRINCIPLE

The social development of people under capitalism is undeniable. In spite the alienation it causes and the high degree of exploitation, the system of capitalist production is a superior way of cooperation when compared to previous forms, this is because the product in capitalist society is more socialized and has a more considerable influence on the life of mankind in society.

This socialization of mankind is a primordial condition for the transformation of capitalism and its historical surpassing as a way of life and production. Under capitalism, social wealth is, on the one hand, represented by things and goods, and, on the other hand, it is characterized as a value of the amount of work to be commanded. Human evolution cannot merely be conceived as the development of this social wealth, in the sense of universalization of the goods and the faculties of all the individuals (Coriat 1976). Therefore, the development of human faculties in the work of the domination of nature is a profoundly pedagogical movement.

Marx integrates education and professional training—concepts which, in the idealistic German pedagogy, were always separated. He criticises the social division of work, which subjugates humans to machines, and launches the bases of a theory of personality which erases specialization. People's faculties should be developed in all areas of social life—that is, at work, in politics, in economics, in culture, and so on.

He developed these ideas in three different periods. The first was in the *Manifesto* (1847–1848), which was preceeded by a draft made by Engels in 1847, entitled *Principles of Communism*. Afterward, in the "Instructions to the Delegates of the International Workers Association Congress" in Geneva in 1866, his main topics were taken up again in *Capital* (1866–1867). Finally, came his *Critique of the Program of Gotha* in 1875. These explicitly pedagogical writings of Marx are always connected to political programs, and these three texts are the essential texts of Marx on teaching.

Right from the writing of *Manifesto* (1848), Marx and Engels understood that education and work were closely linked. They stated that, when the workers took power, they would introduce *free public education*, they would eliminate the factory work of children, and they would unite education with production.

As Marx observed in his *Critique of the Program of Gotha*, large-scale industry in its present form makes the prohibition of children working a "pious desire," and he added that "the combination of productive work with teaching, from a tender age, is one of the most powerful means of transformation of present-day society." (Marx-Engels 1977a, 2:224). Work is a valuable instrument of moral and physical training, as well as serving as a motivation for technical, scientific, and cultural formation, and developing the sense of social responsibility. It is through work that the young person becomes prepared for social life.

Marx recognizes that, in capitalism, the work of children is exploited, and that it should be forbidden by observing a certain age limit. However, he doesn't deny its social virtues because each individual will exercise this activity throughout life.

Bourgeois pedagogy had also worried about establishing the relationship between school and practical activity. However, as it was founded on idealistic philosophy, it could only understand this generic relationship abstractly as a relationship between school and life, and between study and the natural environment.

For Marx, work has a *formative character*. Because of this, he proposes creation of polytechnical, agricultural, and technical schools. *Polytechnical teaching* should take place with a synthesis of theoretical study and practical productive work, and it should transmit the necessary knowledge as well as technical and scientific abilities to understand the production process. It should make the social characteristic of work clear and—within the perspective of the classless society—it should stimulate the free association of individuals.

Bourgeois educationalists considered work in the school as a *bricolage*. Manual work was thought of as a game, a pastime. They believed that work was an instrument of training, but always at a lower level than the theoretical activity of teaching. Sport, music, drawing, and manual work occupy an inferior place inside the information systems of the bourgeois education. Marx associates the productive act with the educative act, and he explains that the unity between education and material production should be admitted as a decisive means for the emancipation of human beings. The worker can only study by working.

This does not mean merely learning a profession but understanding the productive process and the organization of work. For this, it is not enough to just know some techniques, or to know how to handle or operate a machine. Polytechnical teaching has, as its aim, enabling people to understand and to live the socioeconomic structure by taking part in the activity of production, and, thus, to intensify their capacity to act.

The integration between *teaching* and *work* results in an emergence from the growing alienation and reunites individuals with society. This unity, according to Marx, should take place right from childhood. The triple base of education for Marx is intellectual teaching (general culture); physical development (gymnastics and sport); and multiprofessional apprenticeship (technical and scientific). Marx is opposed to precocious specialization as happens with the so-called professionalization, and which is solely reserved for the working class.

Worried about finding replies to the questions of their time, Marx and Engels did not elaborate strategies, neither for education under mature capitalism nor for the socialist education of the future. They merely left us *three great principles:* public education—that is, education for all; free education—that is, education as a duty of the state; and education through work—that is, polytechnical education.

The critique of education and of teaching in bourgeois education in Marx and Engels cannot be reduced to an analysis which is lateral to the critique of classical political economics. In *A Critique of the Rights of Hegel*, Marx condemns hierarchization, bureaucracy, and exams. In *Critique of the Program of Gotha*, he condemns the state's tutelage of education, in the same way that he condemns specialization in *German Ideology*. In this 1846 work—the result of studies in common with Engels—Marx develops the thesis according to which, under the capitalist system of production, the accumulation of wealth and science develops at the same time as does misery and ignorance. The division of society into antagonistic classes makes the working class specialize, and develop no more than one faculty, to the detriment of all human potentialities.

It is in *German Ideology* that Marx and Engels establish the first principles of a *class conception of education*. Bourgeois education is necessarily elitist and discriminating. In order for the children of the dominating classes to be able to study, it is necessary to fail all the others. The so-called high drop-out rate is nothing more than the guarantee for the dominating classes that they will be able to continue to have the power of the monopoly of education.

As the workers do not have the free time for study and research, they are unable to get through the stages of study that the children of the well-to-do classes easily manage to accomplish. As Marx demonstrates in *Capital*, the working conditions in the factories drain the workers of all their physical and intellectual force. "But the intellectual desolation, artificially produced by converting immature human beings into mere machines for the fabrication of surplus value, a state of mind clearly distinguishable from that natural ignorance which keeps the mind fallow without destroying its capacity for development, its natural fertility. . . . " (Marx 1906, 1:436)

These working conditions and the craftiness and swindles of capitalism in relation to compulsory education and workers' education are amply described by Marx in *Capital* from the reports of factory inspectors in England. "Previous to the passing of the amended Factory Act, 1844, it happened, not infrequently, that the certificates of attendance at school were signed by the schoolmaster or schoolmistress with a cross, as they themselves were unable to write." (Marx 1906, 1:437)

As one of these reports stated:

> But it is not only in the miserable places above referred to that the children obtained certificates of school attendance without having received instruction of any value, for in many schools where there is a competent teacher, his efforts are of little avail

from the distracting crowd of children of all ages, from infants of three years old and upward; his livelihood, miserable at the best, depending on the pence received from the greatest number of children whom it is possible to cram into the space. To this be added scanty school furniture, deficiency of books, and other materials for teaching, and the depressing effect upon the poor children themselves of a close, noisesome atmosphere. I have been in many schools, where I have seen rows of children doing absolutely nothing; and this is certified as school attendance, and, in statistical returns, such children are set down as being educated." (Marx 1906, 1:438)

In opposition to the specialization and professionalization which the dominating class reserves for the working classes, Marx puts forward the concept of *multisidedness*. Here we find certain references to the integral being of Aristotle. For Aristotle, education has, as its aim, the development of all human potentialities. These are potentialities which already exist in people and just need to be activated. For Marx, multisidedness is not the development of inactive human potentialities. It is the creation of these potentialities by individuals themselves through work. Marx also conceives education as a phenomenon which is connected to the whole of social philosophy. He doesn't conceive it in the same way that Greek individualism conceived it as the personal and competitive development of individual natural gifts. Education is a social phenomenon, which is both the product and producer of society.

Refuting the accusations that the communists would want to finish with the exploitation of children by their own parents, Marx and Engels, in the *Manifesto*, confess this crime and explain why education is social.

You say that we destroy the most sublime of relationships when domestic education is substituted by social education. But what about your education? Isn't it also social and determined by the social conditions under which you bring up your children, by the direct or indirect intervention of society, by means of schools, etc? The communists didn't invent the intervention of society in education; they just tried to transform the characteristics of this intervention, pulling it out of the influence of the dominant class. The bourgeois statements on family and education, on the sublime links between the child and its parents become more and more repugnant as the action of large-scale industry destroys all the family connections of the proletariat and transforms its children into mere articles of commerce, mere instruments of work. (Marx-Engels 1977, 100–101)

The social division of work results in a divided, alienated, and unilateral person. With the increase of work time necessary for self-reproduction and for the creation of the surplus value, the worker has no time free for the full development of potentialities. In these work relationships, there are no conditions for education nor, therefore, for full human fulfillment, which is a privilege of a minority who benefit from the work of the majority. This is what happened in Greece. The free people could develop fully because all the manual work was performed by slaves.

With the division of labor, a superintellectualization of the elites and an increasing brutalization of the working masses occurs. The elevation of the cultural level of the working classes will happen only with the conquest of their political emancipation. Education will consolidate these conquests through the union of philosophical work with intellectual teaching, physical development, and polytechnical apprenticeship.

Marx foresaw that technological development would bring equally high industrial development. He showed that, at each step in the progression of the forces of production, the division of labor would grow at an equal rate and would find a solution only in automatized industry, thereby eliminating specializations and specialists. The nonspecialization of the workers would not merely be possible thanks to modern automatized industry, but it would be indispensable for it. Industry would demand that a worker be nonspecialized, but have a general education wide enough for him or her to move around the industry, passing from one branch to another, and not as happens in the nonautomatized industries in which workers become incredibly alienated as they execute the same movement thousands of times during many years, thus contributing to complete dehumanization and physical, moral, and mental brutalization.

Although Marx states that it would be the development of large-scale industry that would demand the change in work, he also states that it will be only in socialist production that the division of labor will be eliminated and that the worker will have a chance of developing in a multifaceted way. Given its implicit characteristic of the exploitation of the surplus value of the worker, capitalist production is unable to fulfill this ideal of the fully developed universal person. On the contrary, socialist production allows this objective to be reached because it is not founded on exploitation, but on the will to humanize people. What is important for Marx is to make mankind able to confront all the changes that these new demands of the development of work impose. For this, it is necessary to substitute the specialized and alienated unilateral individual by the omnilateral, nonspecialized one, who is, above all, free from the exploitation and alienation of the force of labor.

Today, at the end of the twentieth century, many of Marx's early visions might not have been fulfilled. Crises have affected not only capitalism but also socialism. It doesn't matter whether Marx was right or wrong in these visions. What is important is that he looked for reasons for a more dignified existence for a human life on the planet—with hope for all. The socialist ethics which oriented his vision of the world continue to be valid.

It is in this sense that the appearance of the so-called *"new man,"* the historical individual who so frequently appears in the texts of contemporary Marxist philosophers and politicians such as Mao Tse-tung, Fidel Castro (1967) and Ernesto Guevara (1967), and who is so unfashionable today. This theme appears frequently in the speeches of Salvador Allende, Amílcar Cabral, Samora Machel, and others. The so-called "European scientific socialism" forgets this human aspect of Marx which was taken up by the Afro-Asian and Latin American socialists. It is not about looking for a lost human nature or of getting near a preexisting essence in man. On the contrary, it has to do with foreseeing the man who will exist with the simultaneous transformation of the conditions of his existence.

THE EDUCATOR AS AN ORGANIC INTELLECTUAL

Antônio Gramsci, called the theoretician of the superstructures, made a decisive step in the understanding of the dialectic conception of education and of culture.

Marx, in the preface to *Contribution to the Critique of Political Economy*, seemed to place all the weight of the social transformation on the infrastructure, conceiving the superstructure as being determined by the infrastructure. The thinking of Marx is not really mechanistic, and he conceives these relationships in a dialectic way, and in reciprocal action. However, there is no doubt that Marx doesn't give the same weight that Gramsci gives to the contradiction of the superstructure in the process of the transformation of society.

Marx showed how the thinking of a period translates the real conditions of material production of existence. However, in no way can one deduce from this that he reduced the intellectual philosopher to a mere emanation, or a reflection of material production. Marx never believed that social reality was divided into two hermetic areas. All his thinking turns on the interrelationships between the spiritual and the material, and between theory and practice.

In brief, what Marx wants to show in the preface to the *Contribution to the Critique of Political Economy* is that it is impossible to perceive the intellectual production of a society without a clear historical reference to its means of production, or to the way that men produce and reproduce their existence. In the same manner, it is also impossible to understand the reciprocal action between the two if we consider them merely unilaterally. There is no economic determinism in Marx's thinking, as some of his critics have stated. On the contrary, he understands the *process of hominization* as an effort of solidarity between individuals, as the result of a collective action of people. Only in this way, can people bring about changes, producing the material and intellectual conditions of their existence. What Marx finally wants to show is that the bourgeoisie has a science, culture, and education that are dominant because it is the economically dominant class.

Nevertheless, it must not be concluded that Marx doesn't consider that the conquests that have been obtained by the working classes inside the society of classes under the domination of the bourgeoisie are valid—including the conquests inside the educational system, such as the democratization of teaching, free education, and more. However, it was Gramsci who was better able to define the pedagogical socialist strategy inside bourgeois society, beginning from the analysis of the bourgeois state.

The two visions of the process converge and complete each other as both start from the same presupposition that the taking of consciousness is not spontaneous—that is, the formation of the individual consciousness is not innately inactive. It demands effort and the help of elements which are both internal and external to the individual, such as education as a contradictory process of subjective elements, and of internal and external forces. Both begin from the critique of spontaneity. If education were a spontaneous process—natural and not cultural—there would be no need to organize nor to systematize it.

The roots of Gramscian thinking are found in works by Marx and Lenin. In order to understand the economic structure and the production relationships in Russia, Lenin begins from the social formation of Marx, demonstrating the particular necessity for Russia to depend on the urban proletariat, as this was the only politically active social force which had its own political organization. It is in this context that Lenin uses Marx's expression of "dictatorship of the proletariat," referring to the direction of a determined type of alliance. In a wider sense, Lenin uses the term *hegemony* as a synonym (Gruppi 1978, 15), understanding by *hegemony* the surpassing of the spontaneity of the revolutionary movement.

The multiple reactions, rebellions and oppositions are not necessarily revolutionary. They might even be conservative or corporativist. It is the job of the proletariat to unify this process, to give it direction—that is, to take to the masses the consciousness of the real content of its own demands by politicizing these demands. The workers don't invent the struggle nor the social movement. They just politicize it. They should join their discontentment with their negative positions, and transform them into positive politics.

This thinking of Lenin appears clearly when, on making a commentary on the newspaper *Iskra*, he states that a revolutionary newspaper must not "forget for a moment its class character and the political autonomy of the proletariat . . . it should make all the democratic demands of society . . . and never be narrowly limited to a proletarian horizon." (Lenin in Gruppi, 1978, 39)

The revolutionary action is extended to all society as an organic unit, reaching all its levels and segments. The proletariat does not conquer its class consciousness by merely operating on itself, but by making politics. However, this is not a spontaneous process. The proletariat and the worker in general cannot spontaneously reach a class, political, and revolutionary consciousness. Therefore, there must be an education—and especially a political education. For Lenin, class consciousness means the domination of revolutionary theory, and this is born from the critical assimilation of the most advanced positions of the bourgeois culture and from the consequent surpassing of them. It is for this that the worker needs the school, and, today, it is precisely this bourgeois school that he is denied. Here, we find the *strategic role* of the school, educators, and intellectuals in societies in transition, and in a determining role in the construction of the consciousness of the working class.

Lenin can be accused of elitism, and of believing that the working class consciousness comes from outside. Gramsci overcame this critique when he thought of the new intellectual as an organic intellectual of the working class, the worker-intellectual. For him, the party is not outside the working class, and it is not the intellectual who thinks and the worker who does things. It is only by direction of the workers that the contradiction between manual work and intellectual work can be surpassed—that is, between those who think and those who do.

> The intellectual organically connected to the proletariat, a new cement between the infra- and superstructure is born, we repeat, from a transformation of the old way of thinking and knowing, and his intellectual being, as a specialist, is expanded into a political being, transforming his action into an engagement which is totally lived in historical action, which he reforms as an intellectual and a militant. (Machiocci 1976, 198)

Gramsci doesn't just "follow the path which was opened by Marx and Lenin, but he was also the . . . Marxist thinker who, in the highly developed state of society that we know, stated as a hypothesis the need to recognize manual and intellectual work at the heart of the same individual. The organic intellectual of the proletariat, whose advent goes through the self-destruction of the old intellectual." (Machiocci 1976, 226) He doesn't need to show the superiority of the intellectuals in relation to the simpletons. His effort is in the elaboration of a new conception of the intellectual. "All men are intellectuals . . . but in society not all have an intellectual function." (Gramsci 1968, 7–8) They are intellectuals because, regardless of their profession, "Every man exercises a certain intellectual activity, he adopts a vision of the world, a deliberate line of conduct and thus contributes to defend and make prevail a certain vision of the world to produce new ways of thinking." (Gramsci 1968, 7–8)

Gramsci understands that the revolution to be performed is an intellectual and moral revolution. In this point, he distances himself from Lenin, distinguishing the concept of *hegemony* from the concept of *dictatorship of the proletariat*. The dictatorship of the proletariat has a place in political society through the conquest of the state. It is the ability to direct or conquer alliances, and the ability to form a social base for the proletarian state. Hegemony, as Gramsci understands it, has a place in civil society. While the dictatorship of the proletariat represents the supremacy and political domination, hegemony represents social consent.

The bourgeoisie imposes its conception of the world on the workers and the peasants, and keeps this social block united, although it is marked by profound contradictions. In order to do this, it uses the school, the church, military service, and the press. It has elaborated its own political and cultural hegemony and its intellectual leaders, who are its organic intellectuals, technicians, and scientists.

> Each social group born in the original ground of an essential function in the world of economic production creates for itself, at the same time, in an organic way, one or more layers of intellectuals which give it nomogeneity and awareness of its own function, not just in the economic field, but also in the social and political fields. The capitalist entrepreneur creates with himself the industrial technician, the scientist of political economics, the organizer of a new culture, of a new kind of law, etc. It should be noted that the entrepreneur represents a superior social elaboration which is already characterized by certain technical and leadership abilities, that is, intellectual. He should have a certain technical ability, not just in the area related to his activity and his initiative, but also in other areas. At least in those which are nearest to the economic production he should be the organizer of the masses. He should be an organizer who has the confidence of those who invest in his factory, of the buyers of his goods, etc." (Gramsci 1968, 3–4)

For Gramsci, the relationship between the superstructure and the infrastructure is not mechanical but dialectic. The two make up a block, whose contents are *socioeconomic* and whose form is *ethico-political*. The ethico-political form of society is made up by civil society and political society. It is what Gramsci calls the "ethico-political state," a political society in addition to a civil society, that is "hegemony covered by coersion." (Gramsci 1978a, 149)

The hegemony is, at the same time, the ideology of directing class, a conception of the world which is spread through all the social layers and is also the ideological direction of society (Portelli 1977, 22). The hegemony of the dominating class supposes that this class produces its intellectuals, whose function is to dominate the consensus of society.

Political society and civil society are separate only methodologically. In the practical reality, both make up a dialectic unit in which consensus and coersion alternate. Both political society and civil society collaborate with each other at the heart of the state, and are, thus, instruments of the dominating class to exercise its hegemony. Gramsci takes the parliament as an example of the collaboration between political and civil society. Parliament is, on the one hand, the organ of a political society in its function of making laws. On the other hand, it is also an organ of civil society, as it is the official representation of public opinion.

Gramsci joins classical Marxist theory when he states that the state is something transitory which is on the way to a "regulated society"—or a socialist society. On the other hand, he innovates, as he makes it clear that the end of the state, as Marx intended, is only possible when the working classes take over the ideological control of all the civil society, or the whole of the organisms that he calls private.

The connection between the superstructure and the infrastructure of classes is made by the intellectuals who try to reach the agreement of the masses through ideological coersion. When this is not enough, the state enters the scene and ensures the agreement of the masses, either through legal or repressive means.

It is through civil society that the dominating class will exercise its hegemony over the classes that it improperly calls "subaltern" in order to obtain their consent, adhesion, and support. In order to *direct* and not just be *dominant*, the economically dominant class must convince the whole of society that it is the most apt and most prepared to exercise power, and that it represents the interests of all of society. This hegemony will be exercised through culture and ideology. In order to stay in power, it will not recur just to strength, but also to moral means.

THE UNITARY SCHOOL

In order to overcome the contradiction that each class has its own type of school—a humanist school for the dominating classes and a professionalizing school for the popular classes—Gramsci puts forward the thesis of a unitary school.

This idea had been defended before Gramsci by the German educator Clara Zetkin (1857–1933), the founder of the pedagogical Marxist movement in Germany. Under the influence of the writings of Marx and Engels, she defended a unitary school with a socialist base. For Gramsci, this school would be mainly formative, and would allow the development of the abilities of the individual for both manual and intellectual work.

After reaching a certain level of cultural development or the formation of a general culture, each individual would be directed and placed in the productive process by learning a profession. In order to avoid the formation of castes or privileged groups, this education should also be the same for everybody, this being a principle that is the foundation of the relationship between school and the social environment.

The unitary school should develop the intellectual self-sufficiency of the pupil and the awareness of his rights. It should be active and creative, the exact opposite of the uniform and bureaucratic school.

> The unitary school, whether it has a humanistic training—and I understand by this term *humanism* in the wide sense and not in the traditional sense—or whether it has general culture, should propose for itself the task of fitting young people into social activity after having taken them to a certain level of maturity and ability, intellectual creativity and practice and a certain self-sufficiency in orientation and initiative . . . the unitary school requires that the state take on the expenses that are today made by the family as regards the maintenance of the schools, that is, that the budget of national education be completely transformed, increasing it in a way that has not been foreseen and making it more complex. The whole function of education and of the formation of new generations becomes, instead of being private, public, as it is only in this way that it can involve all the generations, without divisions of groups or castes. (Gramsci 1968, 121)

The path signalled by Gramsci is still very relevant, not only as regards the content of education, but also in the struggle for democratization, which is the only way possible to overcome that which he calls privileged groups or castes. He believes that the unitary school should have a collective, autonomous life, both in the day and at night. It should be free of the present kinds of discipline. Study should be performed collectively, under the supervision of the teachers and the more advanced pupils. One should not have to wait for higher level studies at a university to learn to study on one's own, or to acquire reading habits and intellectual discipline. This more creative phase is a natural continuation of the collectivization phase which would be the phase of basic teaching, in which a more dogmatic type of teaching would predominate.

In this critique of the organization of bourgeois schooling, Gramsci emphasizes the lack of connection between the different levels, especially in the leap between high school and university.

From the almost purely dogmatic teaching, in which memory plays a large role, one passes to the creative phase or the phase of autonomous and independent work; from the school with its study discipline imposed and controlled in an authoritarian way, one passes to a phase of professional study or work in which intellectual self-discipline and moral autonomy are theoretically unlimited." (Gramsci 1968, 23)

The critical and creative school "does not mean a school for inventors and discoverers; it indicates a phase and a method of investigation and of knowledge and not a predetermined program that forces innovation and originality at all cost. It indicates that learning takes place mainly thanks to spontaneous and autonomous effort on the part of the pupil, where the teacher has just the function of a friendly guide, as happens or should happen in the university." (Gramsci 1968, 124)

The advent of the unitary school means the beginning of new relationships between intellectual and industrial work, not just in the school but in all social life. The principle of singleness should be reflected in all the organisms of culture, and, thus, give them new content.

Gramsci gives great importance to what he calls "clubs" and *nuclei of popular culture* organized from small communities. Ranging from local, urban, and rural groups to regional and main centers, these clubs should be connected to the schools and universities. They would have a more flexible organization than schools and should try to develop individual abilities. Each local club should have a moral and political science section and should slowly organize other special sections to discuss technical aspects of industrial and agrarian problems and the problems of the organization and nationalization of industrial, agricultural, and bureaucratic work. Gramsci gave these clubs the function of undermining the capitalist structures of society, and strengthening the organization of popular movements.

Gramsci's interest in education originally appears in the speeches he made in his youth. However, it was only in his years in prison, spent in writing letters to his family, that he speaks more specifically about pedagogical themes.

Initially, in *Letters from Prison* (1978), he reflects on the education of his children, nephews, and nieces, and this leads him to study the theme of school and the training of the child. Moving away from this more family atmosphere, he extrapolates his considerations to the political scene. He thinks, not just about the training of individuals, but rather the training of a new type of person who is able to take an active part in the transformation of society and nature.

The aim of school and the formative process is the harmonious development of the different types of behavior of the pupil, without attempting to develop his natural gifts. What determines the options of the individual is not generic human nature, but the historico-social training.

One theme dominates Gramsci's preoccupations when he examines the educational process—coersion versus spontaneity, which, in today's terms, would be the debate between authority and freedom. In a letter he sent to his sister-in-law, Tatiana, on 22 April 1929, this worry was present when he wrote of the plants which he was growing in the tiny garden in the prison yard.

> Every day, I'm tempted to prune them a little to help them to grow, but I remain in doubt between the two conceptions of education: acting in accordance with Rousseau and letting nature, which never goes wrong and which is fundamentally good, work; or to be strong-willed and to force nature by introducing into evolution man's clever hand and the principle of authority. I am still uncertain, and the two ideologies are in conflict in my head. (Gramsci 1978, 128)

What worries him is how to overcome the contradiction between liberal ideology and the ideology of strong-will. This doubt vanishes with the education of his son, Delio, who was then five. He begins to condemn *spontaneity*, which only apparently respects the nature of the child and is really, for him, a complete abandonment to the hands of the authoritarianism of the environment, and for the educator, a refusal to educate.

Gramsci writes to his wife telling her that the child should be left to act alone at the beginning of his childhood. However, the child's initial behavior should not be idolized by the parents. On the contrary, the child should be matched with his new logical and social possibilities. He warns of the risk of puericentrism, which ends up by making the child into a tyrant. "Children like it and are happy when they are considered to be equals." (Manacorda 1977, 80)

In other extracts from *Intellectuals and the Organization of Culture*, Gramsci is even more incisive in his battle against spontaneity. He is clearly in favor of a certain coersion. "Would a 40-year-

old scholar be able to stay 16 hours on end at a desk if, as a child, he
had not gained, through mechanical coersion, the appropriate psy-
chophysical habits?" (Gramsci 1968, 133)

Gramsci distinguishes two distinct phases in the life of the
child—namely, before and after puberty. In the first, the personality
still has not been formed. It is the time for the acquisition of work
habits and intellectual discipline. After puberty, any type of coersion
becomes strange and insupportable. "It seems to be something ba-
nal, but the habit of being seated from 5 to 8 hours daily is something
very important, which is easily possible to make someone acquire
until he is 14, but not after that." Gramsci in a letter to his brother
Carlo on 25 August 1930 (Gramsci 1978, 165)

Coersion must not be confused with authoritarianism. Only
self-coersion is educative, and only that which is desired and freely
accepted. However, on many occasions, with children, it is necessary
more than desired.

> All kinds of pedagogy that hope to use a principle of freedom to
> train an individual, isolated from other people, are abstractions
> and illusions. Freedom is not a metaphysical principle, but a
> way of the individual behaving through responsibilities, in
> such a way that the concept of freedom cannot be separated
> from responsibility. The free individual is not he who acts spon-
> taneously, that is, arbitrarily, but he who acts in a responsible
> way, that is, in accordance with a conscious direction." (Lom-
> bardi 1971, 65)

Education is a contradictory process a totality of action and reflection. Once authority has been eliminated, we fall into spon-
taneism. Once freedom is eliminated, we fall into authoritarianism.
The educative act takes place within this dialectic tension between
freedom and necessity. Gramsci on criticising the traditional oligarchic school, says that it "was not oligarchic in its way of teaching." (1968, 136) He doesn't criticize the methods, which were
efficient, but he criticizes the ends, that is, the setting up of oligarchic directing groups. He adds

> It is not the acquisition of directive abilities or the tendency to
> form superior men which defines the social characteristic of a
> type of school. The social characteristic is given by the fact that
> each social group has its own type of school which is destined
> to perpetuate a determined traditional, directive or instrumen-
> tal function in these groups.

In order to surpass the type of education that trains the bourgeois, it is necessary to attack the ends and not the means, to train a man able to think, study, to direct and to control those who direct." (Gramsci 1968, 136)

It does not mean merely qualifying the manual worker or training him for participation. It means making each member of society a part of the governing system.

3

A Critique of Critical Pedagogy

In the first half of the present century, especially in the 1920s and 1930s, in which Gramsci formed and developed his thinking, together with the enormous technical, scientific, and industrial growth, the belief in the possibilities of education grew. The struggle for free public education gained the consensus. The introduction of new methods and techniques and a school actively directed toward life renewed the hopes that social peace and a full development could be reached by education.

However, the world wars and the social convulsions showed how fragile the contribution of the school was, and that education could not offer any hopes of better days.

With the development of active methods, the advent of the means of communication—such as radio, cinema, and television—along with the ensuing difficulty which the majority of people had to form reading habits and with the growing devaluation of the teacher, contemporary pedagogies centered their discussions on the question of authority.

The movement of the new school, reacting against the authoritarianism that characterized the function of the teacher in the traditional school, sought methodologies that looked to the possibilities of the child. Dialogical pedagogy, with a humanistic basis, attempted to reestablish the idea of meeting as a basis of education. The pedagogy of existence defended an individualized education. In addition, the new pedagogies defended the autonomy of the pupil, the conviviality of the teacher-pupil relationship, nondirectivity, and self-management. The 1960s and 1970s were the years of revolt against authority, beginning with the authority of the schoolmaster.

These pedagogies were inspired by the struggle against authoritarianism and Colonialism in which liberation movements, mainly those in Africa, were involved. The political revolt against authoritarianism had a profound influence on the so-called critical pedagogies which more recently were included in the antiauthoritarian movement of nondirectivity.

EDUCATION AT THE SERVICE OF SOCIAL SELF-MANAGEMENT

Nondirective pedagogies are as numerous as nondirectivist pedagogies. It would, therefore, be difficult and arbitrary to include them all in a single theory. Ironically, George Snyders, professor of Educational Sciences at the University of Paris, classifies them into three categories in his study *Où vont les pédagogies non-directives?* *(Where Are the Non-Directive Pedagogies Going?)* (1974).

1. The pedagogy of "elder brother," in which the teacher is fraternal, liberal, and helpful;
2. The pedagogy, in which the "present becomes absent"—the pedagogy based on psychotherapy; and
3. The pedagogy of the "absent teacher dreaming of always being present"—the psychopedagogue who abandons power, on the absent teacher.

This classification helps us to understand the fundamental themes and worries of this stream of critical pedagogy. For nondirective pedagogies, the role of the teacher is not that of guiding and directing, but of creating an accepting atmosphere in which the pupil can fulfill his or her wishes. The teacher reformulates that which takes place in the group through a taking of consciousness by the participants. He or she places themself as a specialist at the service of the group.

Nevertheless, it is impossible to set up groups in the school where the teacher refuses to take any initiatives. A constant and vigilant help will be necessary in order to set up these groups. In this way, nondirectivity fixes on the main problems of group activity—the participation of each pupil in his training, and the blocks in the way for pedagogical communication. The central objective of these pedagogies is *self-management.*

Anyone who studies the history of education will see that educators and pedagogues have always conceived of education as a process aiming at the development of the human being, and respecting the individuality of each person. One could also say that the great majority of educators have always thought about developing the autonomy of the human being.

However, the question of the autonomy of the pupil has never been as widely discussed as it is today. The best-known example is that of the so-called *institutional pedagogy,* whose main representative is Michel Lobrot, a French educationalist who has taught in the Universities of Vincennes and Geneva. He formed a number of self-managing workgroups, whose objective was to recreate the school as a nonalienating institution. Snyders defined it as the model of a subversive anarchist agent.

In his main work, *Institutional Pedagogy,* Lobrot makes a long analysis of the origins of school, of the present hierarchical and bureaucratic systems, and of the new pedagogies, of which he makes a critical analysis. In the second part, he proposes political, therapeutic, and social self-management, and, as the title of the book announces, an institutional pedagogy, which proposes to modify the existing pedagogical institutions by using self-management. This would result in a modification of mentality, making schools open and autonomous, and then, modify the institutions of society. Lobrot believes that school alone is enough to make people less dependent.

This pedagogical trend began with a group that separated from the pedagogy of Célestin Freinet (1896–1966) around 1963, and which developed an important struggle against the bureaucratic pedagogy dominant in France. It introduced new pedagogical techniques, such as the free text and the school press. Institutional pedagogy was also inspired by the social psychology of Carl Rogers (1902–1987), and by the analyses of school institutions and of self-managing Marxism along the lines of Georges Lapassade.

One can say that the basis of Lobrot's theory is in the interpersonal relationships at school. For Rogers, the individual can use his own resources as long as he is in an atmosphere that favors the growth of freedom. The relationship between the teacher and the pupil has failed in traditional pedagogy, because the vital energy existing in each individual is systematically massacred and repressed by the school. Rogers maintains that there exists in every man all that is necessary to solve all of his problems.

In order to reestablish and free this energy, certain conditions are necessary, such as the search for each person to assume individuality, accepting themselves as he or she is, and accepting the other in a nonthreatening way. Institutional pedagogy proposes congruency, empathy, reflection, and respect for the other. This is because everyone is ontologically equal, as stated by Henri Hartung, an educational philosopher, pioneer, and finally critic of the movement of permanent education. In his work, *The Children of Promise* (1972), Hartung concentrates on analyzing the relationship between governors and the governed. He dreams of a society with no leaders, a society in which everyone would have the same privileges and could govern themselves. He believes that only an autonomous being is able to exercise democracy, and that only an interior search can lead people to this autonomy.

In institutional pedagogy, the teacher should renounce the hierarchy in favor of cooperation and freedom of expression. It is a pedagogy without a pedagogue. As Reboul states when writing about Rogers, "As long as he is made to study, the student doubts his experience, he is no longer congruent and therefore a creative being; and, in a period which has needed creativity more than ever, traditional teaching only trains conformists or rebels." (1974, 47)

In another work, *Pour ou contre l'autorité? (For or Against Authority?)* (1974), Lobrot analyses the phenomenon of authority. The main thesis of this book is that authority is of a psychological nature. He says that authority is, more than anything, a human reaction and behavior when faced by nature and by other people. This in no way prevents it from being structural and institutional—that is, giving origin to structures and institutions. Quite the opposite. It is structural and institutional because it is psychological.

Lobrot makes the point that, in the educational sciences, only the psychological discourse on authority is innovative and revolutionary. Political, sociological, legal, and administrative discourse is conservative, because it adopts the language of power. The author refuses these ways of focusing on the problem of authority in order not to fall, as he says, into the trap that consists of speaking about authority by placing oneself inside one's own point of view. It would be like making a critique of metaphysics from within a metaphysical point of view. He refers to Marxism, which intends to surpress exploitation by placing the means of production, and the means of exploitation, in the hands of the workers. He believes that, by doing this, Marxism will introduce a new form of authority—namely, bureaucratism. Although the intention of Marxism is to introduce social justice, Lobrot believes that, in reality, this applies only to the investment of the surplus value which is engendered in production.

Authority is a system which allows one to alter the will of the other and the psychological field in which one wishes to act. The technocrat who holds knowledge also holds power and authority. There is no distinction between the domaine of knowledge and the decisions relative to this knowledge. In fact, it is not just a scientific piece of data that is in question when one takes a decision, but also a system of values.

From where does this growing influence of authority and authoritarianism in our society—which looks as if it will perpetuate itself into the endless future—come? According to Lobrot, the most direct authority that people suffer is the educational authority of parents and school teachers, who have a more precise aim than do other types of authority. Educational authority aims at preventing access to higher forms of instincts and impulses which are considered to be dangerous for the individual. Thus, education causes a certain psychological effect that is part of the origin of the refusal and fear which prevent any positive experience that is profoundly desired.

Lobrot concludes that authority is essentially transmitted through education. In this case, it is here that action must be taken to train free individuals.

How?

Lobrot believes that the fact of understanding the limitations to individual freedom which already exist in society gives the individual power over repressive structures. It is from here that one can work for one's own freedom—and for the freedom of the other.

The aim of institutional pedagogy is not scholastic, but, rather, social and political. The aim is to unleash, from the teacher-pupil group and on the perimeter of the classroom, a process of the transformation of the scholastic institution, and, thus, a transformation of society itself. "Pedagogical self-management is just a preparation for social self-management. This is its final objective." (Lobrot 1972, 259)

How can this process be initiated in the classroom?

First, the teacher must no longer exist as an authority but will only give technical help. To use the expression of Lobrot, the teacher will declare power to be vacant. "The power renounces his attitude of power." (1972, 215) Individual pupils or the group can refer to the teacher when they feel the need. The teacher can inform, reply to questions, and even make expositions as long as this need has come from the pupils. However, the teacher can neither interfere nor direct the group.

The abstention of the teacher aims at making the groups and the individuals that form them acquire autonomy and a sense of responsibility by attempting to find the solutions to their problems for themselves, and by making their own rules and structure with no invidulance or protection. It is the group which, through its own initiative, will determine tasks, make up programs, give their opinions on courses, and control their duration, frequency, evaluation, and so on.

At the beginning, there might be conflicts or anguish when the group seems impotent to establish a common plan, an adequate work method, and sufficient access to information. These conflicts are natural as the group loses the habitual security which is given by the presence of the teacher. At this moment, the role of the teacher will be that of stimulating the awareness of the situation, and elucidating the experience which has been lived through by the group. If the teacher takes a directive posture, he or she could return to taking the role of the guide, the protector of the group, with the worse problem that, now, his or her authority will be recognized because the group is now aware that it is they themselves that are requesting the intervention of the teacher rather than the teacher imposing it. The group would, thus, end up by welcoming the teacher's authority. The exterior authority would become interior.

Once this phase has been overcome, the teacher should become absent again, in order to benefit the learning, and not give advice or orders nor evaluate the group. As Gilles Ferry, professor of Psychopedagogy at the University of Paris, states,

> The success in the transmission of a piece of knowledge presupposes an act of appropriation of knowledge on the part of the student . . . transmitting is not limited to emitting. And also for the teacher, abstaining from emitting in order to receive, in turn, a message concerning the good or bad reception of what he has just emitted in order to adjust his further message. (Ferry in Snyders 1974, 159)

Groups of students are, in general, very heterogeneous. How then can the dictatorship of the majority be avoided? How can the submission of the minority by the majority, and the subsequent substitution of one kind of authority by another kind be avoided?

The nondirective pedagogues cannot theoretically manage to solve this problem. They just recommend, as does Carl Rogers, that all the interventions be listened to and examined with the same attention, that everyone should be able to make himself heard, and that no one try to usurp the functions of the others or to impose himself in an authoritarian way. The solution is, therefore, ethical. The system is blocked if an authoritarian and tyrannical leader manages to impose his authority.

It is always admitted that the group will progress with extreme difficulty, running risks, and making mistakes. The consolation is that these mistakes and imperfections will be "fecund and formative for the pupils," in the words of Irving Rogers and Barrington Kaye, quoted by George Snyders (1974, 98). The pupils will know how to take advantages of these mistakes; they will know how to surpass them.

YOUNG POWER AND THE GENERALIZATION OF INFORMATION

The aim of institutional pedagogy is to reach social self-management. Education would not be an end in itself, as John Dewey suggested. It would be at the service of a project of society. Where would the power of education be to fulfill this dream of a new society? Some put all the emphasis on a new social class—the young—others on the generalization of information. For some, power would be in the youth, and, for others, it would be in the generalized diffusion of information.

Gérard Mendel is one of the scholars of the phenomenon of authority. In *Decolonizing the Child* (1971), Mendel proposes to make a social psychoanalysis of authority. This book is an analysis of the sources of conditioning to authority. In another work, *The Educative Manifesto* (1973), written together with Christian Vogt, Mendel makes a sociopedagogical analysis of student protest and approximates it to the phenomenon of socialism. He writes about a pedagogical revolution of youth. What is new is the reply he makes to the question of education within Marxism.

He makes the point that, in the same way that the industrial revolution brought about the working class, the technological revolution helps to create new forms of protest against the principle of efficiency and authority. Among these forces are *youth,* either as an age class or as a social class. The fact that this new class would act constructively or destructively in political terms would depend in part on adults. In effect, youth would not be able to organize itself, define itself in relation to precise objectives, and become completely responsible unless they form part of a true pedagogical revolution.

Mendel believes that the natural state of man is that of *conflict* and *guilt*—a feeling of guilt when faced with one's parents and society. Revolutionaries feel subconsciously guilty, and this can lead to an attitude of self-destruction or the temptation to appeal to an outside authority. Political analysis should take into account the educational methods which have been received from present-day adults. The pedagogical revolution, understood by Mendel as the establishment of equality between adult and child, is the means of partly freeing the child from his guilt and allowing him to live with his conflicts. Mendel's central thesis is that the dominant social ideology uses, in order to exercise its abusive power, a phenomenon of grassroots authority, which has its roots in the psychofamily life. The conditioning to authority begins the biological inequality, which is the adult-child inequality. The inequality between child and adult has psychoaffective repercussions in the child, such as fear of being abandoned, identification with the father, submission to an adult model, and a feeling of guilt. This fear and feeling of dependence is exploited by the dominant social ideology to exercise an abusive authority over the dominated. This phenomenon is even more penetrating as it is a subconscious phenomenon. This allows the dominant ideology to mystify the real power relationship that exists between all the members of society, among whom one finds teachers and pupils. Therefore, what is important in the educational process is to become aware of what authority is, to show that it is masked by authoritarian ideology, and to make it possible to decondition people to authority.

Today, the protest of the young is because they have become aware of institutional power. *Protest* is the engine of the pedagogical revolution. The pupils are struggling to recover their part of institutional power. Mendel believes that the socialist school will be, in the medium term, the place in which the various institutional classes will exercise power in a complementary manner. This school would have two *main objectives* as outlined by Mendel and Vogt (1973, 276):

1. To teach children to exercise the power to which that their institutional activity gives them a right; and
2. To acquire certain knowledge, in a project of continuous elaboration, as long as it takes into account the wishes and interests of

the children and their reality. This project should be negotiated between the teachers and children.

Mendel believes that the young have become an ideological class. Although they are not a class that has been economically exploited, there are three elements that help to characterize it socially as an ideological class (Mendel-Vogt 1973, 108).

1. The repression coming from the adult. What is repressed in the young person is not just sexuality, but equally what he calls archaism—that is, ludism, nature, creativity, the desire to live in a group, and more.
2. The awareness that youth finds from its total absence in institutional power. Before, teachers and pupils lived a parental relationship, and authority served to hide the institutional power of the teachers. Now, young people become aware that the school aims at taking away the best in them—such as like the pleasure of living collectively—and will not give them anything back.
3. Finally, the absence of the mechanism of the identification with the adult. The adult mercantile society and its ideology clearly appears in the eyes of youth as a strange and objectively dangerous, destructive, absurd, and inhuman universe.

How can and why should the struggles of the youth branch out into antiauthoritarian or self-managing socialism?

According to Mendel, a self-managing form of socialism becomes possible only when the youth channel all their antiauthoritarian ideology into the left-wing forces. Mendel establishes three conditions for this to be accomplished—unity among the young; adhesion to self-managing socialism; and unconditional support of the left-wing forces. In synthesis, what youth should impose on the adults in the short term, is, according to Mendel and Vogt:

1. The opening of the school for a new mode of acquisition of knowledge closely connected to institutional power, therefore, participation in the management of the establishment, in all the organs;
2. An opening of politics, both in the particular way in which youth expresses itself, and in the deepening of the problems of a political school directed toward socialism; and
3. An opening of society through daily awareness at a local level of all that concerns young people. The young person belongs neither to the adult nor to the state. (1973, 274)

In the medium term, the objective of the pedagogical revolution is the socialist school, uniting the transformation of all society.
He says

> In the same way that protest will disappear in quicksand if it
> doesn't join the socialist project, every pedagogical project will
> represent a step backward in relation to present day education
> which just aims at the training of technicians, if this project fails
> to include that which protest expresses: the demand of youth for
> its part of power in society where other types of social and hu-
> man relationships may exist. (Mendel-Vogt 1973, 302)

In a different perspective, but struggling for the affirmation of
the same self-managing ideas, a third author stands out. Henri Laborit was trained as a biologist, but his thinking extends through sociology and politics. We shall look just at his work, *Informational
Society: Ideas for Self-Management.* (1973).

According to Laborit, recent progress in the field of the biology
of behavior and the theory of information supply important elements for the elaboration of a new, more complete network for the
interpretation of social relationships. Marxist and Freudian analyses
should be rethought in light of this new knowledge. Laborit believes
that the desired change for the present society is more along the lines
of a total inversion of the present values, as it is these values that
serve to maintain the dominant power. There should be change in
the levels of organization, allowing self-management.

Laborit understands that, in order to reach a new organization
of society, it would be necessary to structure it as a *human organism* which is, he believes, self-managed. In the human organism
there is no centralization of decision making. The nervous system
is not a dominant class. It doesn't decide for the whole of the organism. Instead, it expresses for this whole the behavioral decision that
is necessary in order to seek well-being and to flee from negative
situations.

What are the conditions that are necessary for a self-managing
society?

Laborit believes that it will be necessary to abolish the hierarchy of values, and put, in their place, a functional hierarchy—that is,
a functional union among all people, creating an interdependence
through levels of growing complexity of organization. It would be
necessary to abandon the primitive behavior of the power groups,
through the structure of functional classes which gives each class,

according to its function, not a hierarchical place, but, rather, a competitive part of power. Through this measure, Laborit understands that *paternalism* and *infantilism* will disappear in interclass relationships, and their places will be taken by an awareness of functional class.

Another measure that Laborit indicates for the formation of a self-managing society is the *generalization of information.* "The only thing left is to look for the means of generalization and diversification of information and their sources on one hand, and on the other, to look for an aim which will be an internal part of the system and connected to its structure and not to its thermodynamics (production)." (Laborit 1973, 60)

Laborit believes that the key to the problem of modern societies is the generalization of information, and such generalized information is possible only with the reduction of production, as it is necessary to have time to be informed. Information will allow every individual to ponder the philosophical question of the aim of the human species, to know the aims of the whole range of men, and to take part in the choice of this aim.

Laborit's thesis is a transposition of the method of analysis of natural sciences to social sciences. He believes that the contradictions of the social world can be seen by beginning with an analysis of the individual. From a biological point of view, he concludes, the dynamic that rules a society is analogous to that of the individual.

The strategy of the surpassing of a thermodynamic society—a society based on production—for an *informational society*—is generalized information. As he says, at the moment when power is generalized, no more power will exist (Laborit 1973, 37). At the center of his thinking, one finds the problem of power and authority. The solution is not to control it, but to dissolve it.

THE DIRECTING ROLE OF SCHOOL AND OF THE TEACHER

This is the central nucleus of the theses on nondirectivity and pedagogical self-management, and of the relationship between authority and freedom presented by these three authors.

In what follows, we shall ask ourselves whether the question of authority was not looked at ingenuously, and whether the conclusions of these three authors, in spite of their scientific foundations, are sufficiently valid to found a new pedagogy.

What do other educators say about these critical theories?

George Snyders (1974) says that nondirective pedagogy is skeptical in relation to the question of truth. He believes that the theoreticians of nondirective pedagogy refuse to look at the question of truth. He justifies this refusal because, in this pedagogy, the problem of the content is unexamined. It concentrates solely on the methods, and the methods become the central content of the pedagogy.

What is important in nondirective pedagogy is the success in interpersonal relationships, group life, the ardour of the discussion, and the pleasure of letting off steam. Snyders doesn't hide the fact that this can easily lead to conservatism. If it is enough just to communicate, and if expressing oneself is all that matters, then all opinions are true.

On the contrary, a pedagogy inspired by Marxism should, first and foremost, consider the content which is to be taught, because it is through this that the consciousness of pupils can be renewed. It should also take care to ensure that this knowledge stays close to the experience of the pupil. Snyders believes that the knowledge of the pupil is normally fragmentary, chaotic, and stereotyped—all characteristics of common sense. The teacher needs to reorder this knowledge—as well as his own—and elucidate it to make it coherent. It is from this directive task that teacher and pupil together gain awareness of the quality of their knowledge and of how it is produced. The teacher has a directive role. It is only in this manner that the old can be broken and the new built.

The socialist educator is, therefore, an organizer who breaks with the idealist antihistorical training, as well as with formalism and with academicist training. This break is possible only with work, collective and historical *praxis*, and the taking of positions, which are renewed both by the teacher and by the pupil. Snyders says that, "In spite of appearances, non-directive methods form part of the extension of bourgeois school politics. . . . A pedagogy inspired by Marxism is possible today and proposes an open, declared, coherent line of conduct which does not fall into drilling and conditioning. It can be presented to the great majority of pupils without being seen to be coercive or arbitrary." (1974, 323).

The critique of Gaston Mialaret in the preface of the polemical book of Lucien Morin, *The Charlatans of the New Pedagogy* (1976), is even more crushing.

> One must have lived in certain North American environments where a certain interpretation of Rogers' theories, a certain way of practicing group dynamics, are no more than caricatures, in

order to appreciate the lucid critique that Lucien Morin makes of these degraded and decadent forms of contemporary education . . . To set up as a pedagogical principle, the necessary ignorance of the educator is the greatest pedagogical monstrosity of our time. Pedagogy becomes demagogy and the educator has only one path: to ask for reform to be brought forward, to leave room for the charlatans. (Mialaret in Morin 1976, 5–6)

Snyders points to the risk that educators run when they think that, before the social revolution, the children of the exploited class will be able to escape from their exploitation, thanks to a liberating school.

However, the contributions that institutional pedagogy made to educational sciences and to pedagogy in our times have attracted attention to the problem of self-management, the lack of participation, and bureaucratism. These problems are all extremely relevant and have been definitively incorporated into the history of pedagogical ideas.

Self-management pedagogies always seem to be moving from theory toward practice. They aren't able to listen to the practice. This is not a question of moving the axis of pedagogy exclusively to practice, under the pretext that this would be richer than theory. It is more a question of not dichotomizing an act that essentially involves theory and practice—that is, the educative act.

Self-management pedagogies have their foundations in a metaphysical anthropology and in religion. They suppose that, through self-management, people will finally have access to an authenticity and will reach transparency. Their relationships with each other will finally become true. On the one side, the is good, embodied in transparency, respect for the other, and the like. On the other side, lies evil, as in the institution of school and authority. The saviour in this would be the pedagogue who freed the pupil from violence and from sin, and who opened the classroom as a new space for purity. As our late friend Claude Pantillion said at the University of Geneva in 1976, the schoolteachers would be transformed into mythical heros, able to break the circle of good and evil, losing themselves in each of the members of the group.

The scientific bases of nondirective pedagogies are found especially in psychology, sociology, and psychoanalysis, and they have the merit of giving importance to the affective element at a moment when education was centered on information and learning, taking these as the whole and not just as part of human development.

Children of classical humanism and self-management pedagogies start from an ethics of congruency, empathy, dialogue, and mutual comprehension, which are founded on the dignity of the human being. What seems to me to be an error in such pedagogies is, not this basic ethics, but the fact that they propose reaching their objective through techniques—as if man could mechanically equate his deepest problems without touching the basic structures which have been formed throughout his history. They propose doing much more than any pedagogy is capable of doing. In this point they are ingenuous.

This ethics that self-management uses as a starting point is much more than a point of arrival, a horizon toward which one can travel, or an ideal. It is not the daily reality of school practice. This point of arrival—the transparent empathetic, congruent, and participating human—cannot be planned, measured, nor quantified. The quantification of man would be an authoritarian attempt—exactly the trap into which self-management doesn't want to be caught, but in which it ends up anyway. No new rule can make authenticity and the meeting sprout up. On the contrary, they can grow even within a completely traditional pedagogy.

I very much believe in the school and its social role. I believe that its transforming potential has not yet been sufficiently exploited by modern pedagogies. However, we must not lose sight of its limits. It is certainly not the lever of social transformation. Nothing can do everything alone. To intend to change society merely through school seems to me to be a great illusion. It does not take into account the past nor the present, history, or the concrete society. School cannot do everything, but it does urgently need to recover its directing role and value the teacher above everything else.

Self-management pedagogies have nothing to do with historical mankind as they conceive human nature as being essentially good, as did Rousseau. It supposes that the bad lies not in the perversion of human relationships, but is merely a consequence or an effect, and not a cause.

Without reference to a wider context, nondirective pedagogies end up by isolating educative practice, and, thereby, making it ineffective. To maintain the *dialectic tension* between the individual and society would possibly be the basic principle of a pedagogy that intended to transform the human condition.

It is pedagogical practice, then—to a greater extent than these considerations—that can show the limitations of the *critical pedagogies* that use nondirective pedagogy as a basis.

In the following pages, I relate a personal experience of self-management at the University of Geneva, between 1974 and 1977, and in the Section of Educational Sciences. As it is difficult to reproduce integrally every type of practice, it will always be a vision of a practice, and not the practice itself. It will therefore have a limited value. However, it is a significant practical illustration of the critical theory of education.

SELF-MANAGEMENT PUT INTO PRACTICE

In the foyer of the main building in Geneva University there is a frontispiece which attracts the attention of visitors who pass before it and along the Promenade des Bastions. It contains the following dedication:

> *Le peuple de Genève en consacrant cet édifice aux études superieures rende hommage aux bienfaits de l'instruction, garantie fondamentale de ses libertés. Loi du XXVI juin MDCCCLXVII.*

This translates as: In consecrating this building to higher education, the people of Geneva pay homage to the benefits of education, a fundamental guarantee of their freedoms. Law of 26 June, 1867.

This sentence translated the feeling of an age toward education and, more importantly, what was expected of it. Education was the "guarantee of the freedoms of the people." This phrase expresses the belief in education and in its powers. Because of this, the building is "consecrated," like a temple, and "homage" is paid to education. Traditional education, connected to the rites of initiation, retained this sacred character. Until now certain rituals, tests, marks, degree ceremonies, and initiations which remind one of this conception, are maintained. There is a house for education in the same way that there is a house of God.

There was a period in which this sentence could have been written in any school in the world. It is still pertinent even today. The benefits of education—or education itself—are not questioned—or, if they are, it is to a minimal degree. There is an undisguised belief in its neutrality. It has an end in itself, as the North American educational ideologue John Dewey stated. The aim of education is more education. This idea continues to be the paradigm of the education of our age.

Far from practicing the liberalism which they had announced with such pride, the elites used education for hierarchization and social reproduction. Instead of being the "fundamental guarantee of freedom," it ended up by being transformed into a large number of school systems, into an immense bureaucratic machine which devoured both individual and collective freedoms.

It is only natural that the European countries which, in this century, have had an extraordinary development of education, definitively implanting basic schooling for all, question this neutrality and experiment with other models and conceptions, such as pedagogical self-management. This was what happened between 1974 and 1976 in the School of Psychology and Educational Sciences, today a Faculty at the University of Geneva.

Based on the experience—and less on the theory that guided it—I tried to make an analysis that aimed more at clarifying a dialectic posture faced with so-called self-management, which could, on many occasions, translate the caprice of the educators in adapting practice to theory. At the center of this experiment was the idea of participation, the magic word in whose name everything was permitted.

As with all fashions, it aroused great curiosity at the beginning, and even a serious and disinterested search for new forms of teaching, learning, and educating.

At the beginning, there was the will for power, domination, or Machiavellism behind this attempt. On the other hand, there was also a desire to get things right, which was guided by a progressive thinking. The ideas of May 1968 were still very much alive.

However, how can the theory be put into practice?

Initially, there were two *basic tendencies*. The first was those who noisily showed that they were in favor of the experiment, imagining that everything that they wanted to do, but until then hadn't been able to, would from then on be permitted. There was another group which rebelled and wanted teachers in authoritarian roles. There were those that, without the authority of the schoolteacher, became quite desperate and extremely personally insecure.

The presence of a number of the top names in self-management thinking—such as Michel Lobrot, Bertrand Schwartz, and J. Ardoino—stimulated the search. The rigid structures began to break. Programs were set up together with the students. Class registers, exams, and marks were eliminated. These self-managing ideas then spread to the structure and workings of the school, with commissions instead of bosses, and decentralization through the creation of departments, which were called "sectors." The shout of "Power to the Assembly!" could be heard in the corridors. Confrontation was created, and every question was discussed, with nothing being held back. Self-management was established, but not without long discussions and tumultous arguments, with the eternally discontented and the new leaderships being formed in the process.

The conquests were:

1. Participation and equal right to the word, collaboration of the students, questionings, and more, instead of courses *ex cathedra;*
2. Participation and equal division of responsibilities in the qualifying process. The student took on his or her own graduation, the learning methods became active, and so on; and
3. Participation and division of power and decision—in brief, *self-management.*

There were moments when we thought that we were making democracy work in the school, given that it was so difficult to make it work in society. The benefits began to be felt quickly. The authority of the teacher, which had been systematically questioned, was limited by the greater presence of the student. The students felt that they had support when they wished to question the teacher. Participation was almost an obligation, a new rule, or a regulation of the student. Whoever failed to participate was not considered to be a good student.

After a year and a half of this experiment, there was even a certain terror which had been created around the idea of participation. Little by little, the idea that the nonparticipants should be given a dressing-down came about. The atmosphere of frankness when speaking disappeared. A number of participants dominated the discussions.

We were able to see that participation was not such a simple thing, and that, in self-management, when there are no clear rules to the game, fear and suspicion begin to dominate people, confrontations begin to be personal, and the desire for power, which had been held back, was now violently expressed. Self-management might hide the conflict of agressivity in the forest. It might become the worst type of manipulation because the enemy does not show himself but is hidden inside of each of one's classmates. Responsibility is diluted in such a way that, as there is no one who can take responsibility for anything because everything is decided in the group, one can never advance. We wouldn't want to accept that a pedagogical relationship was contradictory, and that conflict was inherent to any process of change.

Time passed. The assemblies became more and more empty. The problems were listed for discussion at the next meeting, but the credits of the students—even of those who hadn't taken part in any activity—were being accumulated. Thus, the institution was keeping going, without there having been any reflection on its aims and direction and the services that it should provide for the community.

After two years of the experiment, there were still many *questions* in the air. What did educating for self-management mean, as the student would find himself later in a hierarchical society? Is it sufficient to be nondirective and favor the learning of a new kind of behavior so that students can put forward essential questions, allowing them to reevaluate their own lived experiences? Would not the objective of a progressive pedagogy offer the pupils the instruments for the analysis of reality and the means for which the student can act autonomously on the transformation of this reality?

However, we had also collected some good *results*. Even though they demonstrated a certain lack of knowledge and of cultural capital, the students learned how to organize themselves better. They gained a greater speed of reasoning and vision of the whole, and they expressed themselves more easily. They could no longer put up with authoritarian measures. The position of each student ended up by being more personalized. What one noticed was that the freedom of choice, the noncompulsory tasks, or the possibility of rewriting papers that had been badly done, minimized the problems of inequalities. In relation to traditional teaching in which students obey the teacher or else they are punished, and in which there is a controlled knowledge, self-management had brought a certain amount of progress, especially concerning the relationships between teachers, students and ancillary workers. Through allowing the students the power of questioning methods, allowing them to freely express their dissatisfactions, and authorizing them to choose their methods, the class as a whole had evolved, human relationships changed, and they could perceive that it is also possible to change these elements in society.

During this period when everyone was involved, life with Claude Pantillon, director of the Center of Philosophy of Education, showed us to how great an extent pedagogical *theory* is vain, insufficient and even counterproductive, if it doesn't consider the educating *attitude* of the teacher. Pantillon faced every one of his classes with considerable seriousness, in spite of arriving "punctually late" and of appearing so considerably at ease that, to someone who didn't know him, he would appear remiss. The evaluation of each class was sacred. Normally, he would write this evaluation up at home and, in the following class, we had a new text, which would interrogate the group and make them move forward. There was no need to invent a new theory to justify his attitude. He was not a man who would hide behind theories about which he always had certain reserves.

In practice, we ended up by learning all the advantages and difficulties of self-management in the education of the group. We learned that so-called nondirectivity cannot be a system that is opposed to another system of directivity, but that it can only fundamentally be one of many attitudes. Mystified by pedagogues and educators, it becomes an ideology just like any other.

In this same practice—and by studying Hartung, Laborit, Rogers, and Snyders—we learned that the educative act cannot do without authority. It is present even if the educator and pupil don't wish it to be present. The absence of authority is a form of diffuse repression. Many classmates, who were unable to put up with the vacuum of power, either became violently aggressive or ended up by proposing that it should become a therapy group. Thus, we learned that, in practice, a *philosophy of liberation* should run the risk of a confrontation of positions, discussions, and conflict.

Although we all supported the ideas of self-management at the Center of the Philosophy of Education, in practice, we understood it in different ways. We all believed in institutional pedagogy and in self-management, but we recognized that, in practice, this pedagogy obtained no greater results than serving as an alert to the paradox that the act of educating is. On one hand, a praxis is necessary. On the other hand, an action is imperative. However, in order for this educative act to have effect, this action should be surpassed by the action of the other. This is the dialectics of authority and freedom. Without this dialectics, there is no education. Every type of education that attempts to suppress one of the poles of the relationship will, sooner or later, fail. There is still a certain Rousseau-like optimism in this critical and self-management pedagogy. For example, it never introduces the question of evil or finitude, as the philosopher Paul Ricoeur, a visiting professor at the Faculty, would say. At the same time, it can be admitted that evil not being in people is in the relationships of power, dependence, authority, and in institutional relationships. In addition, the authority for this type of pedagogy is always repressive and never emancipating. Thus, it is also an essentialist pedagogy, although it insists on themes that are linked to existentialism.

As the assistant to Claude Pantillion in the academic year of 1975–1976, I coordinated a seminar course on the Philosophy of Education, which was centered on the theme of ideology and education. From the beginning, we had established that we would use certain readings, but that the reflection should be centered on the individual and collective practices of the participants. The previous courses had warned us not to fall into theoretical discourse. It seemed more important to work with a concrete material, and in the way we were implicated as students, the working of the faculty, and so on, and not simply to go through readings.

However, what happened?

Considerable time was devoted to the elaboration of the program, as well as the exposition of the expectations and worries of the participants. When we were ready to develop the program, the problem of the succession of the chairman of our section appeared. It was a concrete, immediate question that involved everyone. The group then began to devote itself to the elaboration of pamphlets, holding meetings and assemblies, and organizing management and institutional analysis seminars. And we took this fact as a theoretical-practical nucleus of our seminars.

This fact made us abandon the programmed readings to study the internal statutes, the regulations, the students' statutes, the distribution of powers, and the problem of participation. The necessity of confronting precise points—the statutes, for example—prevented us from more profoundly reflecting on the theme of participation.

Once the problem of the election of the new president at the end of the winter term (October-March) had been overcome, the group, on returning at the beginning of the summer term (April-June), was divided between those who wished to continue the struggle inside the institution and those who wanted to go back to their books and make the readings. Some said that the evaluation of the participation had not been made sufficiently well, and that the problems continued. Then, the practice took priority over theoretical study. Others said that they needed theoretical foundations, that it was necessary to alternate theory and practice. This was a good time to discuss our internal divisions.

In spite of the protests from some members of the group, some of the readings were taken up again: Habermas (1972), Gramsci, Marcuse (1964), Marx, and even Mao Tse-tung and Confucius, as this was the time of the Chinese cultural revolution and the consequent de-mystification of Confucianism. A certain theoretical knowledge was accumulated—some called it "banking," using the term of Paulo Freire. The most involved forms of expression, such as pam-phleteering, were abandoned and substituted by a highly sophisti-cated and technical language of theories which were of considerably difficult access to the majority of the population and to the students themselves. We reproduced our own scheme of an elite, and of supe-rior knowledge. The apprehension and comprehension of these texts was frequently made individually, somewhat similar to the accu-mulation of capital by the capitalist.

We ended the year, frustrated between the wish to do some-thing new and the feeling of having missed the chance to do it. The proposal of a common learning had failed. We then began to make various evaluations.

We had approached the problems intellectually, either with ref-erence to the so-called Third World, or in relation to the contempo-rary concrete contribution of the great philosophical theories, especially Marxism. We asked ourselves what use there would be in theorizing if this theory had no connection with practice.

The relationships between teachers and students in the Peda-gogy Section of the university were very friendly and cordial. It seemed—at first sight, and at least judging by the classroom—we found ourselves together with a group that was enlivened by the same ideas and the same political options. The rigidity had been bro-ken, the hierarchization had been reduced, and the reciprocity and the equality of conditions had been finally installed. However, deep down, this cordiality was merely apparent. We had unconsciously re-fused our differences, trying to hide the conflicts in order to collec-tively live our experience.

Self-management cannot be a panacea. It can mean many things, and can, therefore, be confused with many things. It doubtlessly represents a radical change, but, in order to put it into action, it should be understood, first and foremost, as an always un-finished radical democracy and concrete utopia.

Pure self-management ignores the existence of concrete human beings. "All the dreams of a perfect society ended in blood and tears, the fanatics have never been able to find men pure enough for their delirium." (Guillerm 1976, 213)

What happened afterward with the experience of Geneva?

The director, who had lost his place during an assembly, re-turned, chosen by the rector from a list of names which fulfilled the demands of the general norms of the university. However, the institution had changed. The working of the institution was now clear for all to see. On the other hand, we were certain that participation could also be mystified. It could be used to accommodate conflicts. The combat ended because of a lack of combatants. We abandoned the experiment, certain that we could not invest everything in self-management and that we needed intermediary steps.

If they asked me today whether I would do it again . . .

I would reply, "*Yes!*" with the dream and the pedagogical knowledge that I had at the time, but "*No!*" with the ideas that I defend today.

At the time, I thought that the small changes prevented the fulfillment of a great change. Therefore, they should be avoided, and all the investment should be made in a radical change. Today, I am certain of something else—I say certain because we need certainties to think and act. Today, I believe that in the daily struggle, in the day-to-day changing, step-by-step, that the quantity of small changes in a certain direction offers us the possibility of making a great change. It might happen as the result of a continuous, patient supportive effort.

Education will always be the domain of the instable, of the order-disorder, as Edgar Morin (1973) states. His theory applied to pedagogy would be a pedagogy in which the appearance of new concepts, breaking the previous equilibrium or order, would become a pedagogy of the unfinished, utopia, disorder, and the unstable, and would evolve toward a new order, which would be more complex than the preceding order, and which would also be unfinished . . . and so on. Education would play a double game. It would supply models and the critical weapons of these models; it would also make a synthesis, a balance between stability and evolution, between order and disorder, between reproduction and creation, and between authority and freedom.

Even if we recognize all of these limitations, we believe that self-management is a fundamental part of a socialist project. However, this self-management cannot be confused with a renouncing of power, nor is it limited to the classroom in a pedagogical self-management. More than simple self-management, we should speak about collective self-management, that is, self-management as a sociohistorical project, as a movement of the surpassing of individualism, of "the peninsular man," as he is called by Morin (1973).

Education has always had this objective: to train individuals so that they can integrally assume themselves, and, therefore, govern themselves and govern. Self-management is the modern translation of *paideia*. Only today, with the social division of work, a mere part of society—an elite—is being trained to take command and is being trained for self-management. What is lacking is to make this training collective. This will be possible only with the democratization of society.

4

Education and the Class Struggle

It is no surprise that capitalist education is dominated by an individualistic mentality. We find a pedagogy that is sometimes concentrated on the teacher and sometimes on the pupil. References to the social and the political elements are very recent, and clearly appear only at crisis times. The theme of the relationship between education and social class is taboo in practice or is theoretically elaborated in a dogmatic way, as was seen in European pedagogy and philosophy in the 1940s, under the influence of Stalinism, and especially in France (Judt 1992).

Even without abandoning an ideological viewpoint—I understand ideology as a general theory of society—it is possible to treat the theme in a less passionate way. This is what I intend to do in this chapter, as I approach the theme of the relationship between education and the class struggle within the dialectic conception of education.

On one occasion, in an adult literacy center in São Paulo, which contained a large number of supporters of the democratic-socialist

Workers' Party, (Gadotti and Pereira 1989), when the role of the intellectuals inside the party was being discussed, a member of the public said that being intelligent wasn't enough to join a Socialist Party. He added that it is obvious that, here, there are social classes. Therefore, one can see who is on one side and who is on the other.

The discussion that followed had nothing in common with academic disputes as to whether or not social classes exist. A university student continued the discussion as he raised the question of "What is a popular class ?" There was an enormous silence until one of the literacy students replied, "A popular class is made up of people who don't ask what a popular class is." He meant that the ordinary people know very well what ordinary people are like, and they don't need to ask.

Class awareness was not understood as a sociological category nor as conscientization, much less as a taking of consciousness of the world, but rather as an taking part, a taking of sides, or a concrete engagement. The brief discussion that followed contradicted the old thesis, according to which the popular mentality is intrinsically "incoherent, inarticulate, degraded, mechanical and simplistic" as the Brazilian educator Dermeval Saviani maintained while overvaluing critical or philosophical consciousness. (1980, 10) If the popular consciousness initially appears to the intellectual to be incoherent, passive, simplistic, or spontaneous, a greater approximation will reveal a behavior which is coherent and unitary with its class interests. This is not completely clear because the social classes, as we shall see, form complex groups. Therefore, there are those who simply defend the nonexistence of social classes, and do not take class consciousness into account.

It is true that there are societies that have reached a high degree of economic democratization and social welfare, and have also created a strong middle class. It could be said that, in these societies, the classes are not struggling against each other. They enjoy considerable stability, thanks to the conciliation of class interests. However, this is not the case in the majority of poor countries nor in the wealthy countries where there are still enormous disparities in the distribution of income. Social classes do exist. Bourgeois society is essentially a class society. It was not Marx who invented social classes. Everything points to the fact that they will continue to exist. If they had been invented by someone, it would be easier to get rid of them. The popular mentality doesn't have the characteristics which were described by Saviani. As we shall see, if this were the case, it would end up by establishing the existence of a class that was entirely unaware of its interests. Saviani positions himself opposite Paulo Freire and Lukács, who both emphasize the need to learn together with the popular masses. Philosophical consciousness cannot be confused with class consciousness. Class consciousness cannot do without praxis. Only at the risk of making an enormous mistake can it place intellectual training as a presupposition for action. On this point, I prefer to refer to Marx's thesis in *German Ideology* (1977b), in which he sustains that liberation is a historical fact and not an intellectual fact.

Philosophical consciousness has little or nothing to do with class consciousness. More than a century ago, Marx made this separation clear when he stated in his *Eleventh Thesis on Feuerbach* that philosophers have limited themselves to interpreting the world in different ways, when what is important is to transform it.

One can notice here that Marx is not referring to the idealistic German philosophy nor to political bourgeois philosophy. He is instead referring to all philosophy. He is trying to show the limits of philosophy, which are the very limits of reflection, by underlining the need for a *praxis*. However, in doing this, he doesn't deny the value of philosophy and theory in the class struggle, but shows the limits of philosophical speculation.

On the other hand, Marx demonstrates the necessity that philosophy, as a radical reflection, with a rigorous and methodologically structure, doesn't serve social transformation a priori. This reflection needs practice, involvement, and concrete engagement. It is what he himself demonstrates in the rigorous work that he performs in *Capital* (1906), which is never abandoned to its class vision. The philosophical consciousness in *Capital* was appropriated by class struggle, and that is what strengthened the analysis that Marx made of the laws of the formation and development of the productive forces for the working class as not the philosophical and methodological rigour of his work, but rather his class position. In Marx, as we have seen, theory has a "critical and revolutionary" role, as he states in the postface to the second edition of *Capital*.

In the idealist and bourgeois conception, these relationships are inverted. Rigor and internal logic preceed praxis, and class vision is substituted by technical competence—that is, it is technical competence that becomes a political pledge. Technical competence and philosophical competence don't guarantee a priori any advantage over common sense.

I would not like to oppose, by using antonyms, neither the so-called common sense to philosophical consciousness, nor these with class consciousness. This would just be a matter of putting certain concepts against others, some philosophies against others, or one conception against another of many. On the contrary, I would like to reflect on this relationship between education and conscientization or education and class consciousness, which shows the extent to which education is not a neutral nor an apolitical process.

The first obstacle that we should reflect upon is the concept of class itself.

SOCIAL CLASSES STILL EXIST

According to Poulantzas, in Marxist theory, "All social classes are groups of social agents, mainly, but not exclusively, determined by their place in the production process, that is, in the economic sphere." (1978, 13) Although the economic element has had the main role in the determination of social classes, the ideological and political elements are also fundamental in the formation of a class. In Marxist theory, social classes don't exist a priori separated from the class struggle. "Social classes include class practices, that is, the class struggle, and can only be positioned in opposition to each other." (Poulantzas 1978, 14)

The notion of class includes a certain totality, contradictions, and the moment, the practices, and strategies of a group of social agents, determined by the place that they occupy in this struggle, either by their own will or independent of this will.

Therefore, Poulantzas distinguishes the *structural determination of classes* regardless of the will of its agents, the *class position*, in the whole of the class struggle.

> Insisting on the importance of political and ideological relationships in the determination of classes and on the fact that social classes only exist as a struggle (practices) of classes, would not be to reduce, voluntarily, the determination of the classes to the position of the classes. This takes on great importance in the cases in which it can be stated that there is a distance between the structural determination of the classes and the class positions in the whole. (Poulantzas 1978, 14–15)

In fact, *layers or class fractions* can, at certain moments have a class position, which fails to correspond to their own interests, as a result of their class determination. A part of the working class can, at certain moments, take on class positions of the bourgeoisie. There is also the opposite case, when sections of the petty bourgeoisie can take the side of the working class in a strike movement. This doesn't mean that they are part of the working class.

By the structural economic determination, one understands the position that the subject occupies in the production process, and his place in the relationships of production—that is, that of a worker, of the exploited class, or of the dominant and exploiting class of agents who live from their work or from the exploitation of the work of others.

In the passage from competitive capitalism to monopolistic capitalism—and as a result of present-day societies—the social groups that comprise the exploited class and the exploiting class are extremely complex and can't be studied in detail here. Their complexity today no longer leads some sociologists to talk about the bourgeois class and the working class, but rather about bourgeois classes and working classes. Harry Braverman (1977) managed to distinguish a new working class from an old working class. In the new working class, he includes new occupations, created with the development of modern productive forces, especially those which serve an "respositories of specialized knowledge in production and in administration, engineers, technicians, scientists, management assistants, administration experts, teachers, etc." (Braverman 1977, 33) In the second group, he includes manual workers, "despite the concrete movement of occupations and the increase of the various categories of work of this kind." (1977, 33)

Although I would not like to completely avoid this complexity, I would prefer to talk about the working and bourgeois classes.

In the Marxist tradition, the meaning of social class was developed by another theoretician, George Lukács, in his work, *History and Class Consciousness* (1969) originally written in 1922. In later editions, Lukács reexamines some of his positions without, however, denying the central thesis of the role of consciousness in the class struggle. According to the Hegelian scheme, Lukács calls a *class in itself* the structural and objective determination of class through the process of production, and *class for itself* to the class which has its own class awareness and an autonomous political organization. This has nothing to do with an unconscious class (class in itself) and a conscious class (class for itself). Lukács doesn't make a formal opposition between them. Nevertheless, it seems that, in his formulation, he failed to give sufficient attention to class practices and to the ideological class elements which are expressed by classes in struggle.

There is a difference between the interpretations of Lukács and Poulantzas. Poulantzas doesn't believe that a class consciousness or an autonomous political organization is necessary so that the class struggle can take place in all the fields of social reality. It is Poulantzas who attempts to make this differentation, showing that it surpasses the concept of ideology of Marx as a system of ideas or coherent discourse, and understands it as a group of material practices.

In reality, the interpretations of Lukács and Poulantzas are not contradictory, but merely express different facets of the same object of analysis. One must agree with Poulantzas when he states that, even when the working class is heavily influenced by the bourgeois ideology, its existence is translated into specific material, political, and ideological practices, regardless of the degree of organization and of awareness. This doesn't mean, however, that the efficiency in the struggle against the bourgeoisie is the same when the working class has an autonomous political organization and a high level in the formulation of its specific interests—that is to say, a class strategy.

What is a class consciousness? How can it be distinguished from a critical consciousness? What is the role of class consciousness in the class struggle? Can the working class act in a determined state of events against its own interests? These are questions that we shall examine in the next section.

CRITICAL CONSCIOUSNESS AND CLASS CONSCIOUSNESS

I shall try not to give a final definition of these questions, but, rather, show their meaning within a certain totality, which is the sociohistorical movement and which is necessary to know in each set of circumstances. All of these questions have no reply in themselves, but in reference to a determined context.

If we examine the question of class consciousness along these lines, it can only be understood in the context of the class struggle. It is not enough for the working class to understand what class consciousness is. For the working class, the question of class consciousness has a particular meaning—not a general one—a definition of the concept, as it is linked to its practice in the class struggle. Thus, it is not an abstract concept. Class consciousness has a methodological meaning for the working class, whose aim is the conquest of a society of equals, and the domination of the interests of the worker over capital—that is, the transformation of the social system.

As this transformation will not take place spontaneously, the working class—and especially the most oppressed segments of the population—must acquire an increasingly elaborate degree of the awareness of their oppression. Here, the progressive school can play a decisive role. The oppressed class will have an ingenuous but closely lived experience of oppression. This, as Paulo Freire says, in the struggle and in the reflection on the struggle, is transformed into *critical consciousness*, gradually surpassing the initial ingenuousness. However, the critical consciousness is still not class consciousness.

The social agents that acquire the highest degree of understanding of their own situation of oppression might commit other ingenuities. Critical consciousness is not a baptism that washes all the sins away. Neither is it an aware avant-garde taking class consciousness to the masses. It is not something that can be handed over like a present, or donated to the popular masses.

In this question, both economicist spontaneity, which conceives class consciousness of the masses as a pure reflection of their material conditions of life, and idealist volunteerism, which conceives this consciousness as an act of donation of the avant-garde, make a mistake on a very simple point—that is, the fact that their wishes don't coincide with historical reality. In the first case, as Lukács observes, any decisive role of the consciousness in the historical process was taken away" (1974, 63), and, in the second case, the historical role of the masses in the transformation of society was seen to be the work of a small number of demiurges.

In political practice, we frequently find an alternation of trends between *economicism*, which moves toward conservatism, and *avant-gardism*, which, instead of contributing to the advance of the consciousness of the oppressed classes, ends up by distancing them from further supportive engagement. In the class struggle, only the vision of society as a concrete whole can lead to a political party or a social movement to reach its objectives.

Class consciousness for the working class is not a moral consciousness, as the bourgeois and religious sectors have been preaching. Neither is it an empirical consciousness of reality, although the working class can begin from this. This question was discussed in detail in an excellent essay by Adalberto Paranhos (1984), using the critical analysis of Lukács and Goldman and working with the categories of empirical-psychological or real consciousness, and class or possible consciousness. Paranhos believes that there is a real class consciousness and a possible class consciousness. "It is from the real class consciousness, historically considered at a determined time and place that elements that are indicative of the possible class consciousness are found. If the real class consciousness of the proletariat is somewhat contradictory as it is a mixture as much of bourgeois and/or petty bourgeois elements as of specifically proletarian elements, it is only from these latter elements that one can advance to the possible class consciousness." (Paranhos 1983, 51)

I would like to talk about class consciousness, preserving this concept from any subjective interpretation. Class consciousness doesn't mean just a taking of consciousness of a reality, above any act of the transformation of society. Here, it is necessary to avoid both idealism and objectivism. Liberation doesn't work inside the consciousness of men, but in the history that they perform.

Besides, Marx had already warned us about this interpretation in the *The 18 Brumaire of Louis Bonaparte*, when he wrote about the petty bourgeoisie as a class of transition, in which the interests of the two main classes come together to such an extent that it feels above the class contradiction and tries, through all the available means, to surpress the two extremes, to attenuate the oppositions, and reestablish the harmony between the classes, ignoring the existence of antagonistic interests.

As different from the petty bourgeoisie, the working class must become aware of its position in relation to the bourgeois class. Quoting Marx's *Mystery of Philosophy*, Lukács states, "The proletariat must become a class not to confront capital but also to confront itself; that is, it has to elevate the economic necessity of its class struggle to the level of a conscious will, of an acting class consciousness." (Marx in Lukács 1974, 91). This is shown by the close connection between the economic struggle and the political struggle of the proletariat.

Although he wishes to avoid the subject, it is Braverman who offers us the most exact conception of class consciousness. He believes that it is

> ... that state of social cohesion reflected in the understanding and activities of a class or of a segment of class. Its absolute expression is a general and lasting attitude on the part of a class, in the sense of its position in society. Its relative expression in the long term is found in the slowly changing class traditions,

experiences, instruction and organization. Its relative expression in the short term is a complex dynamics of state and of spirit and feelings affected by the circumstances and changing with them, at times, in periods of depression and conflict, almost daily. (Braverman 1977, 36)

He then adds that no class can exist in society "without showing to some degree an awareness of itself as a group with problems, interests and expectations in common, although this manifestation may, for long periods, be fragile, confusing and susceptible to manipulation by other classes." (Braverman 1977, 36)

Wilhelm Reich (1976, 94) distinguished two types of class consciousness and articulation. *Mass class consciousness* is not knowledge of the historical or economic laws that rule the life of men, but rather the knowledge of the vital necessities of each person in every domain, of the ways and possibilities of satisfying these necessities, of the obstacles which are imposed by the society of private economy, of the inhibitions and anxieties which prevent every person from clearly seeing the demands of his own life. *Class consciousness in a revolutionary direction*—that is, of a revolutionary party—is no more than the totality of knowledge and aptitudes that enable what the masses themselves can't express to be expressed.

We need yet another word about a frequently used expression of Lukács'—that the class consciousness of the working class would be the last class consciousness. The class consciousness of the bourgeoisie, which has taken shape through various centuries, is opposed to the class consciousness of the working class in a dialectical relationship of unity and opposition. Defending its own class interests, the bourgeoisie has a consciousness which is necessarily false, as it attempts to mystify the historical reality of its class domination. On the contrary, all that interests the working class is a consciousness that reveals the historical reality of oppression. As Lucien Goldman says, it needs "a truly authentic consciousness." (1979, 39)

The working class cannot surpress the society of classes without, in so doing, surpressing itself as a class. Therefore, the struggle is not just against an external enemy—the bourgeois—but, as Lukács says, it is "a struggle against itself, against the devastating and degrading effects of the capitalist system on its class consciousness" (1974, 69). The working class should immediately surpass these effects through a constant critique of its own steps, acts and conquests.

In other words, it is in the interests of the exploiting capitalist spirit to reduce the class consciousness of the working class, and, through emphasizing its contradictions, reduce the working class to infantility. On the other hand, in order to take over the leadership and hegemony of society, the working class must arm itself with maturity, competence and class consciousness, all of which are able to surpass any class domination. This will not take place without the considerable cultural, social, political, and economic training of the working class, nor without the appropriation of methods, techniques, and knowledge, which are today restricted to the economically dominant class.

It is here that education can make an enormous contribution to the working class, by escaping from simplistic schemes which have been prepared by the scholastic petty bourgeoisie, which amuses itself by offering the working class a school with a superficial technical and scientific training. The main thing for the working class is not to increase its technical knowledge to be able to serve capital better, but to gain enough maturity to confront it and to become the directing class.

I often wonder if the casual farm workers in the interior of the state of São Paulo in Brazil are simply rebellious, or whether they are aware of their exploitation, and the answer fails to satisfy me. Nor am I satisfied when they tell me that it is the pressure of their basic need—hunger—that is the engine of their protest movement and their consciousness, or when they attribute their class consciousness to radical "infiltrators." It can be neither one thing, nor the other, but both with, on the one hand, the technical and political help of the rural trade unions, and on the other, the pressure of people who have nothing to lose.

On a certain occasion, at a meeting with Luiz Inácio (Lula) da Silva, who was, at the time, a metal worker's leader, I stated that the place of the worker is at the gate of the factory and the place of the teacher is in the classroom. He replied by saying that the place of the teacher is also at the factory gate. Even today, I have not been entirely convinced by his reply. I understand that an educator, as a worker, should fight at the gate of the school and not at the factory gate. However, if necessary, the educator must go to the factory gate and especially into the streets to understand the struggle of manual workers, because we are a single class and must learn solidarity in the struggle of our class brethren. It is this lesson that teachers must take in and not give. It is necessary to be with them, so that tomorrow we are not against them nor against their children who attend our schools.

STRIKE AND POLITICAL EDUCATION

In *The Grapes of Wrath,* John Steinbeck gives us a powerful narration of the class struggle in the United States in the 1930s, stating that the struggle for an ideal is the basic quality of humanity. He says, "And fear the time when the strikes stop while the great owners live—for every little beaten strike is proof that the step is being taken. And this you can know—fear the time when Manself will not suffer and die for a concept, for this one quality is the foundation of Manself, and this one quality is man, distinctive in the universe." (Steinbeck 1967, 205).

More than 2000 years ago, Socrates asked how one could learn to be virtuous. After hearing from Socrates that virtue could not be taught—as not even the virtuous Pericles, King of Athens, could transmit his political virtue to his own son Menon—his disciple was surprised. If virtuous men existed and virtue is not something that is innate in men, they must have learned, in one way or another, to become virtuous. Socrates replied, "If our reasoning has been correct up until now, we can only conclude that virtue is not something that can be learned."

Thus, Socratic dialogue finishes, without solving the question of the learning of virtue—that is, of education—as had been proposed in the beginning.

Modern educators and pedagogues surpass this contradiction by demonstrating, as Paulo Freire has done, that no one person educates someone else, but that everyone—educator-pupils and pupil-educators—is educated together. This collective education—which is necessarily political, and which a strike movement unleashes— will probably educate toward political virtue much more than school. In fact, for the worker, the strike is his class process of education. As far as education is concerned, no strike can be a failure. All strikes will reveal this "quality-base" that Steinbeck talks about.

The strike is a school for the working class. From the political angle, strikes always have a positive result. They reveal the abilities of some people and the inabilities of others to handle politics. New leaders are formed in the struggle. Whether the demands are met or not cannot be considered as the only indicator of the success of a strike.

In addition, from the point of view of political education, there are other winners who are not the strikers. See how the *political education of the worker,* and of those who support him, takes shape in the relationship which is established as they go from door to door to collect funds to allow the strike to continue. The "strike fund" serves for both—for those who ask and for those who give or refuse— as an instrument of collective learning of the problems.

Questions are asked and explanations are given. A relationship is established that can break and reduce the individualism that the capitalist mode of production creates and imposes. This experience helps the reduction of such individualism. The refusal to contribute is also an educational act for both. It implies a decision, the essence of the pedagogical act, on the part of he who refuses, whatever the motives may be.

To educate oneself is to take a position, to be a party member. Education is the work of a party. Therefore, a strike educates much more than the strikers themselves might think. These merely supply the occasion for many people to be educated. Because of this, one can be sure that every strike is an advance, or "proof that a step is being taken," as Steinbeck says.

The worker is educated as he becomes aware of his situation and rights. He struggles for these. On discovering the humiliation that he is subjected to every day, he becomes aware of the need and of the possibility of surpassing his present limits, because he is creative and a producer of culture. He discovers his capacity of being, not because someone is whispering in his ear, but because, faced with humiliation, he decides to be. School, when not denied to him, did not teach him to be. On many occasions it humiliated him even more, inculcating him with the idea of his inferiority and inability to be. It did not awaken in him any political virtue. Much to the contrary. It might have taught him a profession, because it was the school belonging to the boss, but it did not teach him how to perform culture or history. With the strike, he feels as if he has history in his hands.

EDUCATION IN THE SOCIETY OF CLASSES

Both the pedagogy of the new school and the pedagogy of the traditional school failed to manage to sufficiently exploit the existing connection between social struggle and pedagogical struggle. Socialist pedagogy exhaustively showed the ideological role of education and denounced its pseudoneutrality. However, it didn't manage to make this negative phase into a positive phase of benefiting and exploiting these analyses at a practical level. An attempt of this type was made by institutional pedagogy.

Bourgeois pedagogues exploited the weaknesses of Marxist pedagogy in this sense by saying that it was no more than a contestation,
or the phase of an antipedagogy. Others insist that it is wrong to ask
the political question of education, as this question has already been
answered. It is a question which has already been surpassed.

This phase of contestation—and of pure critique—has already,
doubtlessly, been surpassed, less because the intellectuals have been
criticizing critical theories than because of the strength of development and of the practical involvement of educators. The surpassing
of a historical phase of education doesn't happen because of ideas,
but because these ideas are modified in function of the social practices of educators, and of social and political movements. If they are
not purely a reflection of material conditions, neither are they purely
a reflection of ideas.

The fact that education is political, the fact of not being able to
perform education in a general sense, the fact that every educative act
as a political act is also a class action and practice—none of these facts
result in the dissolution of the political in the pedagogical, as Saviani
proposes (1983, 92). However, it is impossible for me not to agree with
him at least in one point. The educative act cannot be partisan. However, it is not for the motives that he presents—that is, "education,
being a relationship that takes place mainly between nonantagonistic parties, supposes union and tends to be situated in the perspective
of universality." (Saviani 1983, 90) The reason is neither because this
relationship takes place between antagonistic parties nor because it
is universal. It is because there exists another space for partisan political practice—namely, the political party—and the space of the
school would not be efficent for this. However, the working class cannot be afraid of defending its points of view in the school, and in all
the institutions to which it has access. If it intends to be the dominant class tomorrow, it must, beginning right now, exercise power
wherever it can. The school is also a space of power.

What happens in the school, also happens in the factory. Capitalism forms the idea in the popular masses that everything belongs
to the capitalist, including the state, all the other public institutions,
and the school. The role of the revolutionary educator-worker is to
train the consciousness of the worker to realize that the company, as
much as the school and the state, belong to him as well. In order to
reach the present conquests to which all the inhabitants of the planet
today have a right, as an inheritance of humanity, centuries of accumulated work were necessary in all the sectors of human life. This
wealth of humanity or capital cannot belong to just a few.

This should also begin right now! Power cannot be taken to then learn how to use it. "The ideal taking of power, with the help of a concrete preparation, should preceed the real exercising of power . . . And this is valid for any youth organization, any sports club or military regiment. It is this and just this that is called awakening class consciousness." (Reich 1976, 92)

From right now, the worker should feel that he is the owner of history. It is not an easy question to solve. If it were easy to establish justice, so much struggle would be unnecessary. This is not just a question to be solved. It is a complete program and project for humanity.

What is problematic is not that the dominant class preaches the ideology of private property. What is a scandal is that the school covers up, beneath a pseudouniversality of knowledge, this ideology, and through it, penetrates the masses that attend school to a greater or lesser extent. The preparation of the masses for the exercise of power or citizenship is also a political function of the school. It is of little importance whether this is the specific aim of the school which has been dreamed of by the theoreticians of education. It is a claim of those for whom school is still a space of possible struggle.

The liberal bourgeoisie supported the idea of the universality and the universalization of knowledge, although it nourished scorn for this knowledge. Anibal Ponce (1981) tells us how as this universalization of this knowledge was increasing, exploitation was also increasing, reserving technical culture for the mass of workers. Ponce quotes *Politics* of Aristotle. For Aristotle, "To know how to employ slaves is the science of the owner. This science is not, to be true, neither very extensive or deep: it consists of knowing how to order what the slaves should be doing. Therefore, if the owner can get rid of these jobs, he will give them to a superintendent, in order to devote his time to political life or to philosophy." (Aristotle in Ponce 1981, 148)

Exploitation has no home, nor is any one century more privileged than another. In spite of the proclaimed universality, there are schools for the bourgeoisie, and schools for the working class, reproducing the concrete existence of the social classes. With all the democratization of education—which is preached so much these days—we haven't yet managed to eliminate the classist division of schools, not even in the network of public schools, which are apparently so equal.

In order to be a capitalist, it is unnecessary to be cultivated. Ponce says that "in the books in which Carnegie retold his life and his business transactions, we can overwhelmingly see that fantastic ignorance of this steel king in relation to the technical and scientific problems of this metal. Similarly, in the book in which Henry Ford tells the ins and outs of his industry, we can see how much the despised Edison, who, in his opinion, knew too much to be a good capitalist." (Ponce 1981, 141)

The distinction that Marx made between capitalist and personal appropriation of science should be remembered here. By the first, he understood the appropriation incorporated into capital, which doesn't cost it anything in the form of dead work; and, in the second, as individual capital, human capital, in the incorporation of a certain degree of knowledge, able to increase the exchange value of the workforce. Taken in isolation, the best qualified worker could have a better salary or greater bargaining power in the dispute in the job market. Taken collectively, technical and scientific professional training under capitalism gives priority to capital. It is through this that it stimulates and sets up its own schools. I have shown this in my analysis of the so-called permanent education. (Gadotti 1981)

The bourgeoisie, in the era of monopolistic capital, didn't need education to such an extent as did the revolutionary bourgeoisie at the end of the eighteenth century. The interests of the bourgeoisie were not of disseminating knowledge, which, at the time, was guarded jealously by the clergy and by the nobility—its first state. It was, first and foremost, that of disseminating, through the compulsory, lay, free, and universal public school, the bourgeois vision of the world and morality. However, today, there are more efficient ways of forming public opinion than school. To hope that the bourgeoisie extends school to all those who are under its domination is to hope that it, ingenuously, betrays its own interests.

The studies of Harry Braverman (1977) prove that monopolistic capital has no interest in training for work nor in the development of the public and popular school. The fundamental interest of the bourgeoisie in the basic school is, in its role of disciplining the will of the worker, that it should be given only in homoeopathic doses, as Adam Smith says.

For the modern exploitation of work, the competent worker is the disciplined worker, who is able to follow orders. He doesn't need to know much about what he is doing.

> The more science that is incorporated into the work process, the less the worker will understand about the process; the more complicated the intellectual process that makes the machine turn, the less control and understanding of the machine the

worker will have. In other words, the more the worker needs to know, in order to continue being a human being at work, the less he or she knows." (Braverman 1977, 360)

What late capitalism needs is less a trained mass than teams which dominate technical and organizational knowledge. Therefore, to expect that liberal capitalism will spread the public school to all is to expect that it will destroy itself, and that it will use its own weapons against itself. It is to expect that the dominant class will commit suicide.

As Braverman shows, the diffusion of instruction and the spread of schooling have merely served as a means of sifting, increasing the number of qualified workers, and increasing the reserve industrial army—and, with it, the control of the remuneration of the workforce (Braverman 1977, 371).

I cannot forget what Paulo Freire told me on 5 March 1977, in the points he made at the *viva* of my doctoral thesis at the University of Geneva, where he used the recently published North American edition of Braverman's work to refer to the so-called permanent education, which was the theme of my thesis.

There's no way of expecting that an education, with or without adjectives at the service of the preservation of the capitalist means of production, takes the productive process as the object of critical reflection. Such an analysis would end up by revealing the reason of being of the alienation of work, of its degradation. Therefore, the exclusive emphasis should be given not to the political and complete formation of the worker, but to training. (Freire in Gadotti 1981, 18)

Bourgeois theory of education tries to separate the social, political, and educational. As the German philosopher Schmied-Kowarzik states, "The fact that the pedagogical theoreticians believe and make others believe that pedagogy, simply by keeping the pupils away from the struggles and political misunderstandings, can humanize man and improve his relationships, is part of the context of the misrepresentation of bourgeois society." (1983, 108)

This is also the opinion of George Snyders. In the fundamental experience of Marxism, Snyders tells us that the first reality to become aware of at school is the class struggle. "It is precisely in order not to talk about the essential element that attention is given to a mass of useless, superfluous and lifeless knowledge." (Snyders 1974, 323)

Marx merely outlined his theory of education. The dialectical conception of education afterward received the contributions of numerous philosophers and educators. These theoreticians could show, especially in the twentieth century, the unfoldings of the first of Marx's theses in relation to education. On one hand, they showed the class characteristics of bourgeois education and the mystification of its pedagogy. On the other hand, they pointed to the possibilities of associating social and pedagogical struggles, and opening a path for an emancipating pedagogy—that is, for an education directed toward the future with equity and justice for all.

5

A Single School for Everyone

Two elements have always been present in the defense of popular education. On the one hand, there is the large number of supporters of the public school; and, on the other hand, diverse groups, some of them religious, represent the social movements in the democratization of teaching. On the other side, and against popular education, private capitalist initiative has always defended an elitist conception of education. This is what I intend to show in this chapter, while defending the construction of a liberating education which trains participating and enterprising citizens.

THE SOCIALIST CONCEPTION OF PUBLIC EDUCATION

Socialist thinking in education dates back a long time. However, as it has never catered to the dominant interests, it has often been forgotten or relegated to an inferior level. The socialist conception of education, right from its origins, has been directed to the surpassing of the bourgeois classist conception of education, and toward the fulfillment of the ideal of an equal education for everyone. Therefore, a struggle for a democratic high-quality education has been a part of the socialist tradition. Considering an education directed toward the future, it is of interest to look back on this tradition and its main representatives.

Thomas More (1480–1535) was one of the first philosophers to think about coeducation and the relationship between manual and intellectual work. Domenico Campanella (1568–1639), in his book *The City of God,* which was written at the time of the complete domination of clerical obscurantism, defended observation, the scientific method in education, and the end of educational discrimination between the sexes. Similarly, Michel de Montaigne (1533–1592) stated the need to base learning on direct contact with the world, and not just on books. Montaigne's ideas were echoed by François Rabelais (1495–1533), who fought the authoritarianism of traditional education by supporting the freedom of the child and the opening of school for society.

However, it was Jean-Jacques Rousseau (1712–1773) who systematically worked on the political role of education, attempting to base it on the principles of liberty, equality, and justice. His Émile is an ideal type of pupil, and he develops his own nature effortlessly without being prevented from doing anything that he is able to do. Inspired by Rousseau, Graco Babeuf (1760–1796) educated his own children and formulated a number of principles of socialist pedagogy, among them that of a single type of public school for all. In *Manifesto of the Plebians,* Babeuf accused the dominant education of being opposed to the interests of the people, and of instilling them with a subjection to their state of misery.

Étienne Cabet (1788–1856) defended the idea that the school should feed everyone equally, and that it should be the place for the development of the whole community. He believed that educating the people meant politicizing them. At the same time, Charles Fourier (1772–1837), who understood civilization as a war between rich and poor, gave education an important political role.

Henry de Saint-Simon (1760–1825) defined education as the practice of social relationships. He criticized the education of his time that distanced school from the real world and supported a supernational public education.

Robert Owen (1771–1858) is one of the first thinkers to give fundamental pedagogical importance to manual work. He believed that education should have productive work as a basic principle. He contended that the school should present production and social problems directly and concretely.

Victor Considerant (1808–1893) defended public education with the participation of the student in the organization and management of the educational system.

Pierre Joseph Proudhon (1809–1865) conceived manual work as the generator of knowledge. He admitted that a truly popular and democratic education could not exist under capitalism, and that poverty was the main obstacle to popular education. He foresaw that, under capitalism, there would be a great quantitative expansion of trained employees, who would bring salaries down and capital profits up. He denounced the farce of the free capitalist public school in which the exploited classes who need to work don't have access to a better quality of bourgeois school. He believed that it was a ridiculous utopia to expect that the bourgeoisie would keep its promise of free, universal public education. Those who benefit from public education are the rich, as the poor are being condemned to work right from their childhood.

As we have seen, the principles of a socialist pedagogical education were put forward by Marx (1818–1882) and Engels (1820–1895), and developed by Vladimir Illitch Lenin (1870–1924) and Pistrak among others. In their *Manifesto of the Communist Party*, Marx and Engels defend free public education for all children based on four principles.

1. The elimination of child labor in factories;
2. The association between education and material production;
3. A polytechnical education that will lead to the training of an omnilateral man; and
4. The inseparability of education and politics, therefore of the whole of the social, and the connection between free time and work time, study, and leisure.

Despite being more skeptical than Marx, Mikhail Bakunin (1814–1876) proposed the struggle against the educational elitism of bourgeois society, which he called immoral.

Francisco Ferrer Guardia (1859–1909) proposed a rational education which was opposed to the mystical and supernatural conception. This lay education—which would be complete and scientific—would be based on four principles: science and reason;

the harmonious development of the intelligence, will, morality, and body; the importance of example and solidarity; and the adaptation of the methods to the age of the pupils.

Lenin gave considerable importance to education in the process of social transformation. As the first revolutionary to take control of a popular government, he could experiment with the implementation of socialist theses in education. Believing that education should play an important role in the construction of a new society, he stated that even bourgeois education, which he criticized so much, was better than ignorance. Public education should be primarily political. "Our work in the area of teaching is the same struggle to defeat the bourgeoisie; we publicly declare that the school that is at the margins of life and politics is falsity and hypocrisy." (Lenin 1981, 70)

In his decree of 26 Deceber 1991, Lenin obliged "all the illiterate people between 8 and 50 to learn to read and write in their own language or in Russian, whichever they preferred" (Lenin 1981, 10). In his notes written in April and May of 1917, for the revision of the party program, Lenin defended:

1. The annulment of a single language of the state;
2. Free, general, polytechnical education, compulsory until the age of 16;
3. The free distribution of food, clothing, and school materials;
4. The transference of public instruction to the democratic organs of the autonomous local administration;
5. The abstention of central power from intervention in the school programs and in the choice of personnel;
6. To elect teachers directly, giving the population the right to fire undesirable elements;
7. The forbidding of employers to use children until they were 16;
8. The limiting of the working hours of young people between 16 and 20 to four hours a day; and
9. Prohibiting children from working at night in insalubrious factories or mines.

Pistrak, one of the first educators of the Russian revolution, paraphrased Lenin's contention that there was no revolutionary practice without revolutionary theory, by saying that "without a revolutionary pedagogical theory there can be no revolutionary pedagogical practice." (Pistrak 1981, 29) He gave the teacher the role of an active militant. He expected the pupils to work collectively and to organize themselves autonomously. *Self-organization* and *collec-*

tive work were to surpass the professorial authoritarianism of the bourgeois school.

In order to achieve this self-organization, the pedagogue must attempt to show not only the importance of learning for life, but also how necessary it is for the practice of a determined action. The teacher is an adviser. Only the assembly of pupils can decide on punishments, and the mandates of representation are short in order to enable alternation.

The school methods are active and connected to manual work, such as domestic work, woodwork, metalwork, and agricultural work in developing the alliance between city and countryside. In both agricultural and industrial work, it is necessary that each pupil feels as if he or she is taking part in the production process, according to individual mental and physical abilities. The pupil doesn't go to the factory to work, but to understand the entire process of work. Pistrak says that the problems of our times break out first in the factory.

In the socialist conception of public education, work is the fundamental educational principle. It is an instrument of mediation between mankind and the world, and, at the same time, it is an object of study and a means of integration of theory, practice, criticism, and social transformation. The socialist conception of public education is one which is compromised with the interests of the working class. Therefore, it is conditioned by a vision of both class and history. Even if there is no chance of this conception being completely fulfilled in a capitalistic society, this doesn't prevent possible progressive advances from taking place within it. Thus, we can understand the critical and revolutionary critique of Paulo Freire in a society which he calls one in transition. His *Pedagogy of the Oppressed* takes its place in the struggle for a critical and socialist public education, constructed by the popular masses at the same time as they are struggling for the radical transformation of society.

In the words of the great Polish socialist educator, Bogdan Suchodolski, the socialist school should be "A school directed to the future." (1972, 118)

Bourgeois society doesn't fulfill the conditions for a full educative development as it has a divided and compartmentalized school. Discussing the historical development of pedagogies of essence and existence, Suchodolski concludes that the

> . . . conception of the human essence cannot give origin to an existence of the man corresponding to this essence, nor does

human existence necessarily give origin to the essence of man. What is important is to make such conditions possible, provide encouragement, guarantees and organization, which are the basis of development and of training, the basis for creation and of the human essence." (1972, 117)

Why a school directed to the future?
Because the present reality is not the only reality, nor is it an unchangeable reality. The criterion of the popular and transforming school is the future reality.
According to Suchodolski,

Historical necessity and the fulfillment of our ideal coincide in the determination of this future reality. . . . The fetishism of the present that cannot tolerate the critique of the existing reality and which, through this motive, reduces pedagogical activity to conformism, is destroyed by the education that is directed toward the future." (1972, 118)

Even aware that the public school is not the fundamental agent of change within capitalist society, this is why, from a socialist viewpoint, a basic educational program in a popular public school must engage the young in working toward a better future.

The bourgeois school is based on the adaptation of man to his environment. From the socialist perspective that was indicated by Marx, people are not formed exclusively by their environment nor by the development of their consciences, but by a combination of both, through what he calls a revolutionary practice. It is this practice and the reflection on it that enable the conception of the bourgeois school to be surpassed.

Bogdan Suchodolski, in his *Marxist Theory of Education* (1966), analyzes the pedagogical thinking of Marx, and the difference of opinion which he had with Hegel and Proudhon. He shows that, right from Thomas More and Campanella, utopia has never lost its importance in the history of pedagogical thinking. In the socialist conception of education, utopia is a complete project that breaks with the prison of the present. Thus, he insists on the social function of the school that the bourgeoisie doesn't want to alter.

The theoreticians of the bourgeois school have gotten lost in the education-society antinomy. They wonder whether they should first change the circumstances of people, society, or school. Suchodolski show that, starting from Marx's thinking, the only alter-

native is in the pact between the school and the revolutionary practice of the working class.

> This is the only path for the true training of new men. It means
> that many ideas on teaching, many purely scholastic concep-
> tions about educative work and the development of the child
> must be changed. It means that educative work must be ac-
> complished with the spirit of political struggle for the libera-
> tion of men from the prisons of class oppression, and this work
> must be considered from the aspect of the great perspectives of
> a radical transformation which is parallel to the circumstances
> of men. (Suchodolski 1966, 332–333)

A UNITARY, PLURALISTIC, AND AUTONOMOUS SCHOOL

Among the various currents and trends in education, the main
ones are the *single school* and the *pluralistic school.* In general, the
supporters of the former include the defenders of the public school;
and the supporters of the second include the defenders of the private
school. One cannot, however, say that they are antagonistic conceptions. The pluralistic school includes supporters of the confessional
school and the purely mercantile school. It is also possible to talk
about a unitary pluralistic school, which would be the nonuniform,
but differentiated, public school.

All this leads us to examine the question of the dichotomy between the single school and the pluralistic school.

The twentieth century has been characterized in the area of education by the struggle for a single school that is equal for everyone.
However, as Lorenzo Luzuriaga (1934) shows, the idea of the single
school is very old. Among its defenders were Plato, Comenius,
Pestalozzi, Schleiermacher, Condorcet, and Fichte.

Plato believed that education is an essential function of the
state. Through a basic single school, the school would select the
most able to govern. Only the wisest should be the governors. As
a follower of Platonic ideas, Comenius defended the thesis of a
common school, and a general education for everyone. He defended
pansofia—that is, teaching everything to everyone. Pestalozzi was
also inspired by the single school, whose basis is the general primary
school. Schleiermacher believed that school curriculums should be
the same, regardless of social class. The pedagogues of the French
Revolution, such as Condorcet, thought that the primary school
should be universal, public, free, and lay. Fichte, the creator and

inspirer of German national education, thought that education should be given to all, without any exception, so that, rather than belonging to a special class, education belongs to the nation, and none of its members are omitted.

In the modern sense, the expression *single school* is the defective translation of the German *Einheitschule,* whose correct translation should be "school in unity" or "unified school." It has nothing to do with the monopoly of teaching by the state nor with the uniformization of all education. The single school admits all the different varieties of teaching, and, therefore, is a differentiated or pluralistic, school.

According to Lorenzo Luzuriaga, the single school

> . . . essentially represents the extension of the popular educational movement which began in the eighteenth century, on one hand with the enlightened kings of Prussia, who set up the public school, the school which was instituted, maintained and directed by the state, and on the other hand, with the French Revolution, with its conception of national education, that is, education without class distinction, education of the people in general. This movement developed fully in the nineteenth century, which definitively established the free, compulsory and national public school in all the civilized world, and naturally continued through the twentieth century, which has tended to extend this education beyond the limits of primary teaching both by setting up training schools for proletarian youth and with the aspiration of a single school, that is, of middle and higher education in its totality for everyone,. . . . This is the unitary organization of the educational institutions of a people, so that they can be accessible to all its members, according to their aptitude and vocations, and not according to their economic, social and confessional situation. Or, more concretely, the actuation of education according to the intrinsic conditions of those who should be educated. Or, finally, the putting into practice of education according to its own authentic laws. (1934, 15–18)

The movement, *Les Compagnons,* formed by European teachers who had fought in World War I, stands out as a supporter of the single school. The general secretary of this group was Maurice Weber. In a two-volume book published between 1918 and 1919, called *L'Université Nouvelle, Les Compagnons* expounded their *principles of the single school.*

1. A democratic teaching should be established as all children have a right to receive the broadest education that the country can give them. The country, in turn, has the right to exploit all the spiritual riches that it possesses. Teaching conceived in this way is, at the same time, a selection process.
2. The separations between primary, secondary, and higher teaching have no *raison d'être*. Citizens should not be separated, right from their beginning, into two classes, and be fixed in them forever by different kinds of education.
3. The solution is the single school, which, on one hand leads to the humanities, and, on the other, to professional teaching. The single school is the primary school for everyone, whether they be the children of bourgeois, workers, or peasants. It is the free public primary school converted into the compulsory basis for any teaching.
4. The single school is not a single place, but a single teaching, exam, and teacher. It immediately supposes the suppression of the elementary classes from the secondary schools, and, with this, the end of the separation between the teaching of the poor and the teaching of the wealthy.
5. The single school is not compatible with the free, private, and uniform school. (Luzuriaga 1958, 113)

In France, the single school has been supported by the French League of Teaching, and, at the moment, is supported by the General Federation of Teaching, the General Confederation of Work (CGT), and by the left-wing political parties. The program that the left had in common, when François Mitterand was elected President in 1981, foresaw the nationalization of private schools, which was severely criticized by the Catholic Church and by the right-wing parties.

Right from the first days of the Russian Revolution (Pinkevitch 1941), the socialist school was conceived as a single school, as a school of work, a school where all children should have the same type of education, with equal rights to reach the highest levels, with preference of access being given to the poorest workers.

According to Albert Pinkevitch, the single school of work should not merely be socialist and communist. It should also be unified and self-organized.

Antonio Gramsci, the historian who was a supporter of the single school—as we saw in chapter 2 of this book—calls the single school the "unitary school," giving the idea of unity and democratic centralization. Following the Leninist conception of education, he also places work as an anthropological and educative basic principle of training. He criticizes the traditional school, which divides the classical and professional schools. The former is destined for the "instrumental classes," and the latter for the "dominant classes." (Gramsci 1968, 118)

In his conception of the unitary schools, he proposes the surpassing of this division between classical, intellectual, and professional training in a critical and active school.

> The advent of the unitary schools means the start of new relationships between intellectual and industrial work, not only in school but in all social life. The unitary principle will therefore be reflected in all the cultural organisms, which will be transformed and given new content. (Gramsci 1968, 118)

All these theories and concrete proposals for the surpassing of elitism in education have as their backdrop the difficult equation between the freedom of organization of schools, the freedom of teaching, and the political will to extend education to everyone. A single or unitary school, and centralized training of people on an assembly line might be effective in the short term, but it will continue to be elitist and authoritarian, and, therefore, antidemocratic, even though it might be called socialist. As we shall see in Chapter 7, only an autonomous school, which obviously takes the risk of inequality and competition between schools, can make the school a place for the creation of the future.

THE BOURGEOIS CAPITALIST ALTERNATIVES

We began the twentieth century with enormous hope invested in education. However, we are arriving at the end of the century with a worldwide crisis in education, in which the pedagogical optimism of the beginning of the century has been substituted by a lack of belief. It is true, if we compare the education of the last century with that of this century, that we have made enormous advances. The public powers, pressed by popular demand, have been forced to increase the supply of education. No longer do we have, as in the last century, an almost total control of teaching by the private sector, and the average number of years that the pupil spends at school has also increased.

The polemical thesis that scholastic expansion does not correspond to the necessities of capital has already been defended at length (Braverman 1977, and Salm 1980), as we saw in the previous chapter. In the vision of capitalist production, what matters is giving the minimum of education to the majority, and the maximum to a small minority. It seems that this remains valid as long as

> ... the large company has no great need of training and making impositions on the teaching system; in brief, capital is not the greatest force that orchestrates the rhythm of the increase of the number of courses and enrollments. On the contrary, the school even manages to do a disservice to capital as it trains people who are more demanding and less disposed to accept factory and office routine. . . . The company itself decides, in the workplace, most of the meagre experience that it demands from the majority of its employees. (Durand 1980)

So, who needs a public school today? If capital doesn't have so much interest in the school, will it interest the workers?

The school is certainly not, for the worker, the main locus for his resistance and his political training. At least, it hasn't been up to now. It is also not enough to guarantee a high-quality school for everyone. There are other areas of struggle and of training for the worker—namely, the union, the party, the association, the social and popular movements, and so on.

So, what role can the public school play in the defense of popular interests? To where do the struggles of the workers point? The Brazilian educator Miguel Arroyo can answer the question.

> They do point toward the defense of the existence of the school. But never as the fundamental agent of their liberation. There is no use guaranteeing the school as a cultural space and denying the real cultural spaces where the people build themselves, strengthen themselves and construct their vision of the world and their identity. (1986, 143)

In the second half of the twentieth century, the capitalist state has been divesting itself of its obligation to provide educational services, trying to transfer all responsibility for teaching to civil society and citizens. At the same time, the movement against state or nationalized companies has been increasing, attempting to limit the power of the state, and spreading the thesis that the state should do only that which the private sector is unable to do. Many capitalist states—and even formerly socialist states—have been trying to de-nationalize all sectors of the economy that can be guaranteed by private initiative.

The supporters of private initiative in education have constantly tried to show the inability of the state to provide education for all. Many of them have sought support from the theses of the American economist Milton Friedman (1982), according to whom the crisis in the United States public school is due to, first, the movement of the private school, which is controlled by parents and local communities, to the public sector, which is controlled by the government; and, second, by the fact that professional educators have taken the place of amateur educators, who were connected to and controlled by the community. Friedman finds the solution of the crisis in the privatization of teaching.

The theses of Friedman defend the citizen's freedom of choice, and the equality of opportunities. He says that these would be the principles of a democratic school.

In the French magazine, *L'Express,* in September 1984, Jimmy Goldsmith interprets Friedman's ideas for the French reality, but within a more general point of view—that of the theory of the capitalist school today. A summary of his main theses in relation to education were published in the Brazilian newspaper *O Estado de São Paulo,* on 21 October 1984, under the title of "The Power of the State Must Be Limited."

1. The *state* must see that every child can reach the level of learning which is judged to be necessary by the state. In addition to this, it will have to anticipate that the most worthy will need access to higher education or specialization.
2. The state should not integrate *teachers* into the administration nor create a monopoly of teaching establishments.
3. It is the right of every *family* to choose the place where their children will be taught. The family is obliged to continue the education of the child up to the level considered to be the minimum by the nation. The obligation of the nation is to make sure that there is no split in the educational system between rich and poor. The fundamental liberty to choose the school for one's children must exist, but on the condition that schools for the rich and schools for the poor are not organized. The equality of opportunities is a supreme right. Instruction that separates rich and poor would be the negation of this right and would create or consolidate a class system. Naturally, there will always be, and there must always

be, a separation between those who are deserving and those who are not.

4. The state should provide each family with an *annual credit,* in the form of a bonus, to cover the cost of education of each child at the level considered necessary by the nation. The family will be able to chose the places of teaching where they will invest the resources which have been put at their disposal by the state.
5. The state should have the right to ensure that there is a *minimal level of instruction* offered by the teaching establishments involved. With this aim, it should intervene in the determination of the modalities and the content of certain examinations and competitions.

In the same article, Jimmy Goldsmith thus summarizes the *advantages* of Friedman's alternative of establishing and protecting the freedom of teaching; permitting the multiplication of teaching premises; placing the child safely from any indoctrination from the state; teaching him the values of the nation; reducing the enormous legion of civil servants; broadening the choice; reinforcing family responsibility; and promoting freedom.

Friedman's proposals are tempting, and are supported by a historical analysis. One can wonder that, if all his proposals were put into practice—for example, the end of schools for the rich and schools for the poor—would the school continue to be capitalist? Would capitalism continue to be the same? From the theoretical point of view, socialists and neoliberal capitalists have common points in the answers that they make to the educational problems which are common to everyone. This viewpoint is something new in the educational debate, and it helps to instigate a new theory of education. This is also, quite definitely, a postmodern theme which is just opening to discussion, and one that should be followed.

One can see the contradictory dynamics of the capitalist state. It decentralizes the educational services, at the same time as it centralizes economic and political power. Under the appearance of autonomy and freedom of choice, it creates conditions for the progressive death of the individual, and the growth of impersonal control. It is the state that ends up by being autonomous.

As Toqueville says

After having thus taken each individual in his powerful hands and after having shaped them in the way he wished, the sovereign extends his arms over all of society; he covers the surface with a network of complicated, minute and uniform rules, through which the most original spirits and the most vigorous souls were unable to raise themselves above the mass. He doesn't double will power but softens, bends and directs it. He rarely forces people to act but frequently opposes action. He doesn't destroy but prevents birth. He doesn't tyrannize but gets in the way, constrains, unnerves, chills, blunts, reduces. In brief, each nation is nothing more than a herd of small and timid animals, whose shepherd is the government. (1969, 313)

The so-called democratic countries promise *autonomy* and practice *despotism*. Thus, one can hardly expect that the workers will win complete autonomy without a huge change in the economic relationships which now exist under capitalism. This is not a defense of a backward, rickety, and inefficient economic system, centered on state planning, as was implanted on the so-called formerly socialist countries. However, it is important that we don't expect that these relationships change within capitalism so that, only then, can we think about an autonomous society and a school that contributes to it. Remembering the words of Suchodolski, a progressive school today, oriented by a revolutionary project, must be a "school looking to the future." (1972, 118) One can't demand much of the socialist educator within the capitalist school. One can ask him to take a political position in which he clearly announces that he has a compromise to make certain that the capitalist school is not, at least, reactionary. A socialist today must have the same daring as Mikhail Gorbachev, Nobel Peace Prize winner in 1990, who, when visiting Japan as the last President of the now-extinct Soviet Union, said that he could see more socialism there than in his own nation.

The American philosopher and educator J. Adler Mortimer, author of *The Great Ideas*, launched the *Paideia Proposal* a few years ago. *Paideia* comes from the Greek *pais* or *paidós*, meaning the education of the child, a term related to pedagogy and pediatrics in a broad sense, and the equivalent of the Latin *humanitas*, the *humanities*, meaning the general learning that should be the patrimony of all human beings.

The *Paideia* is an educational manifesto which aims at overcoming the main problems of North American education, namely:

1. The enormous *difference in quality of public school.* The schools in privileged communities are good, and the schools in poor and ethnic minority communities are awful.

2. *Excessively early specialization.* Many children are trained for narrow and limited subjects, professions, or jobs.
3. *The individualization of teaching,* resulting in a curriculum that offers a large number of optional, elective and extramural courses.
4. The traditional and static *methods of teaching,* based on memorization and the verbal transmission of content.
5. The arrival of freshmen in the faculties without basic skills, because of decline in the quality of schooling.

Faced with this picture, the *Paideia Proposal* put forward the following ideas: the same quality for everyone; the same aims for everyone; and the same curriculum for everyone.

Mortimer's mistake is to admit, as did John Dewey, that American society is not classist. His social principle is that the people, as a whole, are the dominant class in the United States. He states that, if the United States is a classless society, then it shouldn't be a society with classes as far as education is concerned. This viewpoint demands the same quality of teaching for everyone.

On the other hand, Mortimer's curriculum proposals fail to overcome *technicism* and *pragmatism.* The person—the child—is absent. There is a static and reproductive vision of culture. There is an excessive emphasis on intellectual and mental training, and little space for manual work, affective education, and the concrete experience of society. There is no analysis of the structural problems of schools, such as bureaucracy, hierarchy, and the lack of autonomy, dialogue, and solidarity. He envisions a narrow, nationalist society which idealizes American democracy, the dream of the good life, and faith in technology and in the ability to solve any problem without touching the structure of society.

If these points are not enough to reveal the conservative character of this proposal for a single school, then it will be quite sufficient to mention that Mortimer dedicates the *Paideia Proposal* to, among others, "the military leaders who need well-trained personnel in the troops to handle sophisticated weapons."

THE SCHOOL AS A CULTURAL AGENT

Pedagogical thinking has made considerable development in Brazil in recent years. It is interesting to be familiar with it, as well as to better understand the contribution of Paulo Freire to worldwide pedagogical thinking. One of the themes that has been much discussed is the social role of education.

In Brazil, the idea of the single school has had many supporters, including Lourenço Filho (1897–1970), one of the pioneers of the new school, who prefaced the book *A escola única (The single school)* by Lorenzo Luzuriaga in 1934. Another supporter of the single school was Fernando de Azevedo (1894–1974), who, according to his pupil and admirer, Antônio Cândido de Mello e Souzo, "was already armed with the intellectual instruments in the mid-1920s, which led him to join the great phalanx of the renovators of public teaching at the different levels in Brazil. His teaching was lay, antiauthoritarian, rational, scientific, and adjusted to social changes, which was translated into practice by the first stage of the struggle in favor of modern pedagogical methods, modernization in the training of teachers, and an updating in school administration. His reform has a peculiarly tempestuous side, thanks to the daring and the extent of the modifications and the aura of transforming radicalness that worried traditional groups—the so-called Bolshevization of teaching—and that attracted the strongest of attacks, culminating with the attempt on his life at a moment when he was demonstrating his project." (Mello e Souza 1988, 79–80)

Brazilian liberals defended the public school until the end of the 1960s, when they aligned with the privative policies of the military regime. We can point out two trends within the progressives' policies which were grouped around two central pedagogical orientations— *cultural transmission* or *cultural transformation*. Both deny the discriminatory model of the capitalist school, but they are different, not antagonistic, in their proposals. In many aspects, they are complementary. Cultural transmission cannot be opposed to cultural transformation.

Under the influence of the work of Gramsci, the progressive Brazilian educators took up the defense of the unitary public school. There are few who have used the term *single*, but many support its principles.

Guiomar Namo de Mello—a recognized Brazilian educator and one of the founders of ANDE, the National Association of Education, and later a deputy in the government of the State of São Paulo—talks about the single school as opposed to the regional school. She says

It is also in the name of freedom that the single, national school is rejected for a free regional school. The unitary schools would be standardizing, trampling the local culture and regional traditions. It is the recognition and the assimilation of the diversity as a starting point that really guarantees the homogeneity of the educative process at the point of arrival. The aim is, starting from the local culture, to reach determined universal blocks of knowledge which ensure national unity. By avoiding cultural ghettoes, the world vision of the Brazilian citizens is broadened. In spite of the enormous differences in their levels of national, state, local, and family wealth, all the citizens have the right to a common basic training." (Mello 1986, 155)

Further on, Mello states that the basic and universal school should have both a common starting point and a point of arrival—that is, a training for citizenship.

This controversial educator, as she calls herself, was named Municipal Secretary for Education of the city of São Paulo from 1983—1985, and, transforming "from catapult into glass" (1986, 81), sought an alternative which was between "ingenuous pedagogical activism" and the "immobilistic pessimism of the left." (1986, 27) This alternative would result in "A better school for everyone." (Mello 1986, 155).

Among the defenders of the single school, some support the presence of the state, but without a monopoly, among those supporters are Luiz Antônio Cunha, Vanilda Paiva, and Celso de Rui Beisiegel. Others, such as Dermevel Saviani, reject the tutelage of the state in educational matters, and support the strengthening of the presence of civil society.

Saviani points to the strategy which will take education out of the tutelage of the state. "Instead of centralizing the defense of the public school in the opposition between public and private teaching, it should be centered on the opposition of the teaching of the elite and poplar education." (Saviani 1984, 21). Saviani also wrote "instead of putting the accent on the question of the public school in higher education, one should fight for the popularization of knowledge." (1984, 22). Futhermore,

The comments on the autonomy of the school may make the idea of the single school unfeasible at a national level. The proposal of the single school does not take away the importance of participation at all levels. The community should, however, take an active part in discussing the national question and not propose alternatives that are incompatible with the more general worries. (Saviani in Nogueria 1986, 27)

Both Guiomar Namo de Mello and Dermeval Saviani connect the question of the public school with the question of the *socialization of elaborated knowledge*. They believe that the school is not an agency of the socialization of popular knowledge. For this aim, the school is unnecessary, as the people themselves will take care of it. They are against polarities, such as a reproductive school versus the school as a revolutionary agent; the school can do nothing versus the school can do everything; and the school as an ideological apparatus versus a popular school.

These various positions are summarized in the thesis of Vanilda Paiva.

> Making the school popular doesn't imply that it has to be made substantially different from the school of the elites. And it is this school that the popular classes want to tear away from the state, submitting it to their critique without deteriorating its quality or abdicating from its content." (1984, 39)

This current of Brazilian pedagogical thinking doesn't so much question the characteristics and the social function of the present school as it queries the lack of access for the majority of the population. A popular school would not be different. It would be the same school, but with free access for everyone.

Paulo Freire, Luiz Eduardo Wanderley, Marilena Chauí, and others have insisted on making an equation between the question of the public school and the question of power, distinguishing the popular characteristics of the public school from liberal conception, which was marked, at the end of the eighteenth century, by education being part of the nation or state. They support the idea of the single school, as long as the state doesn't attempt to homogenize it. They also support the idea of a school made by the people and not for the people, or, as Florestan Fernandes said at the First Public Session of the Forum of Education of the State of São Paulo, on 17 August 1983, a school in which the engagement of the educator is able to "link the struggle for the socialization of knowledge with the main struggle of the working class," which is the struggle for the end of political domination and economic exploitation of the bourgeoisie over the workers.

Marilena Chauí sees, in the bourgeois state public school, as she said at the same 1983 Forum of Education, the authoritarian characteristics of knowledge characterized by that which she calls "already thought out, already said, already made for the people." On the contrary, what characterizes the popular public school, she contends, "is the discovery of the thoughts which haven't yet been thought; the discourse and the possibility of saying what hasn't yet been said, inaugurating a new way of expressing reality, in which action is the creation of its own possible self."

So, these educators insisted enormously on the political training of a new educator who can conceive and create the new school together with pupils, parents, and ancillary staff.

In the functionalist liberal bourgeois conception, the function of the public school is already defined as the diffusion of knowledge. Florestan Fernandes says that in this conception

> . . . the teacher interests inasmuch as he is pure and simply an agent of cultural transmission. His relationship with his pupil is not even a creative relationship. It was that of preserving the levels which had been reached in the realization of that culture by imitation. In this context, the intellectual was, so to say, domesticated. Whether his origin was noble or plebian, he was automatically qualified as a member of the elite and, when this didn't happen, as in the case of elementary school teachers, he was an intermediary element in the interminable chain of political and cultural domination. (Fernandes in Catani, 1986, 16)

Florestan Fernandes also believes that it is vital that the educator

> . . . go back to thinking how he may combine his roles inside the classroom with those he has in society, so that he doesn't see in the student someone inferior to himself, so that he untie once and for all any link he has with cultural domination, and so that he stop being an instrument of the elites." (Fernandes in Catani, 1986, 23)

Discussing the question of the *national* and the *regional*, of the *state* and the *popular*, Marilena Chauí (1986) analyzes the different confrontations and contradictions in the capitalist state and its institutions. She recognises the presence of contradictions in the capitalist school; and the motive for which it may be an agent in the class struggle and, therefore, can be popular and transforming, even within the bourgeois state. She understands, as an example of this, the critical presence of popular culture, demonstrated by the living practice of the pupils who resist the cultural inculcation of the capitalist school. The term *popular* should be understood here as something which takes effect through the dominating culture, although it resists this dominating culture. It is opposed to the illuminist ideas, defended today by mass culture, that the elite posses sufficient organized knowledge to communicate it to everyone, and to show the different cultural manifestations which have been conditioned by the opposition of classes.

Chauí believes that the popular is as ambiguous as the national. The authoritarian and centralized state, in banalizing and domesticating culture, identifies the popular as the regional, labelling everything it produces as typical and folksy, and combating the regional diversities in favor of a national identity. It considers the national as cultivated and illustrated, the popular as romantic and uncultivated.

I believe that these analyses of Marilena Chauí are important because the current tendency of the bourgeois state is to become more and more centralizing and authoritarian. Therefore, the question of the hegemony of the working class passes through the direct organization of the masses, through the workers' councils, and through the *autonomy* which is the refusal of centralization and, at the same time, the refusal of the dominant ideology.

The school is an important part of the conquest of the autonomous, cultural, social, and political power of the workers.

The single, popular, and democratic school, in its different interpretations, has always represented the point of view of the educators and of the workers, and not of capital and the capitalist state. However, it is just one point of view, an abstract idea, created from the theory or the practice of some particular educator. It is part of an active movement, which was born from the immobilism of the even progressive authoritarian theories of education and practices. For a number of years, we have been seeing its birth in various countries, regardless of the parties that are in power. Therefore, we believe in its historical viability.

6

School As a Sociocultural Project

In order to provide foundations for our present action on the vision of an education directed to the future, it is not enough to merely understand the school of today. In order to comprehend the present-day perspectives of education, it is necessary to know about the developmental origins of the school.

EDUCATION AND FORM OF PRODUCTION

In the *primitive form of production*, man maintained a direct contact with nature, and appropriated the goods it offered. He collected what was necessary for his subsistence and reproduction. The formal school did not exist. It was mixed with life. The transmission of culture—which today, is the task of the school—took place spontaneously in day-to-day relationships.

The schoolteacher was, therefore, the one who accumulated the most experience and taught his or her own children, friends, and other children. The method used was oral communication, with memory being used a great deal. There was a climate of living together as well as cordiality in the transmission of culture and its reelaboration. It was not yet possible at that time to talk about the school in the strictest sense or, as it is termed, *strictu sensu*.

The school *strictu sensu* was born in the passage from the primitive form of production to the slavery form of production. This took place in the neolithic period, with the economic revolution which had been initiated by women. In the primitive form of production, the men were nomadic. The women, who didn't take part in the hunting or fishing, were more sedentary. They planted and cultivated the land, and were obliged to wait for the harvest. This made the men become less nomadic, substantially changing the way of life of people and groups. The form of production of society is essentially a way of life.

On frequent occasions, more was produced than could be consumed in a few days. This excess of production resulted in disputes that gradually created a hierarchy that had not existed before in the primitive form of production. It submitted the weaker to the stronger, and, thus, began the slavery form of production.

The formal school was born from within the *slavery form of production* with the birth of inequalities and the division of social functions in society. At this time, the teacher was born. These individuals were in charge, in the division of labor, of guiding children toward adulthood, through the initiation rituals, the religious ceremonies, the teaching of manual skills, body expressions, and the development of arts and culture. The priests themselves exercised these functions. However, this took place slowly. As Everett Reimer has said,

> School is a stage in the succession of specialized institutions. Rites, myths and prehistoric spells; temples and religious castes; Sumerian, Greek, Alexandrian and Roman schools; monastic orders; the primitive universities, public and elementary schools—all play a role in the history of the today's national and international school systems. One of the most instructive trends is that of the progressive specialization of content, methods, personnel, and place in socially organized human teaching. Originally, this included much more than what we today call education. As we know, scholarization includes much less." (1983, 73)

In primitive society, the social division of work, which was to predominate later, did not yet exist. However, it began to be structured inside primitive society through rules and norms which were elaborated by specialized priests, schoolmasters and professional teachers. Slave society developed in this context, and reached its peak in Greece and Rome, where there were many more slaves than free men. School was reserved just for free men and they had an excellent curriculum, which took into account the humanistic ideal of the formation of the man of the slave society called the *"orator."*

The orator is he who knows how to defend his rights, and is, therefore, he who can be free. The zenith of this school of antiquity, however, had revealed certain tendencies—for example, the difference between the Spartan and Athenian schools.

The Spartan school was based on the ideal of *efficiency*, which prepared people more for action. The Athenian school, on the other hand, was based more on valuing thought, the *logos*, and, therefore, reflection. It was a school based more on the idea of *freedom* than on the idea of efficiency. The great difficulty of education today is to find the right balance between the efficiency of the Spartan and the freedom of the Athenian model.

There is a third model of a school, that which appears with the birth of the feudal form of production. The historical development of the *feudal form of production* is marked by the presence of the Church, which, for the first time, transformed school into an ideological apparatus. It realized, from very early on, the importance that the institution of school had as a vehicle to spread its message—that is, its good news of the Gospel.

From Constantine (306–337), the Catholic religion became the official religion of the Roman Empire, which entered into a period of decadence until it died out in the fifteenth century. During all of this long period, the Church dominated the state, and the state became the educator, director, and organizer of society around a *single religion*. Everyone had to submit to a single way of thinking. Anyone different was persecuted and treated as a heretic. The ideal of the orator left the public squares and shut himself in the churches.

The Church thus took education out of the streets and threw it into a closed, holy place, where the word was policed and homologated by his Holiness the Pope. *Difference* was punished and stigmatized. There was an attempt to impose this doctrine, not just on the regions dominated by Imperial Rome, but afterward, on all the known world, with enormous consequences for the development of education and cultures. The type of educational ideal continued to be that of the orator, but now it was that of the holy orator or the *cleric.*

In the first centuries of the Christian era, the Church had set up a network of *parish schools* and cathedrals for basic education and catechism. These schools trained the Christian. The *monastic schools* were destined for the training of the clergy, and played an important role in the Middle Ages in the preservation of the Greco-Latin culture. The rich and prosperous monasteries sheltered idle and curious monks who discovered "pagan" texts and preserved them, even though some had been mutilated by papal censure or by the Inquisition.

The intellectual monastic movement prepared the intellectual renaissance of the twelfth century which culminated in the founding of the first universities, and, with them, freedom of spirit, as we find it in the work of Pedro Abelardo (1079–1142), who tried to free himself from lordly and episcopal tutelage.

From the fifteenth century onward, with the Renaissance, Greco-Latin culture was taken up again by the lay intellectuals, whether they were aristocrats or not. These intellectuals, like the monks of other times, had leisure time, and began the bourgeois way of thinking.

The *bourgeois way of thinking* brought about a cultural renovation with the ideas of progress and that everything should be proved and verified. Dogmas should, therefore, not be accepted. This had begun with Martin Luther (1483–1546), who was the first to worry about the public school in the form in which we understand it today.

> Luther and his followers, coinciding with the invention of moveable type by Gutenberg, gave an enormous stimulus to the development of primary schools in northern Europe. The large-scale printing of Bibles, and the doctrine that salvation came directly from them, made the teaching of reading a moral imperative for Protestants who could afford it. The industrial revolution, which came on the heels of the Reformation, supplied the last necessary condition for the rapid proliferation of schools, supplying both the means and the rational secular basis for the diffusion of literacy" (Reimer 1983, 77)

The bourgeoisie revolutionized society, and also elaborated a *new conception of the school.* It took this apparatus away from the

Church in order for it to also express its own good news, which was now not the Gospel, but the ideas of progress and individual freedom. In order to overcome slavery and feudalism, the status of free men needed to be created, in the sense that they could buy and sell their workforce, free slaves and give society another direction—that is, a lay direction.

More than 200 years ago, the French revolution defended the free, public, lay, compulsory, and universal school for everyone in terms of basic education. We passed from the confessional school to the lay school—or rather, to the semiconfessional school. The revolutionary bourgeoisie invested in the project of the school, because it was interested in using it as a vehicle for spreading its way of thinking and as an instrument of training manual labor to drive its economic project forward. With this—at the end of the last century, which was also the century of the bourgeoisie par excellence—school was universalized in the countries which are today the most developed. At the end of the last century and during the beginning of this century, enormous educational investments were made in Europe, the United States, and Japan. The school was no longer submitted to the doctrine of the Church, but was, rather, at the service of the national states. "The bureaucratic, legal and processual measures which amalgamated dozens of thousands of district schools which were nominally independent, and thousands of secondary schools and universities into a national system are the logical result of a philosophy which considered the school to be subservient to national aims." (Reimer 1983, 79)

In the nineteenth century, important changes were introduced into the aims of teaching. Which now was oriented by the future, and attempting to "train adaptable and usable men." (Lobrot 1972, 23) Compulsory, lay, and free education became the right for all. The objectives which, from then on, marked teaching and pedagogy were defined through official texts, and the teaching staff was, for the first time in history, made up hierachically, in function of the interests of the class in power.

According to Lobrot, there were now five educational aims: general culture; acquisition of elementary automatisms, such as reading, writing, spelling and arithmetic; preparing the child for a profession; practical teaching; and a new pedagogy of learning to learn. All these objectives are based on the bourgeois conception of education that teaching is, first and foremost, a productive and necessary social investment.

Why did the bourgeoisie value education so much?

Because it needed the school and the teacher to erect the new bourgeois and capitalist society. We can say that the *capitalist form of production* completely renewed the school. However, in the middle of the twentieth century, capitalism began to invest less and less in basic teaching and more in higher education because the development of science and technology interested it more than the dissemination of the liberal ideas which were already hegemonic in the developed countries. Society was becoming united around the much more powerful *mass media.*

Those countries which had spread the school for all, putting its roots in the community, managed to, at least, maintain its quality. However, in the countries which had not done this, there was an enormous decline in the quality of the school in the second half of the century. This was the case of Brazil, which had not managed to implant the bourgeois school, and where the interests of the Church had dominated in educational matters. The semicapitalist Brazil reached the 1950s without having made basic education available to everyone, and with a high illiteracy rate. The bourgeoisie invested more in the area of social communication—in the culture industry especially in television—than in the school. Today, Brazil and the countries of Latin America are living through a profound school crisis, as educational investment no longer interests the national elites. The school has, as at the end of feudalism, once again become a popular demand.

The countries which implanted the *socialist model* developed the educational sector much more completely. They broadened access to basic education much more widely than did the dependent capitalist countries. Today, this model is also going through a crisis, with the crisis being of socialism itself. This is probably connected to the crisis in capitalism. For the past thirty years I have been following the situation of the school, and its increasing deterioration in Brazil and Latin America. However, in Latin America, Chile, Argentina, and Mexico—as well as other countries such Uruguay and Costa Rica—have managed to advance much more than Brazil. The rate of school attendance is much higher in those countries.

Without the pressure of society, there is no development of school. Society must defend the school. In Europe and in the States, society pressurizes the state to offer a high-quality education. In Japan, for a number of years, the state invested some 40 percent of its annual budget in education because society demanded it.

HAPPINESS AS A SCHOOL PROJECT

Faced with the crisis of the bourgeois school, we can anticipate the appearance of another type of school which George Snyders calls "the school of the socialist vision," a nonauthoritarian school and which I have frequently called a *"popular public school."*

Today, this school must have three essential characteristics:

1. It must be *democratic*—that is, it must be for everyone and in quantity.
2. It must be *autonomous.*
3. It must have a *new quality.*

This new school cannot be the present bureaucratic school, but it can come from within the present school, working with its internal contradictions. The school council, for example, can be an important step in this direction, but it is not the only instrument. The bureaucratic school is the opposite of the autonomous school. Liberating education today has a new name—autonomy. Education for autonomy is the cradle of liberating and antiauthoritarian education.

I would like to draw attention here to the third characteristic of a new quality. Many people get lost with that concept. They accept the first two characteristics, but not the third. They believe that quality is what we had in the past. A new quality is not a return to the past of the ancient parish schools, as Milton Friedman would like to see. A new quality must be built. It is this question that Snyders develops in his book *Happiness at School.* I would like to comment on it, as one of the presuppositions to rethinking the project of school today.

First, a word about the title of this book of Snyders's is in order. It tells us that, both in religious and bourgeois society, happiness is to be found *after* school. The child is always told: "Don't be sad . . . school has got to be sad because tomorrow you'll be full of happiness. Today, school has got to be sad, serious, because knowledge is something difficult to acquire, and tomorrow you'll get the rewards for the sadness of today. You've got to put off your sadness for after school." This type of school allows the children to be happy just in the breaks.

Snyders believes that happiness at school means not leaving it for afterward, and not putting it off. His central thesis is that happiness and satisfaction are fundamental for the school to accomplish its task of the transmission and elaboration of culture. It first surpasses the position of the *traditional*, religious, and confessional school, which insists on sadness and external discipline. However, it also surpasses the *new school*, because the new school tried to react to the traditional school by innovating methods and making them more pleasant. However, it is not just a question of making methods more pleasant. There is also the question of discovering how much satisfaction and happiness people have as they build and elaborate on their cultures. This is the central thesis of *Happiness at School*.

Snyders introduces the book with three themes.

First, He initially states that renewing the school means transforming its cultural content. He questions the content of today's school. Today, those who emphasize content—the functionalists—fail to understand this thesis of Snyders. They think that he is defending the content of the traditional school.

Second, He contests the idea of the new school by saying that school should prepare for the future.

The school of today tries to leave the most essential elements for the future.

Q. Why do you study?

A. To get through the year. Now I've got to study a lot to pass to the second year, then to the third, then to the fourth, and so on.

Q. But why will you carry on studying afterward?

A. Because I need to study to get into university. And at university they say that we've got to study a lot for afterward. So, if we pass the exams, we might be able to take graduate studies.

Q. And why are going to take graduate studies?

A. No reason . . . Maybe they'll be useful for later. Who knows . . . to be happy.

School tries *to put off happiness*. One reaches the end, and one always puts off for tomorrow the happiness that we can have today. The aim of life is happiness. The school cannot lose sight of this aim in its own objectives. The time and place to be happy are now and here.

Snyders quotes Engels and Marx. He tries to show that this idea of happiness is the Marxist vision of school—of a school full of happiness, joy, and contentment.

The source of joy, however, should not be sought through more agreeable methods, nor in the friendly relationships between teachers and pupils. The new methods propose choices: a free text, a school magazine, a choice of content and activities, free drawing, and the like. None of these should be left aside. However, they are the consequences and not the primary causes. Happiness is a consequence, and not a cause. Snyders wishes to find happiness in the school, and in the particular things that it can offer which can't be substituted. This is a type of happiness that only the school can offer us, and which it is in the best position to give us.

It would be a school that really had the courage to bet everything on the satisfaction that is given by the culture which is elaborated to its highest cultural demands.

Third, Snyders asks another question in this introduction when he talks about this cultural enthusiasm. Would this school not be elitist? Isn't satisfaction only for some people?

It is interesting that Snyders, who, years ago, criticized nondirectivity so much, is now discovering that, in the movement, there was the profound idea that the school must be satisfying. When the students in May 1968 shouted *L'imagination au pouvoir"* ("Imagination to power"), and "Let's be realistic and ask the impossible," they wanted to completely renew the content of the school. They wanted to change the school.

Snyders is rethinking the May 1968 movement, and is also indirectly rethinking the work of the educator Ivan Illich, and the theory of nondirectivity, without renouncing the critique of it which he had previously written, but looking at them with a more positive point of view.

I believe that *Happiness at School* is Snyders's most mature work. He ends this work by stating that his school is not elitist. Happiness is not a product reserved for the few. This school of happiness can be built right now, inside a nonhappy school, and it can be a school for everyone.

THE SCHOOL AND POPULAR MASS CULTURE

There are many cultural products that are acquired outside school, because school is not the only place where culture can be appropriated. Culture is assimilated through the direct experiences of life. We absorb it without knowing. We move in the direction of the culture that impregnates our environment, following our curiosity and wishes. This is what Snyders calls "first culture," the culture of desire, satisfaction, and curiosity.

I am that which I desire, that which I am curious to be, that which I do, that which I work, that which I see and observe, that which I assimilate day-by-day. The result of this lived experience is *first culture*, that which I make use of and which gives me happiness in daily life when, for example, I watch television, read a newspaper or magazine, watch a game of soccer, listen to music, and so on. What most surrounds us today, says Snyders, is *mass culture.*

Snyders doesn't devalue mass culture, but he does demonstrate the extent to which it is insufficient. This first culture promises a lot but accomplishes little of what it promises. It must be extended into elaborated culture. Elaborated culture can, better than first culture, reach the objectives and the satisfaction of the first culture. The first culture—the daily and mass culture—can leave one dissatisfied. Only elaborated culture can fill this gap.

First culture aims at first and real values. It partly reaches them and, in part, it also fails.

Elaborated culture offers us a much greater chance to fully live these same values, which leads to a reflection on the relationship between this first culture and elaborated culture—a relationship which can be seen as a synthesis between continuity and rupture. Elaborated culture is part of the first culture. It continues, but, at the same time, breaks with first culture.

Marilena Chauí, in *Conformismo e resistência (Conformism and Resistance)* (1986), a critical analysis of mass culture, states that this form of culture uses what is best in *popular culture,* weakens it, and then gives it back to the people in the form of prescriptions and precepts. She defends the genuinely popular culture, as opposed to mass culture.

Snyders thinks differently. He believes that the culture of our times is mass culture. He sees great possibilities in mass culture—for instance, the possibility that it offers us of connecting to the whole world. For example, when an actor whom we frequently see on television dies, we feel his death as if it were the death of a member of the family because, through television, he had spent a long time in our homes. Little by little, we accept a large number of new members into our family, including people from other cultures and countries. Snyders believes that this is a positive element of this culture of the twentieth century. It unites us to the whole world. We feel like the inhabitants of a single world.

Television instantly and simultaneously connects us to the planet. In the last century, this means of communication didn't exist. It is not that school of the last century that we must rebuild. We must build the school of the day-to-day, of the people of today, and the citizens of the future. Mass communication has enabled us to feel that we are members of humanity and the human community, not just a group. This feeling has been basically constructed by television and radio.

However, on the other hand, mass culture brings some risks—among them the risks of cultural atomization, simplification, and stereotypes. It doesn't explain complicated matters, but, rather, gives us simplified and momentary results.

The fact that school does not take mass culture into account contributes to the failure at school of children from popular backgrounds. As Snyders says,

> One can't shut up the disquiet that these children feel in relation to the culture of the school. This begins with the language at the school, as it is not theirs, and serves the interests that are not theirs. The school wishes to make them accept the values of others. Added to this is the fact that school will separate them from their families: progress at school takes children away from those whom they love. It may be a way of betrayal." (1988, 57)

School seems to be alienated in relation to the culture that is there. This mass culture that cultivates the affective side, makes the body vibrate and penetrates the mind. School takes the child away from this environment where he is constantly bombarded by mass communication, and takes him to a boring place where his language isn't used, and where his wishes are not satisfied.

Madalena Freire (1983), one of the Brazilian educators who has worked with the relationship between the affective and the cognitive at school, has shown how important this relationship is, not only to rescue the identity of the child, but also for his own intellectual development.

The body is also one of the fundamental themes of the Marxist pedagogy of happiness. To feel good inside one's skin, to feel the other, to feel the look, to understand the tear of the child, to feel the embrace . . . these are all values that the traditional school forbade and which must be rescued. Ana Maria Freire (1989), writing her doctoral thesis on the prohibition of the body in the history of illiteracy, showed how the school in Brazil was born from the prohibition of the body, as the body was considered to be a sin. Nowadays, the means of communication break with this, and young people and children can see this rupture. However, they arrive at school, and they don't see this rupture there. School doesn't continue what they see at home.

School needs to make the synthesis between continuity and rupture in relation to mass culture. The immediate, and the first culture, must serve as an *appeal* in the direction of the more elaborated.

The activity of the pupil must be both free and directed. There is a great risk in allowing the child a free choice. Why? Because the first culture is limited. However, at the same time, there is no way in which we can avoid beginning from its freedom of choice. We must begin from it, but from a choice complemented by the orientation of the teacher.

This synthesis is particularly necessary for the children from the popular classes. Snyders says,

> One will not progress by inviting popular children to contest the frequent devaluation of their cultural habits by a counter-devaluation of theoretical culture. If our culture and ideas are really permeated by the class struggle, how can we suppose that culture can be just in the hands of the dominant class and only determined by the interests of the dominant class? And, there-fore, would the factory worker betray his class if he dominated the abstract level? Renouncing the possibility of guiding chil-dren from the popular classes to elaborated and difficult cul-tural forms—and substituting them by any children's comic or any text, or the most infantile texts of certain adults, is to scorn the people." (1988, 125)

Greek schools took this popular mass culture into account. When I read Snyders's book, I remembered the Greek school that used Homer as the basic content. *The Iliad* and *The Odyssey* were used for the study of language, history, geography, and even for mathematical calculus. Literary works, as they were known and re-cited by everyone—at least the nonslaves—were used as a basis for teaching.

Snyders develops other fundamental themes in order to under-stand his project of a happy school. Among these are *love, optimism,* and *progress.* These are just the themes that are most present in mass culture. He proposes that these themes are also part of the school curriculum, in order to show that school is not chaos, but that it pro-gresses, and that it is not a succession of caprices, chances, and noises. The history of society is a producer of meaning. According to Snyders,

> History possesses a unity, a coherence, a continuity. It forms a total process: the diverse orders of happenings take part in a joint movement. They aren't dispersed in a succession which is simply juxtaposed. Therefore, there is a possible intelligibility

in the historical transformation and a possible control of men over their historical transformation. The world is such that it offers approaches, points of support, both to our action and to our thought." (1988, 170).

What school must show, then, is that there is a continuity in history and a direction for progress.

THE PROJECT OF A NONAUTHORITARIAN SCHOOL

Difficulty and effort will be continually present in the school. Learning for satisfaction and not through satisfaction doesn't exclude the painful. If the school wishes to rival leisure—with the distraction and the entertainment that mass culture offer us—it will always be a loser. It is not through satisfaction, as the new school insists, that one should learn, but for satisfaction. Elaborated knowledge offers us an intense satisfaction which is *cultural satisfaction.*

The school will get tired, in vain, if it wishes to put itself on the same footing as the enjoyments to be found outside school. It can't bring the way of being of the television inside the classroom. Each has its own specificity.

What would the specificity of the school be?

The specificity of the school is in its *systematic* and *progressive* elements, or the antichance, as Snyders says. The first culture takes place, on many occasions, by chance, and through daily life, without a program of continuity. You go to the theater or see a film. Both finish. They might be very instructive. They could be very entertaining, but they have no continuity. The enjoyment that you find at a party has no continuity. When the party is over, it finishes.

On the contrary, at school, the activities are systematically organized, foreseeable, and continued. On such-and-such a day, at such-and-such a time, it's math! You know that this moment is reserved for it. So, there is a continuity, a series, and you know that knowledge will progress little by little, and systematically. This is the specific element of the school.

School doesn't claim a monopoly over elaborated culture. It has never had this monopoly, and it has it less today than ever. Outside school, the multiple forms of entertainment, of further education and self-training, finally put the presence of a culture on the same level as that of school culture. There are theatres, concerts, museums, lectures, scientific experiments, television, cinema, video, and more. The precise difference is in the systematization. What seems to me to characterize school is a systematic and continuous organization of situations. There are prerequisites—that is, a degree of preparation considered to be indispensible for what one does. Therefore, there is a certain homogeneity of training, knowledge, the proper age, and other factors. One proceeds by stages, step by step. There is a progressive program.

However, the coherent and obligatory succession should not be the opposite of happiness. The systematic, the difficult, the obligatory—all these characteristics can obviously also be applied to the traditional school.

> The dream of my school is not to surpress them absolutely; I would like to maintain them in a determined way, even extend them, faced with certain inverse temptations of many innovators: my school is the paradoxical gamble of imposing mathematics on everyone on a certain day, even on those who don't want it, and modify the situation in such a way that everyone can experiment the satisfaction and feel that they are progressing toward freedom." (Snyders 1988, 210)

Snyders values the teacher as a professional worker. He also describes the teacher who yearns to be a teacher, adding that this craving can even reach ridiculous proportions. This particular teacher strives to do the impossible with his pupil, intending that his pupil can surpass him or her. Then, the teacher needs to begin the same journey again with every new pupil.

The pupil will notice how ridiculous the teacher is. However, it is with the ridiculousness—this sublime ridiculousness, this engagement—that the teacher enabled the pupil to, indeed, surpass him or her.

How is it possible to build a happy school, with so many demands that society makes on school, and with so many obligations that don't depend on the free choice of the school and of the educator?

It is very difficult to make an equation for us teachers of the relationship between freedom and obligation. For example, do we know how to maintain discipline as freedom, with a certain camaraderie? How can the school be free, and, at the same time, maintain all of the obligations of both the teachers and pupils?

The conquest of freedom doesn't mean that there will initially be an interminable period of lack of freedom, nor that it will be necessary to wait until later for it to be transferred. At each moment of the school day, there is, in varying proportions, freedom, independence, and progress toward greater freedom. The active methods center on the thesis of the freedom of choice. However, this is just the beginning. The fact of choosing doesn't mean that all the options are valid. This can lead to skepticism. The idea of this free choice in which all the opinions seem to be true makes the child become skeptical—that is, instead of taking a position, it accepts them all as true. The child is not free to choose everything—to choose to be racist, for example. Although the school should be a place for freedom, a teacher should never allow the choice of racism, as this choice would injure fundamental human rights.

I believe that Snyders is on the same track as many other educators, such as Bogdan Suchodolski, Paulo Freire, Francisco Gutiérrez (1984), Amílcar Cabral (1977), and a series of modern thinkers, who anticipate the vision of a school which is the surpassing synthesis between, on the one hand, the religious, confessional, and classical *traditional schools*, and, on the other hand, the lay bourgeois school, toward a school which I sometimes call socialist, sometimes popular, and, more and more, the citizen school. I don't have a definite name for it. Suchodolsky calls it the "social school." He is a socialist, but he prefers to speak about a social pedagogy and a social school. Amílcar Cabral, one of the greatest of African educators, talks about a school of conversion.

Even so, it is not important what name it has. What is important is that the future is sought with the ethics and hope that are the food of the educator. The progressive educator, in spite of the crisis of the school and the difficulty of his work, will always be optimistic, as he believes in history as a possibility. Therefore, it has equity and autonomy for everyone. As Paulo Freire has said, "I don't understand human existence and the necessary struggle to make it better, without hopes and dreams. Hope is an ontological necessity. . . . I am not hopeful out of stubbornness but because of an existential and historical imperative." (1992, 10)

7

Citizen School

The school that loses its autonomy also loses its possibilities of educating for freedom. This is the thesis that I intend to defend in this chapter.

To discuss the theme of autonomy is to discuss the very history of education as we can see that as the history of the struggle for the intellectual and institutional autonomy of the school, which is linked to freedom of expression and teaching. Although autonomy is not the term that is frequently used, its essential content is found in all of the *history of pedagogical ideas.*

AUTONOMY AND THE NATURE OF EDUCATION

The present debate on school autonomy is rooted in the dialogical process of teaching at the beginning of Greek philosophy. In the dialogue between Socrates and Menon in a square in Athens about the possibility as to whether it is possible to be virtuous—to the master, Socrates, insisted that the slave, Menon, should look for the answer within himself. Thus, educating means capacitating, qualifying, and potentializing, so that the pupil can look for the answer to what he is asking. It means training for autonomy. The school, in the ideal of Socrates, should be centered around autonomy. Its method should be dialogue. The disciple should discover the truth. Therefore, education is self-education.

The word autonomy comes from the Greek *autos* (oneself) and *nomos* (law), and means "the ability to determine oneself, to fulfill oneself." Autonomy also means self-construction, and self-government. The autonomous school would be one that governs itself. However, there is no absolute autonomy as it is always conditioned by circumstances. Therefore, autonomy is always relative and historically determined.

The Italian humanistic educator, Vittorino Da Feltre, is a precursor of the modern antiauthoritarian school. In his school, *La Casa Giocosa* (Happy House), and in a period in which authoritarian scholastic methods centered on the schoolmaster, Da Feltre proposed active methods such as the direct participation of the pupils. Similarly, the satirical critique of François Rabelais (1495–1553) of scholastic methods, contributed toward the development of the ideas of self-government in pedagogy. These ideas influenced Montaigne (1553–1592), John Locke (1632–1704), and Jean-Jacques Rousseau (1712–1778). Montaigne believed that the central problem of education is the interest of the pupil in his study, which is greater according to his participation in the choice of content.

As did other modern educators, the Czech humanist, Jean Amos Comenius (1592–1671), emphasized the importance of action, and the auto activity of the pupil. In Locke, we find, for the first time in the history of pedagogical thinking, the expression *self-government,* which is considered to be both the aim and means of education. The self-government of Locke has a moral idea of self-control. In Rousseau, the expression *self-government* has a socioeducative meaning. Rousseau's pedagogy is centered on the autonomy of the child, wherein the child is a complete and perfect being, just like the adult.

The *new school* movement was formed around a new educative paradigm, and was headed by John Dewey (1859–1952), whose principles of "learning by doing," "learning through life," and "learning through democracy" are still very much alive. As well as Dewey, the works of Maria Montessori (1870–1952), Pistrak, Jean Piaget (1896–1980), and Célestin Freinet (1896–1966) consecrate the principles of autonomy and the auto-activity of the pupil. However, they have different visions. The work of Pistrak, for example, insists more on the self-organization of the pupils, and considers the management of the educative activities to be a fundamental educative activity.

Adolph Ferrière (1879–1960), one of the principle figures of the new school, and Jean Piaget devoted various studies to the theme of the autonomy of pupils and school. In *The Autonomy of School Children in Communities of Children*, Adolph Ferrière, after a long study of communities of children and teenagers, and after presenting various examples of public schools that practice the so-called self-management, concludes by stating that "both social and moral life, the feeling of good and bad in collective life, can only be learned in practice." (Ferrière 1950, 143). Thus, the important role of self-management arises in the process of the gradual socialization of culture. Piaget states in his little known book *Autonomy at School*, "Autonomy is a preparation for the life of the citizen, which will be all the better if the theoretical and verbal lessons are substituted by concrete exercises and the experience of civic life." (1950, 26) He warns that autonomy can both train for parliamentary democracy and subordination to one's bosses.

Janusz Korczak (1878–1942), a precursor of the rights of the child and teenager, demonstrates his support of education for autonomy when he believes that "the first incontestable right of the child is that which allows him to freely express his ideas and to take an active part in the debate on the evaluation of his behavior." (Korczak 1983, 67)

The discussion around the theme of autonomy has played a critical and mobilizing role against vertical and bureaucratic power, opposed to centralism in a social practice based on participation.

The antiauthoritarian movement in education is not recent. According to Jesus Palacios, the opposition to authoritarian relationships and methods "has as its central axis the exaltation of the freedom of the child and of the group into which the child is integrated." (1978, 14) The idea of autonomy is always associated with the idea of freedom. The antiauthoritarian movement in education introduces the difference between the traditional school, centred on the schoolteacher, and the new school, centred on the pupil.

One of the most important antiauthoritarian pedagogues is the Spanish educator, Francisco Ferrer Guardia (1859–1909), the founder of the Modern School, a rationalist, and a libertarian. Another educator, the Englishman A. S. Neill (1883–1973), with his experience at the free school of Summerhill, took the principle of freedom and autonomy right to its final consequences. In Summerhill, all the organization of the school is controlled by the pupils. According to Neill, in order for self-management to be possible, the teacher should renounce all forms of authority, all hierarchical pretensions, and all types of strong leadership. On the other hand, the North American therapeutician, Carl R. Rogers (1902–1987) transposed the principle of psychotherapy based on the patient to teaching. Teaching based on the pupil should be based on empathy, authenticity, confidence in the possibilities of being human, the pertinence of the subject to be learned, participative learning, the totality of the person, self-evaluation and self-critique.

It was the new school that lifted the flag of autonomy in the school the highest, understanding it as the free organization of pupils and self-government. Many pedagogical experiments of this type have been made, and there is abundant literature existing on this subject. However, the movement of the new school, which introduces active and free methods into education, emphasized autonomy more as a factor in personal development than as a factor of social change. However, it has the advantage of seeing that autonomy and self-management are part of the nature of education. As Olivier Reboul says, "Authority is doubtlessly necessary to prevent a child from doing harm and harming himself; but education only begins at the moment when authoritarianism ceases. The only educative coercion is self-coercion." (1974, 52)

In the second half of the century, along with the critique of education as a factor of social reproduction and the debate surrounding self-management, the theme of autonomy has been associated with an emancipating conception of education.

The word *self-management* appears at the beginning of the 1960s in political language, and particularly in the intellectual *milieux* of the left in France which were dissatisfied with concrete results of bureaucratic socialism, especially in the Soviet Union. It translated the Serbo-Croat word, *samoupravlje*, literally into self plus management, in describing the socio-politico-economic experience of the management of companies by the workers in the Yugoslavia of Josip Broz, otherwise known as Marshal Tito (1892–1980).

Self-management is not *participation*, as participating means being involved in an activity that already exists within its own structure and aims. Self-management aims at transforming and not at participation. Self-management should also not be confused with *co-management*, which means the joint direction of a company, maintaining the same hierarchical structure. The cooperative is nearer to self-management, as the directors are paid by the workers themselves, partially overcoming the antagonism between capital and work.

In the educational field—especially in Europe and more particularly in France—the theme of pedagogical autonomy has been associated with the theme of *social self-management* since the 1960s. Autonomy means, above all, rupture with centralized schemes. It opposes the autonomy of the workers to the conservative partisan state bureaucracy. It is a form of rethinking social practice, which is an essentially political movement, a movement of rebellion against mechanistic political movements, especially the socialist models that preached a correct line against other lines that were considered to be deviations.

The theme of self-management is responsible for a discussion that began in the 1960s, and still continues, linking *social struggles* with *pedagogical struggles.*

These ideas were inspired by the utopian socialists, among them Charles Fourier (1772–1837), whose phalansteries were autonomous units of production. However, it is Pierre Joseph Proudhon (1808–1865) who is considered to be the father of self-management. He, Jean-Jacques Rousseau, and Michael Bakunin (1814–1876) all proposed, in their own ways, a society made up of freely associated producers. The experiments of societies based on this principle began in the last century with the Commune of Paris (1871); and, from 1917 in Russia, with the Factory Committees; and, more particularly, with the experiment in Yugoslavia, which was begun by Tito in 1951.

In self-management, the worker directly exercises power, rather than having a representative. As Fernando Motta says, "Autonomy is not participation. By self-management, a system in which the collectivity administers itself is understood. Therefore, it is not a question of taking part in power but about having power." (Motta in Fischmann, 1987, 73).

It is not a question of collectively administering capital better in order to produce more and distribute it in a more equable way. The practice of self-management makes a major change in relationships at work, and establishes a considerable contradiction between these relations and the capitalist relationships of work. Lúcia Bruno 1985:32 says that

> . . . self-management, as a radicalization of autonomous struggles, means that it is the workers themselves who manage their production. It is a rather advanced form of struggle, where the workers appropriate space and time, redefining, destroying the hierarchies, eliminating the directors-directed duality and the division between manual and intellectual work." (1990, 32)

Self-management attempts to do in the school what self-management does in the company, or it tries, at least, to open up a free, autonomous space so that the school, by introducing self-management, can play a significant role in the transformation of social relationships in this direction. The concept of self-management has been broadened and is able to take in contradictory experiences. It is also spoken of, without any distinctions being made, in the same way that one speaks of autonomy, freedom, self-formation, self-government, and so on.

However, in the pedagogical field, self-management is a theme which is inseparable from a certain understanding of society. Thus, it is to be found in libertarian pedagogies as much as in active pedagogies. However, in libertarian pedagogies, especially beginning from the work of Lobrot, self-management is mentioned more, and active pedagogies emphasize teaching of the child to be autonomous. Maria Montessori (1870–1952) believed that real education consisted of making the child—and not society—free. Thus, one can establish a great difference between the self-management understood as Rogers's individualization of learning, and self-management as the embryo of Lobrot's social self-management.

The failures of the early experiments in pedagogical self-management showed that the pretensions of institutional pedagogy were too idealistic. They failed to take into account the limits of education and the historical context in which the monopoly of the school over the acquisition and transmission of habits and knowledge had disappeared. It could be asked whether self-management is possible only when the whole of society is also controlled by the principle of self-management. Nevertheless, if the techniques suggested by self-management were shown to be insufficient to reach their objectives, the libertarian principles that institutional pedagogy defends are still alive today. In addition, although, their concept and practice failed in basic education, they were efficient in higher education and, in particular, in permanent education (Hartung 1975).

AUTONOMY OF THE SCHOOL IN RECENT EDUCATIONAL REFORMS

Europe is reforming its teaching systems by reorienting the public schools and by training teachers better—thus, making schools autonomous, and introducing greater participation. On 9 November 1990, the Council of the autonomous province of Trento in the north of Italy passed provincial law November 29, which established the "Norms regarding the autonomy of schools, collegiate organs, and the right to study." Through this law, organizational, financial, and administrative autonomy was recognised for individual schools. Curiously, the accent is not on pedagogical autonomy, which seems to already have been conquered in the Italian school system.

By *organizational autonomy*, one understands the possibility of *making agreements:*

1. With other schools, in order to organize educational, training and sporting activities; and
2. With the province, local bodies, centers of professional training, research, educational recycling and experimentation institutes, universities and institutes, public or private companies, cooperatives or associations, in order to contract or offer services or organize study-work exchange experiments for middle school pupils.

By *financial autonomy*, one understands the possibility of the individual school receiving resources not just from the state, but also contributions from other public or private bodies or from agreements and services rendered.

Administrative autonomy understands that the school and its finances will be managed administratively and didactically by the school council. Budgeting will be made with the help of banks. Payments are made by the director of the school. The law also establishes the possibility that public schools can be legal entities so that they are even more autonomous.

Obviously, all this autonomy will be made possible by a system of supervision, follow-up, and permanent evaluation of individual schools, together with the generalization of information. Aided by accountants, the school submits its annual accounts to the Provincial Junta to evaluate its productivity. The Provincial Junta exercises a role of equalizing opportunities in order to reduce the differences between those schools which, because of local circumstances, have more financial resources than do others.

It is still early to have an exact idea of the consequences these measures bring to the level of the quality of teaching. However, one can foresee a considerable incentive for the initiatives taken by the schools themselves. These changes might definitely establish greater differences among schools, but this would be a difference upward, not downward, and rewarding quality, not the bureaucracy or inertia of the system. Autonomy allows for greater flexibility and responsibility, with the result that plurality is not a synonym of poor quality, but, rather, of transparence, coordination, and organicity.

What is happening in Italy is no different from what is happening in other European countries. The last Spanish Constitution (1978) defines a model of the state based on regional autonomy. The seven Spanish regional communities have complete control over educational matters. This process of decentralization is being extended to municipal autonomy over schools. The same is happening in Portugal. The Portuguese Minister of Education, Roberto Carneiro, said, "Today we have a totally free and democratic educational system. Schools are autonomous, the community has taken control . . . the school must reflect the community and be an agent of differentiation and affirmation of plural educative projects. Everything that is monolithic and uniform violates freedom and is oppressive." (Carneiro in Frare 1991, 22–23) In Portugal, one also finds businessmen on the school councils.

However, the greatest gain from such a single decentralized system is that it breaks out of the unproductive ideological dispute between the public and the private, which, as Mario Malossini says, "responds to an obsolete scheme which is inadequate to explain today's reality and respond to its necessities." (Malossini in Trento 1990, 3)

The Trento experiment brings the public school nearer to the private school. It allows citizens to choose a public or a private school, not simply through a question of ideology, but by giving them the possibility to directly participate in the construction of the public school which they wish for their children—a choice which they found before only in the private sector. This surpasses the state centralism of the previous model. The Trento model experiments with the shifting of a state school to a public-private-social school. In Italy, there is an insignificant number of private schools.

Behind the Trento proposal, there is the global policy of the Province, which is to look to the future beginning with the valuing of the culture of its own community, a "synthesis of the history which is on our shoulders and that which is surrounding us," as Tarcísio Grandi says (Grandi in Trento, 1990, 6). Broadening the autonomy of the school also means stimulating social creativity and inventiveness.

One cannot make a major change in the teaching system without a social project and a project for schools. What Italy is experiencing today, not only in the Province of Trento, is the result of a long road taken with many meetings, debates, attempts, and political confrontations between opposite theses. A good result has been reached.

It can also be seen that the extension of school autonomy is not opposed to the unity of the system. As Remo Albertini says, "Before, the system was unitary in the sense of it being centralized and now it continues unitary and homogenous, but in the sense of decentralization." (1991, 61)

The British educational reform of the Education Reform Act of 1988 is one of the widest and deepest which has taken place in this century in the administration of teaching systems. It can also be seen as an important contemporary example of the application of the principle of school autonomy. It is true that this reform centralizes the common core of the curriculum, but it also implants school autonomy, especially in the financial and personnel areas. In practice, this reduces the role of the state to two basic functions: handing over the budget directly to the school, and evaluating performance.

This reform foresees the possibility of each school being able to opt out of direct financing by the central government through an agreement that frees it from local power and educational bureaucracy. This option would depend on a decision taken at an assembly by the majority of teachers and parents. Schools choosing the new system become entirely independent and autonomous, somewhat like private schools. Each of these schools now has its own budget, which is negotiated annually with the central government.

Without privatizing public schools, the British reforms have the advantage of joining the efficiency of the private school with the democratization of teaching, which has been the greatest conquest of the modern public schools (Tedesco 1991, 33). The schools are motivated to look for alternative sources of funding, and they have the freedom to apply their own pedagogical conceptions, to decide their spending and personnel policies, and to even make agreements with other social organs to diversify their sources of income.

The new British system has the advantage of attributing the responsibility for teaching to the teachers, parents, and pupils, avoiding the paternalism of the state and bureaucracy. This reform, which is still being implanted, questions the old myth that all public schools should be the same. *Decentralization* and *autonomy* go together. There seems to be no turning back from this path toward the school of the future.

Autonomists are people who are dissatisfied, not because they feel frustrated, but because autonomy, as is freedom, is always an unfinished process, a horizon which we never definitively reach. Autonomy is real, as George Snyders says, especially in the pedagogical field, but one "to be conquered incessantly. . . . It is much less a piece of data to write down than a conquest to achieve." (Snyders 1977, 109) Snyders insists that this relative autonomy must be maintained by the struggle, and that "it can only become reality if it participates in the whole of the struggles of the exploited classes." (1977, 109)

The struggle for the autonomy of the school is part of the struggle for autonomy which is at the heart of society itself. It is, therefore, a struggle within the institution, and against the institution, in order to instigate something else. The efficiency of this struggle depends, to a great extent, on the daring of each school to experiment with the new, and not just to think about it. However, in order for this to be done, it is necessary to take the long path of building up confidence inside the school, and to have the ability to solve its problems alone, and to govern itself. Autonomy is about the creation of new social relationships which are opposed to the existing authoritarian relationships.

Autonomy does not mean uniformization. It admits *difference*, and, therefore, supposes *partnership*. Only equality in difference and partnership are able to create the new. Because of this, the autonomous does not mean an isolated school but one which is in constant interchange with society. Right now, struggling for an autonomous school—as we conceive it—means struggling for a school which projects, together with itself, another society. To think of an autonomous school, and to struggle for it, means giving a new sense to the social function of the school. It also requires educators who don't consider themselves to be merely guard dogs of an unchangeable system, but who also feel responsible for a possible future with equity.

The principle of this democratic management and the autonomy of the school implies a complete change in the system of teaching. Our present system of teaching is still based on the principle of bourgeois centralization, contrasting with the social principle of the democratization of management.

In Latin America—and particularly in Brazil—the struggle for the democratization of the management of the public schools has resulted, in recent years, in the creation of *school councils*. Participation and democratization in a public teaching system is the most practical form of training for citizenship. Education for citizenship takes place in the participation in the decision-making process. The setting up of school councils represents a part of this process. However, they will fail if they are introduced as an isolated and bureaucratic measure. They are efficient only as part of a number of *political measures* which aim at the participation in and democratization of decisions, within a broader strategy which supposes:

1. *Autonomy of social movements* and their organizations in relation to public administration. This has nothing to do with co-opting leaderships or adopting a paternal stance with the movements. It is more a question of making alliances and partnerships based on the equality of conditions, while preserving both the specificity of the state and civil society.
2. Opening of the *channels of participation* by the state public administration. It is quite true that the administration is not always disposed to let some of its autonomous ability to take decisions go. It usually makes technocratic decisions. It is easier to decide on the base of technical reports. However, this runs risks, among them the chance of making the totally wrong decisions and ones which have nothing to do with reality. These are the famous cabinet decisions.
3. *Administrative transparency*, that is, democratization of information. The population needs to effectively to get hold of information to be able to participate. In order to participate, the population needs to be able to understand the working of the administration—especially that of the budget—and the laws that control public administration and limit transforming action. In order for school councils to be efficiently created, it is necessary that popular participation, both inside and outside the school, take the form of an explicit strategy for administration. It is also necessary to offer all the conditions for participation. The population is normally invited to take part at inconvenient times, in uncomfortable locales which are difficult to get to, and more, with no care having been taken over these choices. The population needs to take pleasure in exercising its rights.

However, all of these conditions are no good if the population is merely called upon to ratify decisions taken in cabinets. Participation must be translated into concrete results. In the political tradition in the majority of modern democracies, participation has become an instrument of manipulation, resulting in tiresome and interminable meetings or assemblies at which the only decision taken is, frequently, that of arranging the next meeting.

In many municipalities, participation is often confused with the creation of councils. The number of councils multiplies, but the number of participants goes down, and the same people are on all of these councils. A council should not have to meet to make minor technical decisions. Councils exist to make policies, and not to execute these decisions. This is also valid for school councils.

The school council—in which parents, teachers, pupils, and the members of the community participate—is the most important organ in the autonomous school. It should deliberate on the organization of work in the school, and on all aspects of its functioning, including the choice of its directors.

In order to really construct the autonomy of the school, it should deliberate on the curriculum; the school calendar; the setting up of classes, dates, and timetables; and cultural activities—in short, on the governing of the school as a whole.

It is the job of the council to pinpoint solutions to the problems of the interests and wishes of the entire school, such as investments, the streamlining of timetables, the elaboration of a school plan, enrollment, and the general functioning of the school. The council should also be charged with decisions upon the political and pedagogical project of the school. The greater the number of people who are involved with the business of the school, the greater the possibility of strengthening the autonomous project of each school.

The democratic choice of the members of the council should examine specific problems of each school and each region, and it should incorporate the most adequate democratic practices for local conditions. More complex systems of education will need school collegiate councils in order to improve communication channels between the administration and the schools.

From my experience, which was acquired in the administration of the public school system, I can state that the school director is the main partner and interlocutor to the Secretary of Education, so that communications between both should always be direct. As we shall see later, one of the principles of the educational system, built on the basis of the autonomy of the school, is that direct communications between the person responsible for the educational organ and the director of the school should be a top priority.

However, one shouldn't think that proposals of the school council eliminates tension between the school and the community. The council also becomes a school for the parents, providing the possibility for a double learning experience. The school extends its pedagogical function to society, and society influences the destiny of the school.

The council is an example of school-community integration, but it doesn't eliminate any risks. Many parents have a wrong view of school. They might suggest the adoption of authoritarian measures, or they could simply and qualitatively not represent the whole of society. Because of this, we insist that the school council is not the only democratic instrument, but that it is part of a broader strategic plan.

DECALOGUE OF THE CITIZEN SCHOOL

I am borrowing the expression *citizen school* from Genuíno Bordignon (1989), so that I can use his proposals and ideas to give a synthetic reply to the question of "What could the school be like, in a single system of public education, when it is freed from uniformization? What would a citizen school be like?"

It would be an autonomous public school, synonomous with the popular public school, and integrating a single public and popular decentralized system.

Let us see what this means, first, through a brief historical examination of the question.

Opposing the traditional school, the new school began with Rousseau, who thought about separating school from society because he believed that society perverted the child, who was born good. Émile Durkheim (1858–1917) took the opposite view, that only society could make a creature who was born selfish, cooperative, and altruistic.

Dewey proposed a synthesis between these two positions, approximating school and life in order to form democrats or citizens acting in society. Gramsci supports Dewey's thesis, but his aim is different. Training governing people is, for him, the true meaning of preparation for life.

However, people who govern society cannot be trained if they are not intellectually autonomous subjects. Lenin supported this thesis, but, in practice, Stalin suppressed it in his country. Thus, socialism had to follow the long path of state idolatry to discover a simple truth—that is, the bureaucratic school does not train people who govern, but, instead, it trains the governed.

What is important is to build a universal public school, one which is unified and equal for all, but which, at the same time, respects local and regional differences—in short, *multiculturality*, which is an idea so fundamental and dear to the theory of popular education.

The great challenge of the public school is that of guaranteeing a level of quality for everyone, and, at the same time, respecting local and sociocultural diversity.

The bourgeoisie nationalized the school. In order to construct the popular public school, the national must be united with the regional, and the popular must be included in the public, thus surpassing the national state school to arrive at the popular school.

What would this school be like?

The citizen school is, without doubt, a project of "historical creation" (Castoriadis 1991), but it can also be considered to be a horizon, or a belief. Therefore, I have no hesitation in speaking of a decalogue. An educator must believe in the school, and believe in exercising his function, which is that of educating.

1. The autonomous public school is first, and foremost, democratic— for everyone—democratic in its management, and democratic in terms of access and the possibility of remaining there for everyone. It is also popular—that is, it is, characteristically, a social community, or a public space for the elaboration of culture.
2. In order to be autonomous, the school cannot be dependent on intermediary organs that make policies which the school merely executes. Therefore, in the single decentralized system, the technicians of the central organs should carry out work in the school themselves. A school—all schools—can, just as the universities do, have more than one building or campus.
3. The citizen school should value the full-time contract of teachers, and give each of them the maximum of four classroom hours daily and four hours of other activities in the school, at home, or substitutions, perhaps in an interdisciplinary team). Valuing the school means not taking work home unless, during the school session, there is no adequate place. In this case, teachers should keep to this school timetable at home until the school finds an adequate place for such out-of-class teaching activities. This means the end of the part-time, merely filling-in teacher, and greater professionalization.
4. Direct action is a further principle. This means that personal initiatives and projects in the schools should be valued. The problem is not in the crisis of the school, but, rather, in the crisis of the system, in the routine that it produces in the school through its excessive control. The crisis of the system imprisons and standardizes the school under the pretext of the democratization of opportunities.

5. The autonomous school cultivates curiosity, the love of learning, the enjoyment of reading, and the production of written or oral texts. It is creative, rather than mechanical, learning. It proposes spontaneity and lack of conformism.
6. It is a disciplined school. The discipline comes from the specific role of the school, which is systematic and progressive.
7. The school is no longer a closed space. Its connection with the world is through work. The autonomous school attempts to join the external world through the social spaces of work, the professions, and the multiple human activities. It is a laboratory of the world by which it is penetrated.
8. The transformation of the school cannot take place without conflicts. It takes place slowly. Small, but continued actions, are better for the process of change than spectacular, but fleeting, events. Only the direct action of each teacher, class, and school can make education become an enriching process.
9. No two schools are alike. Each school is the fruit of the development of its contradictions.
10. Each school should be sufficiently autonomous to be able to organize its work in the way in which it wishes, including contracting and exoneration of the criteria of the school council.

PUBLIC ADMINISTRATION AND THE CITIZEN SCHOOL

The public administration of the school can be based on a systematic and narrow vision which attempts to emphasize the static aspects, such as consensus, adaption, and order, or a dynamic vision that values contradiction, change, and conflict (Sander 1984). We can talk here of a *closed system* or an *open system*. The first camouflages the contradictions and conflicts. The second works with tension and conflict. In the closed system of teaching, the users—parents and children—and the staff—teachers and ancilliary workers—do not feel responsible, and, therefore, do not participate.

The two opposite paradigms of the teaching system are never found in their pure states. In practice, eclecticism predominates in the confrontation between a static *functionalist vision* and a dynamic *dialectic vision* of the system. In this confrontation of conceptions and practices, the system tends to move toward a surpassing synthesis, or a single decentralized system.

The administration of a single decentralized teaching system will be based on four major principles.

Democratic Management

I don't understand democratic management as a complicated system of elections of representatives for all functions of the system. On the contrary, elections should be reserved for choice of directors in cases in which the citizens, themselves, cannot directly exercise their citizenship. There should be as few representatives as possible. Neither does this mean a swelling of the teaching system with an enormous bureaucratic body to exercise power in the name of the workers of education. On the contrary, a democratic management that values the school and the classroom would eliminate mediation between directors of the organs responsible for education and the schools.

The present functions of planning, and putting ideas into practice, could be left to the schools themselves. Strictly speaking, there would be no need for a Secretary or Minister of Education, but, rather, for a superintendent of public schools. Whenever one speaks about a secretary, one envisions plans and new projects for, and not of, the schools. Every new secretary or minister who takes office wants to perpetuate themselves in the system, and attempts to leave their marks, thus justifying their political tenures in the office.

On the contrary, a single decentralized system supposes educational objectives and goals which have been clearly established between schools and the government, and which aim at the democratization of access and management, as well as the construction of a new quality of teaching without passing through innumerable intermediary powers.

Democratic management should not be limited to the administration. It should also include budget and finances. Democratic procedures should also be imposed upon the elaboration of the budget and its execution, both of which guarantee administrative and financial autonomy.

Direct Communication with the Schools

If the school is the central locus of education, it should become the irradiating pole of culture, not merely to reproduce it or execute plans elaborated outside it, but to construct and elaborate the culture itself, whether it be general or popular culture. The basic principle of the organ responsible for education should be to work toward the autonomy of the school. Today, the distance between the central organs—especially the cabinets of the Secretariats, and the schools—

is one of the main causes of our educational backwardness. This is the fruit of the power of technocratic bureaucracy.

Direct communication between the administration and the schools has its corollary in the communication between the schools and the population. In order to be able to participate, the population must be well-informed. The bureaucratic school is afraid of the participation of parents, and, as a consequence, fails to use the pupils themselves to establish a permanent dialogue with the parents. The school has an enormous potential for communication which has not yet been tapped by participation or democracy.

Autonomy of the School

Every school should be able to choose and build its own political and pedagogical project. This doesn't mean that every school will be isolated from every other school. Autonomy also means unity and the ability to communicate. School doesn't mean just a building, a single space, or a locale. It means, as we have previously seen, a project which can associate various school units or buildings, surpassing the dreaded problem of the atomization of the educational system. School and government would decide educational policies together.

Permanent Evaluation of School Development

This is one of the crucial points of a single decentralized system of public education. Today, schools are not evaluated, nor are they evaluated bureaucratically. In order for evaluation to be emancipating, it must be included as an essential part of the school project. It cannot be a mere formal act which is executed by technicians outside the school. It should involve the internal community, of pupils and teachers; the external community, of parents and the community; and the public power. This principle of evaluation brings us back to the first principle—that of democratic management.

In the organization of the system of teaching which has been proposed in this work, the schools would no longer be subordinate to central organs. They might be transformed, for example, into teachers' cooperatives, as Cláudio Weber Abramo suggests.

> Some would be formed into individual schools, others would unite schools of the same region. Through this, the teachers would be fixed in the diverse communities, enabling the

communities to make demands and contacts which are impossible today. All the central educational management organs would immediately be abolished, like the Regional Teaching Delegations, whose reason of being is inexplicable, even today. The Ministry of Education and the secretariats would be be thinned down enormously as their function would now be just that of paying the schools. (Abramo 1991:3)

Abramo also suggests that the schools should be paid, rather than the individual teachers, using the school population as a basis. In Abramo's words, "Each school should define how its teachers are to be paid and how to manage the resources that are received, and should be allowed to attempt to obtain additional money in the community, something which is forbidden by law today." (Abramo 1991, 3)

Educational systems are formed by a *layer of bureaucrats* who frequently attempt to spread educational tasks while concentrating the power of decision. Alternatively, they propose the privatization of educational services, throwing all the responsibility upon the individuals. In opposition, we frequently find a corporativist *educational syndicalism* which concentrates almost exclusively on the struggle for improved salaries and on the strengthening of the bureaucratic state. These two forces—although they are supported by antagonistic ideologies—have proposals for identical solutions, which, in their majority, are no more than "fetters of the bureaucracy," as the great Brazilian educator Anísio Teixeira (1900–1971) would often say.

Where can a solution be found?

It can be found in a *utopian vision*, which is stronger than ideologies, because it has nothing to hide. It can be transparent, with no hidden tactics or strategies. This utopia proposes the return to the community, where school first originated. In order to do this, it is necessary that the community defend the school in the same way that it defends access to domestic gadgets, transport, sewerage, asphalt, housing, work . . . in brief, it should defend education as a fundamental necessity for the quality of life.

The essential question of the school today is that of its quality (Glasser 1990). This quality is also directly related to the small projects of the schools themselves. The political-pedagogical project of the school is much more efficient for the conquest of this quality than are huge projects, which are anonymous and distant from the day-to-day existence of the schools. Why?

1. Only the schools with a close knowledge of the community and its projects can give concrete replies to the concrete problems of each school;
2. Therefore, they can respect the ethnic and cultural peculiarities of each region;
3. They spend less on bureaucracy; and
4. The community itself can evaluate the results from near at hand.

This new school is already being built in the concrete resistance of many educators, parents, pupils, and school workers. These are schools in which children are happy to go, study, and build the elaborated culture, as George Snyders says. This school will not be abandoned by the children. No one leaves or abandons what belongs to them and are what they likes.

8

Sociocultural Diversity and Education for All

The universalization of basic education has been a constant theme in congresses for educators throughout the world. However, on the majority of occasions, the question is asked within an extensionist view of education. The universalization of teaching is confused with the extension of a preestablished set of knowledge which has already been systematized, or a type of cultural uniformization, called by Paulo Freire a "cultural invasion" some years ago.

Asking the question of education for all from the politically correct point of view, one must begin with the idea of respect for the first culture. We should, then, ask ourselves how, through culture, we can develop certain themes that will enable people and groups to better dominate their educative itinerary.

Without intending, in this last chapter, to exhaust the subject, which is more interrogative and prospective. I would like to present some ideas, which have been nourished by practice, and which have also nourished practice. This is in order to better understand the relationship between cultural identity and the educative itinerary which is seeking the universalization of basic education.

CULTURAL IDENTITY AND EDUCATIVE ITINERARY

When I introduce myself to someone, and I say, "I'm so-and-so," I am identifying myself. The other person, by saying, "Pleased to meet you. I'm so-and-so," is becoming aware of me. From now on, he will call me by my name. Naming me, he is recognizing me. By recognizing oneself, or naming oneself through saying "I am," one is manifesting the fundamental existential element on which it is possible to construct an itinerary for life, and, therefore, a pedagogical itinerary.

Everything begins with the recognition of one's identity. The first educative act is the recognition or the rescuing of the fact that the identity of the educator, and the pupil, has its own existence, as we saw in the first chapter of this book.

If it is easy to understand what an educative itinerary means, the same is not the case for the expression *cultural identity*.

What is *cultural identity?*

First, we should talk about ethnocultural identity as, when we speak about the identity of a culture, we must locate it within a determined time and space and inside an ethnic group. In turn, this identity would be linked to a national and a regional identity, which are also historically determined.

Some years ago, the philosopher Roland Corbisier (1975) said that the Brazilian national identity began to exist with modernism—that is, at the beginning of this century. Before this, there was just a transplanted identity.

To affirm an ethnocultural identity is to affirm a certain originality, a *difference*, and, at the same time, a *similarity*. Identical is he who is perfectly equal. In the identity, there is always a relationship of equality that cements a group, and an equality for all those who belong to it. However, identity is defined in relation to something which is outside, and which is different. One can say that Brazil belongs to the Third World—an expression that is becoming less and less clear—because it is different from the First World. Yet the simple opposition to the other—self-defense in relation to the First World, for example—doesn't make up the identity of a nation nor a people.

Today we live in a period of an *explosion of differences*—ethnic, sexual, cultural, national, and so on, which ask the question of the possibility of rescuing identity. Increasingly, we are asking ourselves, *"Who are we?"*

Faced by the economic blocks of North America, Europe, and Japan, we Latins—the inhabitants South America, and, in particular, the inhabitants of Latin America, ask ourselves who we are. What does being a Latin mean? On which basis of identity can we fulfill our utopia, which is our Latin American unity? In which ways are we different from other countries and economic blocs?

We are a mixture of Afro-Americans, Indians, whites, and Asians . . . Just this? The Brazilian poet, Carlos Drummond de Andrade said that "No Brazil exists," and he asked himself, "Is it just by chance that Brazilians exist?" What is genuinely ours? Of what is our identity made?

Jacques Lambert (1986) said that there are two Brazils. There might be many Brazils—not only the real Brazils, but also the Brazils described by sociologists and philosophers. For example, the Brazil of the sociologist Gilberto Freyre (1933) is very different from the Brazil of the philosopher Alvaro Vieira Pinto (1960).

Sociocultural identity would be an innocuous concept if it tended to fix cultural patterns in order to just preserve them. Culture is dynamic, and, in the contact with other cultures, it is transformed. Nowadays, it is increasingly difficult to discover a culture that is not intimately interdependent with other cultures. One of the most notable tendencies at this end of century is the *globalization of economies and communications.* (Naisbitt 1990), which makes the global village possible. Paradoxically, other marked tendencies of today all *multiculturalism,* cultural diversity, and, therefore, the valuing of regional cultures, the affirmation of the identity, and the values of small and ethnic groups.

How can we connect cultural diversity with educative itineraries that lead toward equity? I suppose that there is no way to recognize difference if one does not begin by accepting alterity and equality. In order to know myself, I must recognize the other as a partner. Identity presupposes a relationship of equality and of difference, which could be antagonistic or not. There is only dialogue and partnership when the difference is not antagonistic. The dialogue is a relationship of unity of nonantagonistic contrary factors. Between antagonistic factors there is merely conflict.

The theme of the relationship between cultural diversity and the educative itinerary has already been examined by educators such

as Paulo Freire and George Snyders. Each of them has, in his own
way, pointed toward a pedagogy which is based on the respect for the
cultural identity of the pupil.

Paulo Freire builds his pedagogy—his method, as it is known—
on an itinerary which ranges from popular culture to literature erudite
culture, passing through the training of the critical consciousness.

His thinking has its deepest roots in the politico-cultural debate at the end of the 1950s, which was centered on the construction
of a national identity based on political, social, and economic development. According to Paulo Freire, this would pass through the stage
of a taking of consciousness of the Brazilian reality. This process
would not take place without a transformation in the structure of
teaching and the extension of education for everyone. A project of
emancipation and construction of a new Brazilian nation would pass
through the assumption of its characteristics of a Latin-American
and Third-World nation—contrary to what the dominant elites
thought, which was that they were building a new Europe or a new
America in Brazil.

Then, Paulo Freire looks at the question of cultural invasion,
dependence, and alienated consciousness. By denouncing this national reality, Paulo Freire was dialectically announcing its end, and
inaugurating, in our midst, a vigorous movement around an autonomous pedagogical thinking. Paulo Freire reintroduces the reflection on the social element in Brazilian educational thinking, and
pledges himself to socialist and democratic ideas.

Popular culture is, therefore, synomous with conscientization—in other words, of the taking of consciousness of the Brazilian
reality in order to transform it and to create new forms of social and
political relationships. It means a consciousness of rights, the possibility of creating new rights, and the ability to defend them against
authoritarianism and violence—whether it is symbolical or not—
and the arbitrary stance.

Finally, popular culture means culture for citizenship. In the ac-
knowledgements to *Pedagogy of the Oppressed*, Paulo Freire indicates the new actors in this transformation. They are "the
ragged-trousered of the world, and those who discover themselves in
them and, by discovering themselves, suffer together with them, but
who especially struggle together with them." Therefore, not only the
ragged-trousered of the world are actors in history. Those who discover themselves in them, and struggle with them, are actors in history, too. This reminds me of what Pier Paolo Pasolini said in one of

his films. "Solidarity is a very different right from piety. By acting and struggling, it becomes supportable."

The pedagogy of George Snyders, as we have already seen, intends to make a rupture and a continuity between the *first culture,* which we can most clearly see in mass culture, and *elaborated culture,* which is that of the school, and understood not only as the place of the systematic and the progressive, but also the place of happiness.

The school which denies mass culture would be contributing to the failure at school of children from the popular segments of society, as opposed to children from the elites. The school must make the synthesis between continuity and rupture, as Snyders says, in relation to mass culture, if it wishes to respect the cultural identity of the popular children. The immediate or the first culture should be an appeal toward the elaborated.

It is clear that this is valid in the countries in which mass culture is hegemonic, but it is not so evident in relation to the countries in which there are nations and peoples with a considerable cultural diversity.

Today, multiculturalism, or cultural diversity, is an increasingly visible reality. There is also no way of establishing hierarchies between cultures. It would be completely stupid to say that French culture is either superior or inferior to African culture.

As respect for the civil rights of minorities increases, the political and cultural importance of minority cultures also grows. The difference becomes visible and might be a discomfort to some. It might also happen that those who have always found external enemies to justify domination will, today, with the difficulty of finding these enemies, more easily find arguments to internally discriminate against Negroes, Indians, immigrants, children, the poor, and others, simply because they are different.

Elaborated culture doesn't necessarily represent an element that is superior for the vital necessities of all individuals. It depends on the historical context in which they live. It might even destroy their identities through a type of forgetting or rejection of the first culture. It could represent "pure alienation," or the "discourse of the other," in the expression of Cornelius Castoradis (1982), who, lodging within me, ends up by speaking for me.

This is the case, for example, of the drama which certain indigenous communities face today in Brazil. They end up by being neither Indians nor Brazilians. The school of the whites might destroy their Indian identity. As, in this case, contact with the white man is inevitable, what can be done is to set up bilingual schools and help create centers of Indian culture. There are already six hundred of these schools in Brazil. Their objective is to preserve and strengthen the social organization, culture, customs, languages, beliefs, and traditions of these indigenous communities.

Failure at school, which is demonstrated by the high dropout and repetition rate, continues at an alarming level, even in certain countries where basic education has been extended to everyone. Responses given by governments have varied from automatic promotion to the next level, and division by cycles, to full-time schooling. Behind these responses, there is an understanding of the problem which throws the responsibility onto the so-called clientele—namely, the pupils, and especially their economic conditions. The school would try to correct defects of supply and demand for schools without even questioning itself. It would try to promote the equality of chances, making it easier for the less-favored to climb the school ladder through formal and bureaucratic mechanisms, and allowing pupils to be failed only at certain levels or making them stay at school at long as possible. These solutions suppose that the problem is in the pupil, and not in the school.

I would like to look at the problem from another angle, which first questions the school, without ignoring the difficulties that the poor have in order to study. I would like to look at the problem of pupils repeating the year as a problem relating to the school.

Theories of learning put forward the point of view that the retention of knowledge doesn't depend solely on effort and repetition, but more particularly on interest. We can more easily fix in our memory what we are interested in knowing, and what we live more intensely. I proved this through a survey in São Paulo (Gadotti 1993), which showed that those who have been excluded from school have a high opinion of school. If they could, they would soon return to school. They recognized that the teachers were badly paid, that they often didn't turn up, and that the school didn't respect them. However, what most attracted my attention was that they liked school, even though they didn't find in it what they were looking for. They didn't find a knowledge that corresponded to their interests, or their immediate necessities. School activities failed to involve them. Learning was, for them, a dull obligation more than something that was essential for their lives. They didn't feel the need to learn what the school taught them. Yet, despite all that, they liked it!

School hasn't yet solved the question of the transmission of knowledge for the popular segments—that is, it doesn't manage to make the synthesis between elaborated and popular culture, which is the first culture of the pupil. Despite the large number of surveys and amount of research, the curricula have not been able to adequately equate the relationship between *cultural identity* and the *educative itinerary* of the pupils who come from the popular segments of society. Our curricula still present the pupils with a package of knowledge which they must learn, whether it has any meaning for them or not. They are evaluated—passed or failed—according to whether they assimilate this package of knowledge. They are not evaluated according to the development of their abilities to think autonomously, even nearly a century after the first appearance of the theses of the New School.

THE PROMISES OF MULTICULTURAL EDUCATION

Although it is still being developed and is full of contradictions, the theory of multicultural education aims at making an adequate reply to this question as it takes into account the social and cultural diversity of the pupils. The first rule of this theory of education is pluralism and respect for the culture of the pupil. Therefore, democracy is a basic value. It supposes that the task of education is to help establish equity and mutual respect, and overcome prejudices of all kinds, mainly those of race and poverty, as those who are excluded from school are mainly blacks and the poor. Without this principle, one cannot talk about education for all nor of an improvement in the quality of teaching.

Equity in education means equality of opportunity for everyone to develop individual potentials. Equity can also be reached only when the popular classes enter and remain in a school that interests them. "Equal for all" does not mean a monocultural uniformity. Education for all means, regardless of social or economic position, access for all to education, and access to a range of knowledge and basic abilities that allow each person to develop fully, while taking into account what belongs to each culture.

Multicultural education attempts to confront the challenge of maintaining the balance between the local or regional culture of a social group or ethnic minority, and a universal culture, which belongs to humanity. The school which takes on this vision attempts to open up horizons for its pupils, so that they can understand other cultures, other languages, and other ways of being in a world that is becoming closer and closer. It attempts to build a pluralistic and independent society. It is, at the same time, an international education, which attempts to promote peace between peoples and nations, and a community education, which values the local roots of the culture—that is the most intimate daily life in which each person's life takes place. This emerging conception of education is little known. It implies a *pedagogy of human rights* (Best 1991) and respect for the environment: Today, it is part of a large cultural movement for equity, equality of educational opportunities, and the quality of life, particularly in relation to ethnic minorities and the poor segments of the population. Today, many people don't have access to education, either for ethnic reasons, through extreme poverty, of for all kinds of other deficiencies.

Multicultural education intends to make a critical analysis of present-day monocultural curricula and to critically train teachers so that they change their attitude toward the poorest pupils, find instructional strategies which are suitable for the education of the popular segments, and attempt, first and foremost, to understand them in the totality of their cultures and their visions of the world. For example, in the education of young and adult workers, a strategy of literacy, in a multicultural conception of education, should begin with their own experience of work and life—that is, the biography of the pupils themselves and not with the drawing of letters, which is an antiscientific technique. This technique was successfully used in São Paulo (1989–1992). The young people and adults felt more involved in the literacy process when they noticed the importance that the teacher gave to their own lives. As one of them said, he was previously ashamed to tell people about his life, as he considered it to be a failure. He felt that this failure was his own fault, and not the fault of the iniquitous social and economic structure. When he talked about what he had done in his life, he could accept it with greater confidence, understand it better, and look for reasons for a better life. If learning enabled him to live better, he would give all of himself to continue learning. If school was this, then it was all that he was looking for. He felt happy to be at school, as there were so many places of work where he had felt ashamed.

Multicultural education tries to equate the problems which have come about as a result of cultural diversity faced with the obligation of the state to offer an education which is equal for all. It also tries to point to strategies to overcome these problems.

Cultural diversity is the wealth of humanity. In order to accomplish its humanistic task, the school needs to show the pupils that there are other cultures besides their own. Because of this, the school needs to be local as a starting point, but it must be international and intercultural as a point of arrival. School autonomy does not mean isolation and enclosure inside a particular culture. School autonomy means a curious, daring school which attempts to dialogue with all other cultures and conceptions of the world. *Pluralism* doesn't mean eclecticism, or an amorphous cultural patchwork, but, above all, a dialogue with all other cultures, beginning with a culture which opens out to the rest. As José Luiz dos Santos says, "Culture means respect for humanity as a whole and, at the same time, for each of the peoples, nations, societies and human groups." (1984, 8)

In 1787, a new discipline appeared which had *anthropology* as its basis. It was "destined to reapproximate and incorporate data which belonged to different epistomological fields, but which refer to particular entities which have an ethnic base: tribes, peoples, nations or states." (Erny 1982, 26) This discipline is called "ethnology," and it studies different societies using their own cultures as a starting point.

Each society imprints a specific way of being and of thinking on individuals. This is alien to the will of each person. Each society is made up in a different manner, according to particular beliefs, myths, and ways of life of each group. Each culture has its own vision of the world that cannot be judged by standards that are strange or foreign to it. "Cultural diversity has something irreducible," says Franz Boas. (Boas in Erny 1982, 26)

However, it is not very easy to recognize the *differences* between cultures without over or undervaluing them. Therefore, we need a science with objective methods. Ethnology attempts to objectively analyze the culture of a people. Multicultural education surpasses ethnological science, or the pure knowledge of cultures, as it doesn't just try to know them but rather to integrate them, surpassing simple respect for cultural, ethnic, linguistic, or national diversity.

This recent phenomenon of the confrontation of cultures in the same territory, made possible by the industrial and modern urban process—a multicultural society or a multiracial democracy—can be called "multiculturalism." It began with the organization of the so-called minority movements which questioned the hegemony of the white, male, and Western Christian thinking. It is a movement against racial, sexual, and immigrant discrimination. The explosion of the demands of the ethnic minorities, the intensification of xenophobia and the radicalization of the minority lobbies are all demonstrations of this cultural movement which characterizes this end of century.

Multicultural education can be seen as a possibility of understanding this phenomenon, and of achieving a democratic and harmonious way of living together. It becomes necessary, not only in regions where there are a large number of immigrants, but as a fundamental element in today's integral education. Therefore, it doesn't intend to be another kind of education, parallel to present-day education, but a conception of education in which the ethnic minorities, understood qualitatively as nondominant, have the possibility of preserving characteristic traits of their culture, without denying the need to dominate the instruments which are necessary to enable them to have access to the *dominant culture.*

Today, multicultural education can be focused in two ways: (Bennett 1990)

As a Movement

This movement is in favor of the equality of educational opportunities, equity, and justice as opposed to all kinds of prejudice and discrimination. The recent movement of the so-called educative cities can be placed in this line of action. The educative cities which are aware of their roles and the responsibilities in matters connected to education—in addition to developing their traditional economic, social, political, and work functions—also attempt to develop a specifically educative function. This movement is based on the fact that we know the world, first, through our parents, and our immediate circle. Only afterward, do we progressively enlarge our universe. The district, and then the city, are the main educative means that we have. The educative city is a city with its own personality, which is integrated into a country and the world, in a complex system which is in constant evolution.

As a Curriculum Approach

In recent studies in the field of comparative or international education, the theme of multicultural education has been examined more and more frequently. For example, in Europe people are worried about saving the numerous spoken languages from extinction as young people prefer the language that is used by the media to their maternal language. Bilingual literacy schemes for children would be a way of opposing this cultural euthanasia. Thus, there is the necessity of a multicultural curriculum as opposed to the present mono-cultural one.

It is not a case of denying access to the elaborated general culture, which is an important instrument in the struggle for the minorities. It is more a case of not killing the first culture of the pupil. In a world which is getting smaller and more homogenized through culture, the survival of the nondominant forms of culture can become more and more difficult.

Multicultural education, which basically questions white, male, and Western Christian thinking, demands the inclusion of other legacies in the curriculum—such as, African, Arab, Oriental, female, homosexual and so on. It implies concrete changes in the educational system, which, if they are taken to their final consequences, can not only break with the hegemony of one type of knowledge, but can also activate hidden conflicts under the cover of social unity.

Multiculturalism has a considerable dose of ambiguity. It might stimulate, in a contradictory way, the scorn for that which is different, such as racism or self-centrism. Examples of racial violence are very frequent. This also means that multiculturalism can bring divisions, create ghettoes, and be used as a mechanism to coopt any attempts to integrate cultural differences into a single unifying principle.

It is because of this question that multicultural education is still a polemical theme. There are pros and cons, and especially many difficulties to effectively putting it into practice.

How can ethnic and cultural diversity be tackled? Through integration or autonomy? This is the key question for multicultural education.

In the United States, for example, certain groups of Hispanics and Asians prefer to adapt themselves to the dominant North American culture, in which they have better chances of social ascendency, than to remain strongly connected to their cultures of origin. The same can be said of immigrants in the south of Brazil who lost their native languages. These groups are against a multiculturalism that denies them access to the dominant culture.

There is no doubt that multicultural education can, contradictorily, cause *separatism* and antagonism between groups, and fragment society, It can also lead to conflicts and the nonreciprocity of the cultural differences, as well as the possibility of isolation, or of excluding nationalisms. The radicalization of these ethnic and social groups favors segregation and, consequently, it forms isolated groups

or tribes who fight with each other. The difference, or the basic necessity to mark cultural identity, is transformed into exclusion. This
can be overcome only by a grassroots ethics, respect for difference,
and, therefore, a philosophy of dialogue.

There is also a certain risk of *eclecticism*, which would be that
of treating the different cultures superficially, and thereby distorting
them. Multiculturalism can be an alibi to guarantee the hegemony
of one culture or one way of thinking. It would serve, not to give
space to each group to act harmoniously in society, but, rather, to
separate the groups and weaken them so that they could be adapted
to the norms and the customs of the dominant group.

There is also the risk of excessively valuing one culture to the
detriment of others. This is regionalism, which focuses only on the
local or particular culture, to the detriment of the universal whole.

The development of a multicultural education depends heavily
on changes in the educational system, and especially on the training
of the educator. It has often been said that teachers should respect
the culture of pupils—their hidden curriculum—but few instruments have been indicated to help teachers in this task. All educators recognize the problem and the consequences of not respecting
the popular culture of children of the popular classes. However,
speaking more generally, our teaching is aimed at an average pupil
who is an abstraction of the real pupil. Multicultural education helps
the teacher to better go about the task of speaking to the concrete
pupil. It values the point of view of the pupil, thus opening up the
school system, and constructing a curriculum which is nearer to the
pupil's cultural reality.

THE MEANING AND CHALLENGE OF BASIC EDUCATION

The 1990 World Conference of Education for All in Jomtien,
Thailand, unleashed a series of initiatives throughout the world,
especially in relation to the basic learning necessities. (PNUD,
UNESCO, UNICEF, Banco Mundial, 1991) In the preceding years, in
many parts of the world, the theme was widely discussed in various
preparatory meetings.

One of the main consequences of the Jomtien Conference was
to shift the axis of the educational debate, mainly in the so-called
Third World, away from the theme of literacy toward the theme of
basic education. The new vision of education proposed by the Jomtien Conference includes literacy in the concept of basic education,
and, thereby, gives a new meaning to both. Education begins to have

a new focus. Literacy is no longer the main worry of the countries with high levels of illiteracy, and efforts are now concentrated on basic education.

What is the meaning of this *new focus?*

Actually, after the Jomtien Conference, those who had been excluded from basic education continued to be the same. The so-called illiterate continued to be illiterate. However, the new theoretical vision can change educative practices. Are there any really illiterate people? Isn't it true that the development of the intelligence and learning begin at birth? Isn't it also true that the most significant experiences are those that take place in early infancy? Isn't it further true that the so-called illiterates do not recognize themselves as being so, and that, to call them illiterate, is to call them ignorant? No one knows everything, and no one is ignorant of everything, as Paulo Freire often says. According to this point of view, there are no really illiterate people. Rather, there are people who, at the right age, had no access to basic education.

The theme of the meaning of basic education, and the challenge that it represents today, are especially relevant, both in theory and in practice. The declaration for the Jomtien Conference, which was prepared by the Executive Secretariat of the Inter-Agency Commission, and published a month after the Conference took place under the title of *Satisfying Basic Learning Necessities: A Vision for the Nineties*, gave the following definition of basic education:

> Basic education refers to the education which attempts to satisfy the basic learning necessities; it includes primary or fundamental instruction, on which subsequent learning should be based; it includes infants' and primary (or elementary) education, as well as literacy training, general culture and essential skills for the training of young people and adults; in some places it also includes middle teaching (UNDP-UNESCO-UNICEF-World Bank 1990) (UNDP: 1990)

The basic learning necessities refer to "knowledge, skills, behavior, and values which are necessary for people to survive, develop the quality of their lives, and continue learning (UNDP: 1990) These definitions need some *comments.*

1. Basic education should be understood as a basis, as the floor and not the ceiling, of the educative development of each individual.
2. It includes the primary or basic level of formal teaching, but it should not be confused with this teaching.

3. It is not directed just toward children, but equally to young people and adults who have had no access to formal education at the right age.
4. Understood thus, basic education supposes a link between formal and informal education.
5. Therefore, the formal school must make new links with the community.
6. Through its proximity to the community, the municipality is the fundamental actor in these new connections.

The Jomtien Conference attempted to make a definition of basic education, but it must be recognized that it is impossible to work with a uniform concept when faced with the *heterogeneity of cultures and experiences.* Any definition would give problems. The new definition of basic education should, then, be both flexible and operational. Attempts were made to give an integral and integrating vision of the concept—but one which was not a vague definition, as this would be of no use in helping plan for concrete action. Therefore, the Jomtien Conference tried to give basic education a new focus, associating it with the concept of the basic necessities of learning.

Through this new focus, the school will continue to be the main channel of access to the basic learning necessities. However, it will also take into account other training vehicles, such as radio, television, clubs, libraries, and the other forms of formal or informal community education, with the vast range of educational technologies which are appropriate for these modes of training.

When one analyses the meaning of basic education, two essential and complementary categories should be highlighted—equity and autonomy. *Equity* in education basically means justice in the face of the fundamental human right of access to education, at least at a basic level. It can be seen, however, that equity should not be understood only in relation to that which refers to access to education, but also to the permanence and the possibility of taking advantage of the benefits of education as a whole. In many countries today, the problem of equity is not situated so much in access to education, as in the quality of the education which is offered. For a few, its quality is high. For the majority, it is low.

Autonomy—a theme which was only briefly examined in Jomtien—is the possibility for self-determination, and the presence of the universal right of access to education. These two principles put many present-day school systems into check, as they are either unable to offer a quality education to all, or their bureaucracy freezes the creative capacity of the school and the classroom.

To promote equity means giving an opportunity to all to reach and maintain an acceptable level of learning. This equity means improving the quality of education offered today, and eliminating all the stereotypes and prejudices of color, race, gender, habits, customs, and so on. The concept of autonomy is, thus, indispensible as a complement of equity.

To affirm the autonomy of the school means that there are no two schools which are equal. Each school is the result of the development of its own contradictions. Every attempt at the uniformization of this process means the reduction of the quality of the school.

In the discussion of this theme, the arguments frequently fall into two opposing traps. On one side, there is *regional conservatism,* and on the other side, we have *alienated universalism.*

In the first case, one can fall into the arrogance of judging that an absolute autonomy exists, exalting the particular, and refusing both the knowledge which is universally valid as well as universal ideas and values, such as democracy and pluralism. In the second case, regional specificity and local culture are disdained.

These two tendencies are ingenuous. They are moving in the opposite direction to history as, today, there is a clear trend—as we have already seen—toward the globalization of the economy on the one hand, and, on the other, toward the valuing of local cultures. These trends are not antagonistic, but complementary tendencies. In education, we can say that, behind the single and decentralized system, there is another system which includes a range of universal knowledge which is available after being filtered by the local culture and an emerging school into the *citizen school*—the school that trains the governing citizen, and not the citizen who will be governed. In this school of basic education, there is no place for false dichotomies between universal knowledge and local or popular culture. Thus, it operates the synthesis between equity and autonomy.

A renewed vision of the concept of basic education suggests that fundamental teaching should be the basis for a *continued education,* which is integrated into all the aspects of human development as it serves to approximate individuals in the community, concentrating the educative process on people, their needs, and their context.

Basic education should not be understood as a level which is separated from the whole of education. Its connection with higher education and permanent education is inherent to the concept which has been outlined here. It is only a bureaucratic conception of education that dichotomizes levels and series of teaching. Basic education finds meaning in an organic whole, and in a connected educational system, which is oriented by general aims. It is well-known that many national systems of education are no more than unequal parts stuck together. Higher education—as in preparing the teachers of normal basic education and receiving pupils who come from basic education—is necessarily connected to basic education. In this connection, there is a mutual learning.

There would be no sense in opposing the priority of basic education to that of *higher education*. They are complementary priorities, and there is no question of opting for one of the choices and excluding the other. As Juan Carlos Tedesco says,

> Solving the basic problems of the system is vital to guarantee the democratic character of social development. To strengthen the scientific qualification, promoting the training of highly qualified resources and the production of knowledge that allows us to solve social and productive problems is vital to guarantee the growth and availability of resources. (1989, 18)

In the same way that one should not promote basic education by sacrificing the development of other priorities—such as scientific and technological development—basic education should also not be developed regardless of its connection with work and production, especially in the basic education of young people and adults. As Daniel A. Morales-Gómez and Carlos Alberto Torres insist, the promotion of basic education should take advantage of the most recent historical experiments in education in the regions (Morales-Gómez 1990). In Latin America, they point to the original contribution of *popular education*, particularly in the field of the education of young people and adults, and the nonformal education in the 1960s and 1970s. In recent years, popular education has also been developed inside the school system, in the so-called popular public education.

Basic education should have different goals and objectives in its different contexts. This means always searching for and renewing the meaning of education, and not fixing on inflexible theoretical models which are unable to read the great book of reality, in order to learn with it. The basic necessities of learning cannot be considered as the straitjackets of basic education. They are possible paths to be taken, but, in each society, they deserve a concrete analysis, not mechanical nor abstract reproduction.

In order for this new vision of basic education to be efficient, a permanent and carefully studied *curriculum reorientation* is necessary. This should give a theoretical and practical consistency to what is learned. It should eliminate prejudices, and it should recognize the knowledge of the pupil so that he or she can start from there to build a more elaborative knowledge. Individual pupils are the subject of the knowledge, and their experiences whether they are children or adults, are the primordial source of this knowledge. It is necessary to emphasize the process of the construction of this knowledge, and of the acquisition of skills, more than the simple adaptation or acquisition, which translates to a static conception of the learning processes.

Every human being is capable of learning, and of teaching. In the process of the construction of knowledge, everyone who is involved is also learning and teaching. The learning-teaching process is more efficient when pupils themselves take part in the construction of their knowledge. Making knowledge one's own is not just learning knowledge.

A true educative process is not restricted to the acquisition of skills and knowledge, but presupposes the development of the individual, so that the right to actively participate at the heart of society, in work, in leisure, in culture, and more is guaranteed. Knowledge cannot be reduced to the product. It is also the process. It is one thing to assimilate knowledge in a way that contains no type of appropriation, but another thing entirely to recognize the democratic construction of knowledge itself.

Faced with the educational backwardness of many countries, the *responsibility of the university* to engage in a movement of the universalization of basic education continues to grow. In many places, the university is turned far too much inward on itself, contemplating its own crisis, when it might well be better off to look for solutions to its own crisis in basic education for everyone. By doing this, the university could offer many services.

1. It could take another look at biopsychic learning and developmental theories of the child and the adolescent.
2. It could offer permanent programs for the retraining of teachers.
3. It could aid the planning of the organs responsible for basic education.
4. It could produce didactic and instructional material.
5. It could develop documentary and information centers, and publicize didactic and pedagogical material.

6. It could define and experiment with models of formal education.
7. It could develop extramural and cultural activities.

In summary, the university has a debt to the university extension programs and to the service that it lends to the community when, it would seem, that it has been much more worried about teaching and research.

As can be seen, a *reconceptualization of basic education* also implies a reconceptualization of higher education. If we want to renew the challenges of basic education, we must also renew our conceptual instruments. We often work with concepts which were elaborated centuries ago, and in a historical context in which the interests of the elites predominated. This no longer corresponds to the present demands of democracy. The Jomtien Conference took an important step in the direction of the democratization of education, but it didn't map out all of the path. This must be done as we go along, and taking every context into account.

Of what does the *challenge* of basic education consist?

The answer to this question is simple. The challenge to basic education is its own universalization. We already have before us a worldwide situation with almost a billion young people and illiterate adults, and more than 100 million children who have no access to education. What is complex is how this challenge will be accomplished in practice. It is necessary to distinguish the enormous disparity between those countries which have been making an effort to develop basic education for more than a century—and which have already reached a high level of democratization of educational opportunities—and the large number of other countries which have, only a short time ago, begun to make a precarious effort.

What is certain is that, in those countries in which there is considerable educational backwardness, the universalization of basic education will not come about without the *political will* of its governors. In practice, this means that only the state can get rid of educational backwardness. In the socioeconomic conditions in which the majority of the population live in developing countries, the involvement of the public powers in the universalization of basic education is vital. Without this engagement, there will be few guarantees for the success of private actions, unless they are linked to a more global policy. In the opposite case, private initiatives run the risk of being short-lived and atomizing.

Nevertheless, the state would be impotent without the participation and engagement of society. One key concept of this thesis was developed by the Jomtien Conference—that is, the construction of *new alliances* or partnerships, involving, for example, public organizations which are responsible for the teaching and organized movements of civil society.

The contribution of *nongovernmental organizations* within this policy of new alliances is particularly important, as they make contact with the local community easier to accomplish.

Another piece of evidence is that the universalization of high-quality basic education will be possible only through the *normal system of teaching* and the debureaucratized public school—that is, one which has pedagogical, administrative, and financial autonomy.

Experience has demonstrated that, with rare exceptions, it is an illusion to think of the universalization of basic education through future campaigns or episodic movements. It is necessary to make a *permanent effort*, involving both children and adults. Here, basic education should be thought of with appropriate methodologies for every age. The basic education of young people and adults should be offered through curriculum content which is centered on their social practices and their work, and the methodology of teaching-learning should be suitable for the maturity and the experience of the pupil. However, the methodological conception is not enough if it is unaccompanied by huge investments in basic education in those countries where the lack of access—and the dropout and repetition rates—are still very high.

At a number of international meetings, the thesis that the countries with large external debts can transform part of this debt into funds for the development of basic education, under the control of nongovernmental organizations, has been gaining ground. Others recommend the creation of regional funds to channel new resources destined to satisfy the basic learning necessities, which will allow for mutual learning support and the exchange of experiences. So, in addition to the internal effort of each country, regional conditions can be created to make educative efforts in common possible.

The disparity of investment in education is revealed by the cost per pupil. According to Frederico Mayor, director general of UNESCO, in his speech at the opening of the Jomtien Conference, there are countries which spend, based on United States currency, an average of $29 per pupil per year, while other countries spend an average of $1,987 per pupil per year. In many cases, in the interior of each country, the same picture is reproduced. For example, in Brazil in 1987, the direct annual cost of primary teaching of the network in

Rio de Janeiro state was $306, whereas in the state of Piauí only $32 was invested per pupil.

It is along these lines that the thesis of a *new educational order* should be developed, such as that which was defended at the sixth World Conference of the International Community Education Association, which took place in 1991 from the 29 July to 2 August in Port of Spain, Trinidad. This new order makes an inversion of the priorities of present-day education possible. (ICEA 1991)

One of the greatest obstacles to the universalization of basic education is the distribution of financial resources, which privileges the administrative machinery, planning functions, supervision, orientation, and control, to the detriment of end-activities in the classroom. In many cases, the heavy educational bureaucracy has made the expansion of educational opportunities difficult. In this new educational order, a fundamental problem is that of rescuing the role of the teacher in the classroom, and the social function of the school as the privileged locus of education.

In the search for the practical confrontation of the challenge that basic education represents in many countries, one element of education has taken on a new strength—*local power*, especially in the municipalities (Romão 1992). This phenomenon is also associated with the growing vitality which is demonstrated by the emergence of innumerable nongovernmental organizations and popular movements. In many places, local power has begun to want to interfere in the formulation of policies for the sector, although it points to being overloaded with responsibilities which are imposed on it by the legal apparatus and by the administration of the social demands of basic education. In addition, local councils are often technically and financially fragile. Those countries that achieved better results in the expansion of educational opportunities could count on the force of the community as well as the political will of their governors. Centralized systems—such as that of France; the ideological apparatus of the state in the formulation of Louis Althusser; or gigantic teaching networks, as in the state of São Paulo, Brazil, with approximately six million pupils and more than five thousand—school, are ungovernable and become distanced from the population. The municipal organs of education are, therefore, the most qualified, through their proximity to local problems, to plan and manage basic education. Decentralization or municipalization is a necessity, and, in no way, threatens the disintegration of national educational systems, if—at the diverse levels and in the various systems—common objectives are worked toward in collaboration.

The formulation of policies and the elaboration of plans will become efficient only if they attend the concrete demands of society, and if society legitimizes these plans through active participation assured by the diffusion of information, and through channels of communication opened by public power. The community must discuss, propose, and organically participate in the elaboration of educational policies.

I don't believe in educational plans which are conceived in closed offices, even though they might have been created by the best of technicians. New advances in education can take place only when society becomes mobilized, and when it gives priority to education. Therefore, one of the greatest challenges in basic education lies in social mobilization around the value of education, the school, and knowledge.

The state has the duty to offer everyone the opportunity of access to education. However, the deeper meaning that should move us to promote equity in education is the furtherance of humanity—the deep desire to do justice to and to build a human society of solidarity. This solidarity cannot be considered to be a concept that has been surpassed in a world of increasing agressivity, as some people insist on saying. It is an attitude of profound respect for differences and for people. If those who are excluded from basic education enter into our calculations, they don't enter as numbers nor as goals, but as people. We are not donating anything to them. Instead, we are promoting their rights.

All our efforts should be directed to the greater participation of those who should benefit from basic education. They should be constantly heard, and be deeply involved, so that basic education is not a mere desire of well-intentioned educators. It should be—first and foremost—the fruit of the engagement, whether it be called a popular movement or participative planning. It should come from the individuals themselves, those who must make their own decisions when faced with life as a whole. In order to accomplish this, basic education is an indispensible instrument.

Conclusion

EDUCATION AFTER MARX

Today, after Perestroika and the great social and political movements of Eastern Europe and the fall of the Berlin Wall (Blackbrun 1992), we are reaching the end of the last decade of a century under the sign of perplexity and of the crisis of conceptions and paradigms. It is a new moment rich with possibilities.

We cannot escape our period. We cannot talk about the future of education without a certain caution. It is also with this caution that the reader should examine some of the viewpoints that are highlighted here, and which are based on the works of those educators and philosophers who have tried, in the middle of this perplexity, to point toward a path for the future.

Traditional education, rooted in the slave society of ancient times and destined for a small minority, began its decline in the Renaissance, yet it survives until today, despite the average extension of schooling which the bourgeois revolution brought.

The new education, which begins most clearly with the work of Rousseau, has developed in the last two centuries, and has brought innumerable conquests, especially in the educational sciences and in teaching methodologies. The Freinet techniques, for example, are definitive acquisitions.

However, both traditional and new education have the conception of education as a process of individual development in common. The most original characteristic of education in this century has been the shift of focus from the individual to the social, political, and ideological. Institutional pedagogy is an example of this. The experience of more than half a century of education in the socialist countries is another example. Education is this century has become permanent and social.

There are many differences in levels between regions and countries, between the North and South, and between peripheral and hegemonic countries. However, ideas have been spread throughout the world—among them that there is no special age for education, that education extends throughout life, and that it is not neutral.

At the beginning of the second half of this century, educators and educational policies imagined an internationalized education under the auspices of one great organization—namely UNESCO.

The highly developed countries had already universalized fundamental teaching and eliminated illiteracy. The national systems of education had been carried forward with great impetus from the last century, which enabled numerous educational plans to be made which reduced costs and increased benefits. The thesis of an international education had already been in existence since 1899, when the International Bureau of New Schools was founded in Brussels by Adolphe Ferrière.

As a consequence of these international associations of parents, teachers, and educational researchers—as well as the educational theories based on the idea of a single, unitary, and universal school—the subject of Comparative Education began close to the beginning of this century in 1917. The aim of this discipline was the study and research of the comparison among theories, practices, and educational systems at national and international levels. Later, UNESCO gave considerable emphasis to comparative education, publicizing studies and research which, today, are part of the training of educators in many countries. The expressions *comparative pedagogy* and *comparative education* are often used to mean the same thing, although the first has the connotation more of educative theories, and the second carries more of the idea of educational practices and systems.

In 1968—the same year that students rebelled, proclaiming "Imagination in Power!" and "It's forbidden to forbid!"—UNESCO, at its fifteenth General Conference, analysed education, and proposed a new conception, called *"permanent education."*

In this theory, national educational systems should be oriented by the principle that man is educated throughout his life and not just at the beginning. This new conception of education was extremely broad. However, it was considered, in the vision of the United Nations, to be a chance to construct an education which was also an instrument for peace, as it educated adults to live together.

After more than half a century of world wars, it seemed evident to everyone that education was a bulwark of peace. The principle of permanent education—which was taken up again as a key concept in the International Year of Education in 1970—should inspire new education policies in the member countries. However, it was inevitable that such a broad concept did not have the desired effects. In the proclamation that the planning of education should be integrated with social and economic planning, the first contradiction appeared. It was brought about by the differentiation between economic, political, and social systems. This universal principle could hardly be adapted to specific regional situations.

Although they were limited by the fact that they served only as recommendations, the efforts of UNESCO had a certain impact on the countries of the Third World—especially on those that were advancing toward democracy. In these countries, the proposals received a warmer welcome, thus demonstrating that education can receive the appropriate treatment only in a democratic country. Even so—and in spite of all the international efforts—many countries have still not managed to erase illiteracy.

The consequence of the evolution of *modern technologies* has yet to be fully seen in teaching, as McLuhan (1969) foresaw—at least within the majority of nations. Education operates with written language, and our present day dominant culture is impreganted by the new languages of television and informatics.

Education systems have not yet managed to evaluate the power of audiovisual communications, whether to inform or to narrow minds. We still work with traditional resources which have no appeal to children and young people. The methods of teaching must be severely changed in order to preserve for the human brain what is peculiar to it—that is, the ability to think—instead of merely developing the memory. The function of the school consists of teaching how to think critically. It is, therefore, necessary to dominate language, including electronic language.

Japan is one of the countries which has most developed technology in education. Nevertheless, carried away by technological lyricism, it, too, has ended up by creating an educational system that is dominated by fear, and carries a military discipline. Japanese schools have been transformed into teaching and drill machines, resulting in producing narrow, uncritical, and frustrated minds. In order to escape from a system which makes people obsessed with success—and which generates conformism and subservience to an order maintained by symbolical violence, agressivity, and competition—alcoholism is increasing among young people. One is not surprised that this educational model which, on the one hand, is so efficient, has, on the other hand, increased the number of suicides among young people and even among children. This increasingly worries Japanese educators. However, despite the criticism which must be made of these teaching machines, better this than nothing— meaning the lack of any schools at all, which characterizes Third World countries.

Among the new theories which have come about in recent years, there has been a great interest from educators in the so-called *holonomic paradigms*, which have not yet been fully defined. Among them, we can include the reflections of Edgar Morin, author of *The Lost Paradigm: Human Nature* (1973), in which he criticizes modern productivist reason and rationalization, and proposes a logic of the human being. These paradigms put forward a unifying principle of knowing, and of knowledge about man that values his daily life, lived experiences, the personal, the unusual, the odd, the chance, and other categories, such as decision, project, noise, ambiguity, finitude, choice, synthesis, connection, and totality.

These would be the new categories of the so-called holonomic paradigms. Etymologically, the Greek *holos* means *all*, and new paradigms attempt to center on the whole. It would be utopia, rather than ideology, that would have this ability to rescue the whole from the real, or a lost whole. For supporters of these new paradigms—the *classic paradigms*, identified in positivism and Marxism, which are ideological paradigms—dealt with categories which reduced wholeness. On the contrary, the holonomic paradigms intend disorder (Edgar Morin); communicative action (Jürgen Habermas); radicalness (Agnes Heller); empathy (Carl Rogers); hope (Ernest Bloch); happiness (George Snyders); the unity of man against unidimensionalization (Herbert Marcuse); and many more.

Clearly, all these authors would not allow themselves to be placed within the holonomic paradigms. The differences between them cannot be refuted. Still, they all point to a certain tendency— or better, a certain vision of education. The supporters of holonomic paradigms believe that they attempt to find in the unity of opposites, and in contemporary culture, a sign of the times, or a direction for the future, which they call the pedagogy of unity.

On the other hand, the paradigm of *popular education*, originally inspired on the work of Paulo Freire in the 1960s, found its fundamental category in conscientization. Practice—and reflection of this practice—led it to incorporate another no less important category—that of organization. It is not enough to be conscious. It is necessary to be organized in order to transform.

In the 1980s, popular education surpassed the level of the community, local power, and adult as well as nonformal education, to directly influence public educational systems and become established as popular public education. This trend of popular education is becoming stronger and stronger in Latin America, with the emergence of democratic governments and the conquest of important segments of power for popular parties. To restore the wholeness of the individual subject, measuring his or her initiative and creativity by valuing the microcosm, complementarity, and convergence. Proponents of these paradigms believe that the classical measures sustain the age-old dream of a complete society with no borders, and within which there will be no friction and a complete consensus. By accepting the anthropological idea that conceives man as essentially contradictory as fundamental in education, the holonomic paradigms allow us to maintain all the elements of the complexity of life without attempting to surpass them.

The holists believe that it is only the imaginary, utopia, and the imagination that are the basic factors of society. They refuse an order that annihilates desire, passion, looking, and listening. The classical focuses banalize these dimensions of life because they overvalue the macrostructure, or the system in which everything is a function or an effect of the socioeconomic, epistemic, linguistic, or psychic superstructures. For these new paradigms, history is essentially a possibility, whereas, what is worthwhile, is the imaginary.

To be truthful, these categories are not new in the theory of education. However, they are read today and analyzed with more sympathy than they were in the past. They can be found in the works of many intellectuals, philosophers, and educators. There is the sense of the other (Paulo Freire); tolerance (Karl Jaspers); the structure of welcome (Paul Ricoeur); the dialogue (Martin Buber); self-management (Célestin Freinet); However, the demand for popular education in also growing in Africa, Asia, and in numerous other countries that are not considered to be in the Third World. (Gadotti 1990; Torres 1990)

Another important current within popular education today is popular community education (Poster and Zimmer 1992). Based on the same political rationality in force in popular education, community education is more involved in new production alternatives. However, this is not all. Community education is also involved in the education of social and popular movements, in the struggle for civil rights, and against all types of discrimination.

Within community education, the category of production has definitively became part of popular education. Popular community education, working within the category of production, looks for ways to learn by producing, taking into account the reality of marginalized populations, which are excluded from the dominant means of production. The fields of action of popular community education can be both the formal and the nonformal school, economic and popular organizations, productive schools, and even small businesses.

In recent years, educators who have been faithful to the principles of popular education have worked mainly in two areas which have already been mentioned: that of popular public education, in the space which has been conquered inside the state; and in popular community education, especially that which is not under state control.

If previously enormous emphasis was given to the transformation of education through the conquest of the state by populist sectors—or those who had been given illusions by populist politics—nowadays, popular education, especially nonformal education, is being dispersed into thousands of small experiments. Unity is lost, but diversity is gained. These experiments are also mechanisms for democratization, in which the values of solidarity, reciprocity, and new alternative forms of production and consumption are seen. The 1990s are characterized by a post-Marxist and postmodern thinking, as well as by questioning of orthodox and bureaucratic socialist theses and the affirmation of subjectivity in politics. (McLaren 1986) This is expressed through social movements which are more concerned with immediate questions, than with a distant utopia, which we all dreamed of in the 1960s.

Faced with this state of affairs, popular education—as a theoretical model which has had its conceptions changed—can offer a wide range of alternatives for what remains of the 1990s. Among these alternatives is the reform of the public school system. The linking of popular education to local power and to the popular economy also opens new and immediate possibilities for the practice of popular education.

The theoretical model of popular education, which was elaborated from the reflection on educational practice during a number of decades, undoubtedly became one of the major contributions of Latin America to educative theory and practice on the international level. The notions of learning from the knowledge of the popular subject and teaching from generative themes, and of education as an act of knowledge, social transformation, and the political element of education are just some of the legacies of popular education to universal critical pedagogy. (Gadotti and Torres 1992)

At the threshold of the twenty-first century, and a new millenium, education is at a double crossroads. On one hand, the performance of the school system hasn't been able to cope with the universalization of basic quality education. On the other hand, both new and classical theoretical networks fail to present the global consistency which is necessary to point to paths which are really secure in a period of rapid and profound transformation. In this context, whatever the perspective that contemporary education takes, an education directed to the future will always be a contesting education, surpassing the limits which have been imposed by society, and, therefore, an education which is much more directed to social transformation than to cultural transmission. Here, *pedagogy of the praxis*, in its various forms, can offer a general reference which is much more secure than the pedagogies which are centered on cultural transmission.

Education, as we know it today, is deeply marked by modernity. However, modernity and postmodernity are in conflict today. Postmodernity means more modernity and antimodernity at the same time (Bosi 1992). Postmodernity has been talked about since the 1950s, when modernity (1900–1950), at least in literature, conventionally ends. Postmodernity is a name which is given to changes which have taken place in the sciences, arts, and in the advanced societies in the last decades. In the 1970s, postmodernism took on great impetus with critiques by philosophy of Western culture. Today, postmodernism is not considered to be just a fashion in cinema, music, the arts, and in daily life. Rather, it's viewed as a movement that questions the future. Actually, its only real identity is that of questioning modernity. There is no clear definition of what postmodernity is.

Among the elements that reveal aspects of postmodernity is the invasion of electronic technology, which causes a certain loss of identity in individuals. Postmodernity is also characterized by the crisis of paradigms. References are lacking. A *postmodern education* would be one that took cultural diversity into account, and would be, therefore, a *multicultural education*. Postmodernism came about as a criticism of modernity, faced with the disillusment caused by a rationalization which took modern society into the tragedies of the world wars and dehumanization.

Modern mankind is directed toward mass participation in politics, which often results in war, while postmodern mankind is devoted to daily life and the world. People today are involved with minorities and short-term small causes which have personal goals. Modern society is one which is cemented to the social. Postmodern people seek their affirmation as individuals, faced with the globalization of communications.

Postmodern education intends to rescue the unity of history and subjects which had been lost in the modernizing operations of the deconstruction of culture and education. Postmodern education appears to be closely linked to the culture. It is multicultural and permanent. It doesn't lend so much priority to the appropriation of universal knowledge, as to the process of knowledge and its aims. Actually, before knowing, mankind is asking itself, and is interested in knowing. The preoccupation of the postmodern theory also stems from this interest, which is the basis of education. Knowledge has a prospective characteristic.

Postmodernism in education works more with meaning than with content, and much more with intersubjectivity and plurality than with equality and unity. By advancing in this direction, postmodern education can bring a change of content in education which will make the content more meaningful for the pupil. Working with the notion of local power, and working in small groups, postmodern education values movement, the immediate, the affective, relationships, intensity, engagement, solidarity, self-management, and a struggle against the elements of classical modern education which values the content, efficiency, rationality, methods, techniques, and the instruments. The objectives of education are valued more than the use. Its philosophical base is neohumanistic. In it, we also find the themes of happiness, beauty, hope, a healthy environment, production, and more.

In brief, it could be said that modern education works with the key concept of equality to eliminate differences, and postmodern education works with the key concept of equity, looking for justice and equality without eliminating difference.

In order to accomplish its humanistic task, the school must show its pupils that other cultures, as well as visions of life and ideas besides their own do, indeed, exist. Therefore, as we have seen, the school must be local as a starting point, but it must also be international and intercultural as an arrival point. The uniformizing modern school was incapable of constructing the universal from the particular. It tried to invert the process, imposing universal values and content, without starting from the social and cultural practice of the pupil and without taking his or her identity and difference into account. One of the factors of the failure of our educational system lies in the fact that it doesn't take cultural diversity into account in the construction of an education for all.

In general, the philosophical category which has been dearest to modern pedagogy has been *hegemony*. It attempted to make a certain conception of the world and of life, whether it was Christianity, liberalism, or socialism, hegemonic through education. The category that is most dear to postmodern education is seen in the idea of the autonomy of the individual and of the school. As we have seen, the *autonomy* of the school doesn't mean isolation, nor enclosure inside a particular culture. An autonomous school means a curious, daring school that tries to dialogue with all the cultures and conceptions of the world from a culture that opens itself to the rest of mankind.

These ideas are really not new. The new comes from the old. If a postmodern education is possible tomorrow, it is because today, within the modern, and at the heart of its crisis, the elements of a new education are appearing. The challenge that I wish to leave with my readers in this farewell—especially the young people—is that they be impatient and restless, that they look to the past as much as to the future, and that they attempt to identify the new in the old as well as in everything and anything. Here, Marxism, *as a philosophy of the praxis*, which has been reborn from the success and failures of concrete experiences, is still a valid paradigm on which to found a theory of education—as long as it is conceived critically!

Bibliography

Abramo, Cláudio Weber. "A Way Out for Education." *Folha de São Paulo* newspaper, 9 September 1991, p. 3.

Adler, Alexandre. "Gramsci: Lenin in the West?" *Encontros* "Meetings with Brazilian Civilization" magazine, 5. November 1978.

Afanasiev, V. *Fundamentals of Philosophy.* Rio de Janeiro: Civilização Brasileira, 1968.

Albertini, Remo. "Autonomy against the School." *Il Trentino* magazine, 28:170. June–July 1991. 56–65.

———. *In Favour of Marx.* Rio de Janeiro: Zahar, 1979.

Althusser, Louis. *Positions.* Paris. Ed. Sociales, 1976.

Althusser, Louis, and Alain Badiod. *Historic Materialism and Dialectic Materialism.* São Paulo, Global, 1980.

Althusser, Louis, et al. *Reading Capital* 2 vol. Rio de Janeiro: Zahar, 1979.

Alves, Rubem. *Conversations with those who like to teach.* São Paulo: Cortez, 1981.

Apple, Michael W. *Cultural and Economic Reproduction in Education: Essays on Class, Ideology and the State.* London: Routledge & Kegan Paul, 1982.

Aronowitz, Stanley, and Henry A. Giroux. *Postmodern Education: Politics, Culture, and Social Criticism.* Oxford: University of Minnesota Press, 1991.

Arroyo, Miguel. "Against the School." *Leia* magazine. São Paulo, Letra Viva. October 1986.

Astrada, Carlos. *Work and Alienation.* Rio de Janeiro: Paz e Terra, 1968.

————. *Dialectics and History.* Buenos Aires: Juaréz, 1969

Barros, Jefferson. *The Function of Intellectuals in a Class Society.* Porto Alegre: Movimento, 1977.

Baudelot, Christian, and Roger Establet. *The Capitalist School in France.* Paris: Maspero, 1971.

Beachler, Jean. *What is Ideology?* Paris: Gallimard, 1976.

Benavente, Ana. *The School in the Society of Classes; the Primary Teacher and the Lack of Success at School.* Lisbon: Livros Horizonte, 1976.

Benjamin, Walter, et al. *Selected Texts.* São Paulo: Abril (Os Pensadores), 1975.

Bennett, Christine I. *Comprehensive Multicultural Education: Theory and Practice.* Boston: Allyn and Bacon, 1990.

Berger, Manfredo. *Education and Dependence.* Porto Alegre: Difel, 1976.

Berstein, Basil. *Class, Codes and Control: Applied Studies toward a Sociology of Language.* London: Routledge and Kegan Paul, 1971.

————. *Power, Education and Conscience: Sociology of Cultural Transmission.* Santiago: CIDE, 1988.

Best, Francine. *Education, Culture, the Rights of Man and International Comprehension.* Paris: UNESCO, 1991.

Birnbaum, Pierre. *The End of Politics.* Paris: Seuil, 1975.

Blackbrun, Robin, ed. *After the Fall: the Failure of Communism and the Future of Socialism.* São Paulo: Paz e Terra, 1992.

Boltanski, Luc. *Prime Education and Class Morale.* Paris: Mouton, 1969.

Bordignon, Genuino, and Luiz S. Macedo de Oliveira. "The Citizen School: A Municipalist Utopia." *Municipal Education* magazine. São Paulo: Cortez/Undime/Cead, May 1989. 5–13.

Bornhein, Gerd A. *Dialectics: Theory and Praxis: an Essay for a Critique of the Ontological Fundamentals of Dialectics.* Porto Alegre: Globo, 1977.

Bosi, Alfredo. *Dialectics of Colonization.* São Paulo: Companhia das Letras, 1992.

Bottomore, Tom, ed. *A Dictionary of Marxist Thought.* Oxford: Basil Blackwell, 1983.

Bourdieu, Pierre, and Jean-Claude Passeron. *The Inheritors.* Paris: Minuit, 1964.

Bowles, Samuel, and Herbert Gintis, *Schooling in Capitalist America.* London: Routledge & Kegan Paul, 1976.

Brandão, Carlos Rodrigues. *What is Education?* São Paulo: Brasiliense, 1981.

———. *What is Paulo Freire's Method.* São Paulo: Brasiliense, 1981.

———. Ed. *The Educator: Life and Death.* Rio: Graal, 1982.

———. *Lessons from Nicaragua: the Experience of Hope.* Campinas: Papirus, 1984.

Braverman, Harry. *Work and Monopoly Capital.* São Paulo: Zahar, 1977. (New York, Monthly Review Press, 1974).

Broccoli, Angelo, *Antonio Gramsci and Education as Hegemony.* México City: Nueva Imagem, 1977.

Bruno, Lúcia. *What is Working Autonomy?* São Paulo: Brasiliense 1985.

Buber, Martin. *Life in Dialogue.* Paris: Aubier-Montaigne, 1959.

———. *Me and You.* São Paulo: Moraes, 1977. First edition 1923.

Cabral, Amílcar. *Selected Works of Amílcar Cabral.* 2 vol. Lisbon: Ceara Nova, 1977.

Cardonnel, Jean, et al. *Socialism and Christianity.* Rio de Janeiro: Paz e Terra, 1968.

Carnoy, Martin. *Education as Cultural Imperialism.* New York: David McKay, 1974.

Carnoy, Martin, and Joel Samoff, eds. *Education and Social Transition in the Third World.* Princeton: Princeton University Press, 1990.

Carvalho, Nanci Valadares. *Self-management: government by autonomy.* São Paulo: Brasiliense, 1983.

Castoriadis, Cornelius. *The Imaginary Institution of Society.* São Paulo: Paz e Terra, 1982.

———. *The Historical Creation: the Project of Autonomy.* Porto Alegre: Palmarinca, 1991.

Castro, Fidel. *The Cuban Revolution.* Paris: Maspero, 1967.

Cavalcante, Pedro Celso Uchôa, and Paolo Piccone. *Invitation to a Reading of Gramsci.* Rio de Janeiro: Achiamé, 1976.

Catani, Denise Bárbara, et al, eds. *University School and the Formation of Teachers.* São Paulo: Brasiliense, 1986.

Charlot, Bernard. *Pedagogical Mystification: Social Realities and Ideological Processes in the Theory of Education.* São Paulo: Zahar, 1980.

Chatelet, François. *Logos and Praxis.* Paris: Société d'Edition d'Énseignement Supérieur, 1962.

Chauí, Marilena. *What is Ideology?* São Paulo: Brasiliense, 1981.

———. *Conformism and Resistance: Aspects of Popular Culture in Brazil.* São Paulo: Brasiliense, 1986.

———. *Culture and Democracy.* 4th ed. São Paulo: Cortez, 1989.

Cheptulin, Alexandre. *Materialistic Dialectcs.* São Paulo: Alfa-ômega, 1982.

Coelho, Teixeira. *What is the Cultural Industry?* São Paulo: Brasiliense, 1981.

Corbisier, Roland. *Philosophy, Politics and Liberty.* Rio de Janeiro: Paz e Terra, 1975.

Coriat, Benjamin. *Science, Technique and Capital.* Madrid: Blume, 1976.

Cortella, Mário Sérgio. "Seminar on the Philosophy of Education: An Experience with Sisyphus." *Education and Society Journal.* I:1. São Paulo: Cortez & Moraes, 1978. 182–185.

Cutler, Antony, et al. *Marx's Capital and the Capitalism of Today.* São Paulo: Zahar, 1982.

Demo, Pedro. *Participation is Conquest.* São Paulo: Cortez, 1988.

———. *A Lower Form of Citizenship: Some Quantitive Indications of Our Political Poverty.* Pettrópolis: Vozes, 1992.

Descartes, René. *Discourse on the Method.* Rio de Janeiro: Edições de Ouro, 1969.

———. *Rules for the Direction of the Spirit.* Lisbon: Estampa, 1971.

Detrich, Théo. *Socialist Pedagogy.* Paris: Maspero, 1973.

Dewey, John. *Democracy and Education.* New York: Free Press, 1966.

Dommanget, Maurice. *The Great Socialists and Education: From Plato to Lenin.* Madrid: Fragua, 1972.

Drew, Naomi. *Peace Can Also Be Learned.* Preface by Moacir Gadotti. São Paulo: Gaia, 1990.

Dumont, Fernand. *Ideologies.* Paris: PUF, 1974.

Durand, José Carlos. "Companies and School." *Folha de São Paulo* newspaper, 18 December 1980.

Durkheim, Émile. *The Rules of Sociological Method.* São Paulo: Nacional, 1987.

Dussel, Enrique. *Erotics and Pedagogy.* São Paulo: Loyola, 1983.

Engels, Friedrich. *Dialectics of Nature.* Rio de Janeiro: Paz e Terra, 1976.

————. *The Origin of the Family, Private Property and the State.* Rio de Janeiro: Civilização Brasileira, 1979.

————. *From Utopian Socialism to Scientific Socialism.* São Paulo: Alfa-ômega, 1980.

Erny, Pierre. *Ethnology of Education.* Rio de Janeiro: Zahar, 1982.

Faure, Edgar, et al. *Learning to Be.* Paris: Fayard-Unesco, 1972.

Fedosseiev, P. N., ed. *Karl Marx: Biography.* Moscow: Progresso, 1983.

Fernandes, Florestan. *The Brazilian University: Reform or Revolution?* São Paulo: Alfa-ômega, 1975.

————. *The Educational Challenge.* São Paulo: Cortez and Autores Associados, 1989.

Ferrière, Adolphe. *The Autonomy of School Children in Communities of Children.* Neuchâtel, Switzerland: Delachaux et Niestlé, 1950.

Ferry Gilles, *The Practice of Group Work: An Experience of the Formation of Teachers.* Paris: Dunod, 1970.

Fetsche, Irvin. *Karl Marx and Marxiams: From the Philosophy of the Proletariat to the Proletarian Vision of the World.* Rio de Janeiro: Paz e Terra, 1970.

Fischmann, Roseli, ed. *Brazilian School.* São Paulo: Atlas, 1987.

Fougeyrollas, Pierre. *Philosophy in Question.* Rio de Janeiro: Paz e Terra, 1972.

Foulquiè, Paul. *Dialectics.* São Paulo: Publicações Europa-América, 1974.

Frankl, Viktor. *Psychotherapy and Its Image of Man.* Paris: Resna, 1970.

Frare, José Luiz. "Europe Builds the School for the 21st Century." *Nova Escola* magazine, 6:51. São Paulo: September 1991, 18–23.

Freinet, Celestin. *Birth of a Popular Pedagogy.* Paris: Maspero, 1968.

————. *For a School of the People.* Lisbon: Presença, 1973.

————. *Education through Work.* 2 vol. Lisbon: Presença, 1974.

Freire, Ana Maria. *Illiteracy in Brazil.* São Paulo: Cortez, 1989.

Freire, Madalena. *The Passion to Know the World.* Rio de Janeiro: Paz e Terra, 1983.

Freire, Paulo, *Education as a Practice of Freedom.* Preface by Francisco Weffort. Rio de Janeiro: Paz e Terra, 1967.

————. *Pedagogy of the Oppressed.* Preface by Ernani Maria Fiori. Rio de Janeiro: Paz e Terra, 1975.

————. *Education and Change.* Preface by Moacir Gadotti. Rio de Janeiro: Paz e Terra, 1979.

————. *Education in the City.* Preface by Moacir Gadotti and Carlos Alberto Torres. São Paulo: Cortez, 1991.

————. *Pedagogy of Hope: A reunion with Pedagogy of the Oppressed.* Rio de Janeiro: Paz e Terra, 1992.

Freitag, Barbara, *School, State and Society.* São Paulo: Moraes, 1979.

Freyre, Gilberto, *The Big House and the Senzala: the Formation of the Brazilian Family in the Patriarchal Economy.* 14 ed., 2 vol Rio de Janeiro: José Olympio, 1969, First edition 1933.

Friedman, Milton, and Rose Friedman. *Freedom to Choose: New Economic Liberalism.* Rio de Janeiro: Record, 1982.

Froom, Erich. *The Marxist Concept of Man.* São Paulo: Zahar, 1979.

————. *On Disobedience and other essays.* New York: Seabury Press, 1981.

Furter, Pierre. *The Systems of Formation in their Contexts: Introduction to a Method of Comparative Education.* Rio de Janeiro: Fundação Getúlio Vargas, 1982.

Gabel, Joseph, *Ideologies.* Paris: Anthropos, 1976.

Gadotti, Moacir. *Communication of the Teacher: An Essay of the Characteristics of the Education Relationship.* Preface by Georges Gusdorf. São Paulo: Loyola, 1975.

————. *Education and Power: An Introduction to the Pedagogy of Conflict*. São Paulo: Cortez, 1980.

————. *Education against Education: the Forgetting of Education and Permanent Education.* Preface by Paulo Freire. Rio de Janeiro: Paz e Terra, 1981.

———. *The Dialectic Conception of Education: An Introductory Study.* São Paulo: Cortez and Autores Associados, 1983.

———. *A Single School For All: Paths Toward School Autonomy.* Preface by Florestan Fernandes. Petrópolis: Vozes, 1990.

———. *Citizen School: A Class on the Autonomy of the School.* São Paulo: Cortez, 1992.

———. *Cultural Diversity and Education for All.* São Paulo: Graal, 1992a. Preface by José Eustáquio Romão.

———. *Organization of Work at School: Some Presuppositions.* São Paulo: Atica, 1993.

———. *History of Pedagogic Ideas.* Preface by Antonio Joaquim Severino. São Paulo: Atica, 1993.

Gadotti, Moacir; Paulo Freire; and Sérgio Guimarães. *Pedagogy: Dialogue and Conflict.* São Paulo: Cortez, 1985.

Gadotti, Moacir, and Otaviano Pereira. *Why the PT: the Origin, Design and the Consolidation of the Workers Party.* Preface by José Dirceu de Oliveira e Silva and posface by José Genoino Neto. São Paulo: Cortez, 1989.

Gadotti, Moacir, and Carlos Alberto Torres. *The State and Popular Education in Latin America.* Campinas: Papirus, 1992.

Gelpi, E. Hore. *Human Complexity: Research and Formation.* Florence: Mecoll Publisher, 1992.

Giroux, Henry. *Teachers as Intellectuals: Toward A Critical Pedagogy of Learning.* Barcelona: Paidós, 1990.

Giroux, Henry, and Peter McLaren, eds. *Critical Pedagogy, the State, and Cultural Struggle.* New York: SUNY Press, 1989.

Glasser, William. *The Quality School: Managing Students without Coercion.* New York: Harper Collins, 1990.

Goldman, Lucien. *Human Sciences and Philosophy.* Paris: Gothier, 1966.

———. *Dialectics and the Human Sciences.* Lisbon: Presença, 1973.

———. *Dialectics and Culture.* Rio de Janeiro: Paz e Terra, 1979.

Goldsmith, Jimmy. "It's necessary to limit the power of the State." *O Estado de S. Paulo* newspaper. 21 October 1984.

Gorbachev, Mikhail. *Perestroika: New Ideas for My Country and the World.* São Paulo: Best Seller, 1987.

Gramsci, Antonio. *The Intellectuals and the Organization of Culture.* Rio de Janeiro: Civilização Brasileira, 1968.

———. *The Dialectic Conception of History.* Rio de Janeiro: Civilização Brasileira, 1968a.

———. *The Pedagogical Alternative.* Barcelona: Nova Terra, 1976.

———. *Letters from Prison.* Rio de Janeiro: Civilização Brasileira, 1978.

———. *Machiavelli, Politics and the Modern State.* Rio de Janeiro: Civilização Brasileira, 1978a.

Gruppi, Luciano. *The Concept of Hegemony in Gramsci.* Rio de Janeiro: Graal, 1978.

Guevara, Ernesto. *Socialism and Man.* Paris: Maspero, 1967.

Guillerm, Alain, and Yvon Bourdet. *Self-management: A Radical Change.* Rio de Janeiro: Zahar, 1976.

Gusdorf, Georges. *Why Teachers?* Paris: Payot, 1963.

Gutierrez, Francisco. *Total Language Pedagogy of the Means of Communication.* Buenos Aires: Humanitas, 1974.

———. *Education as Political Praxis.* Preface by Paulo Freire. Mexico City: Siglo Veintiuno, 1984.

———. , ed. *Community Education and Popular Economy.* Heredia: Editorialpec, 1990.

Habermas, Jürgen, *Theory and Practice.* 2 vol. Paris: Fayard, 1972.

———. *Technique and Science as "Ideology".* Paris: Gallimard, 1976.

Hartung, Henri. *The Children of Promise.* Paris, Fayard, 1972.

———. *The Time of Rupture: Permanent Education and Self-Management.* Neuchâtel: A la Baconniere, 1975.

Hegel, Georg Wilhelm Friedrich. *Phenomenology of the Spirit; Aesthetics: the Idea and the Ideal: Aesthetic Beauty and the Ideal; Introduction to the History of Philosophy.* São Paulo: Abril Cultural (Os Pensadores), 1980.

———. *Writings on Pedagogy.* Mexico City, Fundo de Cultura Econômica, 1991.

Ianni, Octavio. *Imperialism and Culture.* Petrópolis: Vozes, 1979.

ICEA (International Community Education Association). *Report of the Sixth World Conference.* Coventry, England: ICEA, 1991.

Illich, Ivan. *Deschooling Society.* Petrópolis: Vozes, 1973.

Illich, Ivan, and Barry Sanders. *ABC: the Alphabetization of the Popular Spirit.* Paris: La Découverte, 1990.

Judt, Tony. *Past Imperfect: French Intellectuals, 1944–1956.* Berkeley: University of California Press, 1992.

Knowles, Malcom. *The Modern Practice of Adult Education: From Pedagogy to Andragogy.* Wilton, Conn.: Association Presse, 1980.

Konder, Leandro. *What is Dialectics.* São Paulo: Brasiliense, 1981.

———. *Lukacs.* Porto Alegre Brazil: L&PM, 1980.

Korzcak, Janusz. *How to Love a Child.* Rio de Janeiro: Paz e Terra, 1983. Preface by Bruno Bettelheim.

Kosik, Karel. *Dialectics of the Concrete.* Rio de Janeiro: Paz e Terra, 1969.

Kriesbere, Louis, *The Sociology of Social Conflicts.* N.J.: Prentice-Hall, 1973.

Krupskaia, N. *Communist Education: Lenin and Youth.* Madrid: Nuesta Cultura, 1978.

Laborit, Henri. *Informational Society: Ideals for Self-Management.* Paris: Cerf, 1973.

Lalande, André. *Technical Vocabulary and a Critique of Philosophy.* Paris: PUF, 1960.

Lambert, Jacques. *The Two Brazils.* São Paulo: Nacional, 1986.

Lao Tsé. *Tao tö King.* Paris: Gallimard, 1967.

Lapassade, George. *The Entry to Life.* Paris: Minuit, 1963.

———. *Groups, Organizations, Institutions.* Paris: Gauttier-Villars, 1967.

———. *Pedagogic Self-Management.* Paris: Gauthier-Villars, 1971.

Lebrun, Gerard. *What is Power?* São Paulo: Brasiliense, 1981.

Lefébvre, Henri. *Marxism.* São Paulo: Difel, 1974.

———. *Formal Logic, Dialectical Logic.* Rio Janeiro: Civilização Brasileira, 1975.

Lenin, Vladimir Ilitch. *Materialism and Empirocriticism.* Paris: Ed. Sociales, 1948.

———. *Philosophical Notebooks.* Moscow: Ed. du Progrès; and Paris: d. Sociales, 1973.

————. *Public Instruction.* Moscow: Progresso, 1981.

Lipman, Matthew. *Philosophy Goes to School.* Philadelphia: Temple University Press, 1988.

Lobrot, Michel. *Institutional Pedagogy: the School Versus Self-Management.* Preface by J. Ardoino, Paris: Gauthier-Villars, 1972.

————. *For or Against Authority?* Paris: Gauthier-Villars, 1974.

Lombardi, Franco. *The Marxist Pedagogy of Antonio Gramsci.* Toulouse, France: Privat, 1971.

Lowy, Michael. *Dialectical Method and Political Theory.* Rio de Janeiro: Paz e Terra, 1978.

————. *Ideologies and Social Science: Elements for a Marxist Analysis.* São Paulo: Cortez, 1985.

————. *The Adventures of Karl Marx against Baron Munchausen: Marxism and Positivism in the Sociology of Knowledge.* São Paulo: Busca Vida, 1987.

Ludojoski, Roque Luis. *Self-Management in Pedagogy.* Buenos Aires: Guadalupe, 1967.

Lukács, Georg. *History and Class Conscience: Studies of Marxist Dialectics.* Mexico City: Grijalbo, 1969.

Luzuriaga, Lorenzo. *The Unique School.* Preface by Lourenço Filho. São Paulo: Melhoramentos, 1934.

————. *A History of Public Education.* São Paulo: Nacional, 1958.

Macchiocci, Maria Antonieta. *In Favor of Gramsci.* Rio de Janeiro: Paz e Terra, 1976.

Manacorda, Mario Alighiero. *Marx and Modern Pedagogy.* Barcelona: Oikos Tam, 1969.

————. *The Educative Principle in Gramsci.* Salamanca: Síngueme, 1977.

————. *A History of Education: from Ancient Times to Our Days.* São Paulo: Cortez and Autores Associados, 1989.

Mandel, Ernest. *An Introduction to Marxism.* Porto Alegre: Movimento, 1978.

Mannheim, Karl. *Ideology and Utopia.* Rio de Janeiro: Zaher, 1976.

Marcovic, Mihailo. *Dialectics of Praxis.* Buenos Aires: Amorrotu, 1968.

Marcuse, Herbert. *One-Dimensional Man: Studies in the Ideology of Advanced Industrial Society.* Boston: Beacon Press, 1964.

————. *Historic Materialism and Existence.* Rio de Janeiro: Tempo Brasileiro, 1968.

————. *Ideas on a Critical Theory of Society.* São Paulo: Zahar, 1972.

Markus, Gyorgy. *The Theory of Knowledge in the Young.* Marx. Rio de Janeiro: Paz e Terra, 1978.

Martins, José de Souza. *On the Capitalist Way of Thinking.* São Paulo: Hucitec, 1980.

Marx, Karl. *Capital.* New York: Randon House, 1906.

————. *Misery of Philosophy.* Rio de Janeiro: Leitura, 1965.

————. *A Contribution to the Critique of Political Economy.* Lisbon: Estampa, 1973.

————. *Economic-Philosophical Manuscripts and Other Chosen Texts.* Abril Cultural (Os Pensadores), 1978.

————. *Sociology.* Octavio Ianni, ed. São Paulo: Atica, 1979.

————. *Capital.* 6 vol. Rio de Janeiro: Civilização Brasileira, 1980.

Marx, Karl, and F. Engels. *Philosophic Letters and Other Writings.* São Paulo: Grijalbo, 1977.

————. *Chosen Works.* São Paulo: Alfa-ômega, 1977a, 3 vol.

————. *German Ideology.* São Paulo: Grijalbo, 1977b.

————. *A Critique of Education and Teaching.* Texts organized, introduced, and commented on by Roger Dangeville, Lisbon: Moraes, 1978.

Maturana R., Humberto. *Emotion and Language in Education and Politics.* Santiago: Hachete, CED, 1992.

McLaren, Peter. *Schooling as a Ritual Performance.* Boston: Routledge & Kegan Paul, 1986.

————. *Life in Schools: An Introduction to Critical Pedagogy in the Foundations of Education.* New York: Longman, 1989.

McLuhan, Marshall. *Mutations 1990.* Paris: Mame, 1969.

Mello, Guiomar Namo de. *First Grade Teaching.* São Paulo: Cortez, 1982.

————. *School Education; Passion, Thinking and Practice.* São Paulo: Cortez, 1986.

Mello & Souza, Antônio Câudido. "Fernando Azevedo" In: Revista (Municipal Education Journal). São Paulo: Cortez, Ano I, No 1, jumbo 1988, pp. 79–81.

Mendel, Gérard. *To Decolonize the Child: Sociopsycho-analysis of Authority.* Paris: Payot, 1971.

Mendel, Gérard, and Christian Vogt. *The Educative Manifesto: Questioning and Socialism.* Paris: Payot, 1973.

Mendes, Durmeval Trigueiro, ed. *The Philosophy of Brazilian Education.* Rio de Janeiro: Civilização Brasileira, 1983.

Mialaret, Gaston. *An Introduction to Pedagogy.* São Paulo: Atlas, 1977.

Montero, Antonio Moreno. "Spain Searches for an Autonomous School."Interview by José Luiz Frare. *Nova Escola* magazine. 6:50 São Paulo: August 1991 20–25.

Morales-Gómez, Daniel A., and Carlos Alberto Torres. *Education for All: Prospects and Implications for Latin America in 1990s.* Los Angeles: School of Education, UCLA, March 1990.

Morin, Edgar. *The Lost Paradigm: Human Nature.* Paris: Seuil, 1973.

Morin, Lucien. *The Charlatans of New Pedagogy.* Preface by Gaston Mialaret. Lisbon: Publicações Europa-América, 1976.

Mortimer, J. Adler. *Paideia Proposal.* Brasilia: UnB, 1984.

Motta, Carlos Guilherme, *Ideology and Brazilian Culture (1933–1974).* São Paulo: Atica, 1977.

Motta, Fernando C. Prestes. *What is Bureaucracy.* São Paulo: Brasiliense, 1981.

Naisbitt, John, and Patrícia Aburdene. *Megatrends 2000: Ten New Trends for the Transformation of Society in the Nineties.* São Paulo: Amana-Key, 1990.

Nicol, Eduardo. *The Principles of Science.* México City: Fondo de Cultura Económica, 1965.

Nogueira, Madza J. "Open debate: the challenge of Constituent." *ANDE* magazine, São Paulo: 1986.

OECD–CERI. *Multicultural Education.* Paris: OECD, 1987.

Oliveira, Rosiska Darcy de. *In Praise of Difference: the Emerging Feminine.* São Paulo: Brasiliense, 1992.

Paiva, Vanilda, ed. *Perspectives and Dilemmas of Popular Education.* Rio de Janeiro: Graal, 1984.

Palácios, Jesús. *The School Question: Critiques and Alternatives.* Barcelona: Laia, 1978.

Pantillon, Claude. *What to Do With A Philosophy of Education.* Lausanne, Switzerland: L 'Age d'Homme, 1981.

―――. *Changing Education: the Thematics of Change in Permanent Education.* Preface by Chadly Fitouri. Lausanne, Switzerland: L 'Age d'Homme, 1983.

Pantillon, Claude, and Moacir Gadotti. *Philosophical Manifesto: toward a Philosophy of Education.* Geneva: Faculté de Psychologie et des Sciences de l 'Education, 1976.

Paranhos, Adalberto. *Dialectics of Domination: Domination, Ideology and Class Conscience.* Campinas: Papirus, 1984.

Pereira, Luiz Carlos Bresser. *State Society and Technobureaucracy.* São Paulo: Brasiliense, 1981.

Piaget, Jean. *Where is Education Going?* Paris: UNESCO, 1972.

Piaget, Jean, and J. Heller. *Autonomy in the School.* Buenos Aires: Losada, 1950.

Pinkevich, Alfred. *Modern Pedagogical Theories and the New Education in the USSR.* México City: Fuente Cultural, 1941.

Pistrak, E. *Fundamentals of the School of Work.* São Paulo: Brasiliense, 1981. Introduced by Maurício Tragtenberg.

Plekhanov, G. *Materialistic Conception of History.* Rio de Janeiro: Paz e Terra, 1978.

PNUD, UNESCO, UNICEF, BANCO MUNDIAL. *World declaration on education for all and the plan of action to fulfill basic learning needs.* World Congress on Education for All, Jomtien, Thailand, 5–9 March 1990, Translated by Carmem Emilia Pérez, José Eustáquio Romão, and Moacir Gadotti. Brasilia, UNICEF, 1991.

Politzer, Georges, et al. *Fundamental Principles of Philosophy.* São Paulo: Hemus, 1970.

Ponce, Anibal. *Education and Class Struggle.* São Paulo: Cortez and Autores Associados, 1981.

Portelli, Hugues. *Gramsci and the Historical Block.* Rio de Janeiro: Paz e Terra, 1977.

Poster, Cyril, and Angelika Krüger. *Community Education in the Western World.* London: Routledge & Kegan Paul, 1990.

Poster, Cyril, and Jürgen Zimmer. *Community Education in the Third World.* London: Routledge & Kegan Paul, 1992.

Poulantzas, Nicos. *Political Power and Social Classes in the Capitalist State*. México City: Siglo Veintiuno, 1971.

———. *Social Classes in the Capitalism of Today*. Rio de Janeiro: Zahar, 1978.

Prado, Jr., Caio. *Dialectics of Knowledge*. 2 vol. São Paulo: Brasiliense, 1952.

Reboul, Olivier. *Philosophy of Education*. São Paulo: Melhoramentos, 1974.

Reich, Wilheim. *What is Class Consciousness?* Oporto, Portugal, 1976.

———. *Dialectic Materialism and Psychoanalysis*. Lisbon: Presença, 1977.

Reimer, Everett. *The School is Dead*. Rio de Janeiro: Francisco Alves, 1983.

Ribeiro, Darcy. *The Necessary University*. Rio de Janeiro: Paz e Terra, 1975.

Ricoeur, Paul. *Interpretation and Ideologies*. Rio de Janeiro: Francisco Alves, 1977.

Rockwell, Elsie, and Justa Espeleta. *Participatory Research*. São Paulo: Cortez and Autores Associados, 1986.

Rodrigues, Neidson. *The State, Education and Economic Development*. São Paulo: Cortez and Autores Associados, 1982.

Rogers, Carl. *Becoming a Person*. Lisbon: Moraes, 1973.

———. *From Person to Person: the Problem of the Human Being*. São Paulo: Pioneira, 1976.

Romão, José Eustáquio. *Local Power and Education*. Preface by Moacir Gadotti. São Paulo: Cortez, 1992.

Rossi, Wagner Gonçalves. *Capitalism and Education*. Preface by Maurício Tragtenberg. São Paulo: Cortez & Moraes, 1978.

———. *Pedagogy of Work*. 2 vol. São Paulo: Moraes, 1981.

Rousseau, Jean-Jacques. *A Discourse on the Origin and the Fundamentals of Inequality between Men*. Paris: Gallimard, 1965.

———. *Emile or on Education*. Introduction by Michel Launay. Paris: Garneir-Flammarion, 1966.

Rubel, Maximilien. *Pages of Karl Marx: for a Socialist Ethics*. Paris: Payot, 1970, 2 vol.

Salm, Cláudio. *School and Work*. São Paulo: Brasiliense, 1980.

Sander, Beno. *Consensus and Conflict: Analytical Perspectives in Pedagogy and the Administration of Education*. São Paulo: Pioneira, 1984.

Santos, José Luiz dos. *What is Culture?* São Paulo: Brasiliense, 1984.

Santos, Theotonio dos. *The Concept of Social Classes.* Petrópolis, Vozes, 1985.

Sarup, Madan. *Marxism and Education.* London: Routledge & Kegan Paul, 1978.

Sartre, Jean-Paul. *A Critique of Dialectical Reason.* Paris: Gallimard, 1960.

Saviani, Dermeval. *Education: from Common Sense to Philosophical Consciousness.* São Paulo: Cortez and Autores Associados, 1980.

———. *School and Democracy.* São Paulo: Cortez and Autores Associados, 1983.

———. *Public Schooling and Some Words on the University.* São Paulo: Cortez, 1984.

Schaff, Adam. *Technocratic Society: Ideology and Social Classes, the End of Ideology.* São Paulo: Documentos, 1969.

Schmied-Kowarzik, Wolfdrietrich. *Dialectic Pedagogy: from Aristotle to Paulo Freire.* São Paulo: Brasiliense, 1983.

Schwartz, Bertrand. *Education Tomorrow.* Paris: Aubier Montaigne, 1973.

Severino, Autônio Joaquim. *Education, Ideology and Counter-Ideology.* São Paulo: EPU, 1986.

Sherover-Marcuse, Erica. *Emancipation and Consciousness: Dogmatic and Dialectical Perspectives in the Early Marx.* New York: Brazil Blackwell, 1986.

Silveira, Paulo. *From the Side of History: A Critical Reading of the Work of Althusser.* São Paulo: Pólis, 1978.

Smart, Barry. *Sociology, Phenomenology and Marxist Analysis.* São Paulo: Zahar, 1978.

Snyders, Georges. *Where Non-directive Pedagogies Are Going?* Paris: PUF, 1974.

———. *Progressist Pedagogy.* Coimbra: Almedina, 1974a.

———. *School, Class and Class Struggle.* Lisbon: Moraes, 1977.

———. *Happiness at School.* São Paulo: Manole, 1988.

Steinbeck, John. *The Grapes of Wrath.* New York: Viking, 1967.

Stockfelt, Torjörn. *Pedagogy of the Life of Work.* Stockholm: University of Stockholm, ALPlatim, 1991.

Suchodolski, Bogdan. _Marxist Theory of Education_. México City: Grijalbo, 1966.

———. _Treaty on Pedagogy_. Barcelona: Península, 1971.

———. _Pedagogy and the Great Philosophical Currents_. Lisbon: Horizonte, 1972.

Sweezy, Paul M. _Theory of Capitalist Development_. Rio de Janeiro: Zahar, 1967.

Tedesco, Juan Carlos. _The Regional Educative Liberation and Active Strategies for the World Congress on Education for All_. Consulta de Quito, 28 November to 1 December 1989.

———. _Some Aspects of the Educative Privatisation in Latin America_. Quito: Instituto Fronesis, 1991.

Teixeira, Anísio. _A Short Introduction to the Philosophy of Education_. São Paulo: Nacional, 1975.

———. _Education is not a Privilege_. São Paulo: Melhoramentos, 1977.

Tocqueville, A. _Democracy in America_. São Paulo: Nacional, 1969.

Torres, Carlos Alberto. _The Politics of Nonformal Education in Latin America_. Preface by Martin Carnoy. New York: Praeger, 1990.

———. _Political Sociology of Education_. Preface by Moacir Gadotti. São Paulo: Cortez, 1993.

Torres, Rosa Maria. _Discourse and Practice in Popular Education_. Ijuí: UNIJUÍ 1988.

———. _Nicaragua: Popular Revolution, Popular Education_. México City: Linea, 1985.

Tragtenberg, Mauríco. _Bureaucracy and Ideology_. São Paulo: Atica, 1977.

Trento, Provincia Autona di. _For a Quality School_. Special number of _Il Trentino_ journal, 27:113. November 1990.

Tse-Tung, Mao, _The Philosophy of Mao Tse-Tung_. Belém, Brazil: Boitempo, 1979.

UNDP, UNESCO, UNICEF, World Bank. _Meeting Basic Learning Needs: A Vision for the 1990s_. (background document). New York: UNICEF House, April 1990.

———. _World Conference on Education for All: Meeting Basic Learning Needs_. New York: UNICEF House, May 1990a.

UNESCO. *Self-management in Educative Systems.* Paris: UNESCO (Esdudios y documentos de educación, 39). 1981.

Vasquez, Adolpho Sánchez. *Philosophy of Praxis.* Rio de Janeiro: Paz e Terra, 1977.

Vasquez, Aida, and Fernand Oury. *Toward an Institutional Pedagogy.* Paris: Maspero, 1967.

Vieira Pinto, Alvaro. *Conscience and National Reality.* Rio de Janeiro: ISEB, 1960.

——. *Science and Existence: Philosophical Problems of Scientific Research.* Rio de Janeiro: Paz e Terra, 1969.

Villalobos, André, et al. *Social Classes and Productive Work.* Rio de Janeiro: Paz e Terra, 1978.

Wanderley, Luiz Eduardo W. *Educating to Transform: Popular Education, the Catholic Church and Politics in the Grassroots Education Movement.* Petrópolis: Vozes, 1984.

Weber, Max. *Essays on the Theory of Science.* Paris: Plon, 1968.

Index

A

Abelardo, Pedro, 122
Abramo, Cláudio Weber, 151–152
Africa, 58, 181
Afro-americans, 157
Aquinas, Thomas, 32
Albertini, Remo, 143
Alienation, 38
Allende, Salvador, 45
Althusser, Louis, xx, 24, 174
America: North, 157; South, 157.
    See also Latin America
Andrade, Carlos Drummond de,
    157
Anthopology, 163: political, xxv;
    metaphysical, 69
Antipedagogy, 93
Apple, Michael, xxvi–xxvii, xxx
Argentina, 124
Aristotle, 3, 10–11, 43, 94
Aronowitz, Stanley, xxx
Arroyo, Miguel, 109
Asia, 157, 181
Augustine, 32
Authority, 63–64, 138; and educa-
    tion, 61; and freedom, 75; and
    power, 61, 67; grassroots, 64; new
    form of, 61; principle of, 53; psy-
    chological nature of, 60; question
    of, 57. *See also* Power
Authoritarianism, 54, 58, 61; and
    coersion, 54; of traditional educa-
    tion, 100

Autonomy, 60, 62, 112–113, 118,
    125, 185; administrative, 142;
    and decentralization, 143; and
    equity, 167–169; and the nature of
    education, 135–140; concepctions
    of, xxviii; of school, xxiv, 115,
    140–147, 150–151, 163; financial,
    142; for social moviments, 145;
    institutional, 135; meaning of,
    136; moral, 52; of public school,
    147–148
Avant-gardism, 87
Azevedo, Fernando de, 114

B

Babeuf, Graco, 100
Bakhtin, Mikhail, xii
Bakhunin, Mikhail, 101, 139
Basic education, 166–175; and
    higher education, 170–172; uni-
    versalizattion of, 172. *See also*
    Education
Behavior: revolutionary, 29; pro-
    gressive, 29
Beisiegel, Celso de Rui, 115
Bennett, Christine I., 164
Berlin Wall, 177
Bernstein, Basil, xxvi
Best, Francine, 162
Blackbrun, Robin, 177
Bloch, Ernest, 180
Boas, Franz, 163